A Primer for Benefit–Cost Analysis

To my loving wife Elizabeth and my amazing sons
Aaron and Derek.   A.B.

To the Zerbe Clan and to Arnold Harberger, who is my
inspiration.   R.Z.

A Primer for Benefit–Cost Analysis

Richard O. Zerbe Jr.

University of Washington, USA

and

Allen S. Bellas

Metropolitan State University, USA

Edward Elgar
Cheltenham, UK • Northampton, MA, USA

Published by
Edward Elgar Publishing Limited
Glensanda House
Montpellier Parade
Cheltenham
Glos GL50 1UA
UK

Edward Elgar Publishing, Inc.
136 West Street
Suite 202
Northampton
Massachusetts 01060
USA

A catalogue record for this book
is available from the British Library

ISBN-13: 978 1 84376 897 5 (cased)
ISBN-10: 1 84376 897 6 (cased)

Printed and bound in Great Britain by MPG Books Ltd, Bodmin, Cornwall

Contents

Acknowledgements

The authors gratefully acknowledge the comments and suggestions of David O'Hara, Tim Borders and two reviewers, as well as Scott Farrow, who was the inspiration for this book.

This work was supported in part by the Center for the Study and Improvement of Regulation at Carnegie Mellon University and the University of Washington.

1. Introduction

1.1 PURPOSE OF THE BOOK

The purpose of this book is to provide clear and relatively straightforward guidelines for conducting proper benefit–cost analyses (BCAs) of proposed or previously enacted public projects. Alternatively, the purpose of this book is to allow the reader to critically examine BCAs encountered in the course of work or study. While it might be nice to believe that all analyses are correctly and responsibly done, existing studies demonstrate a great range of levels of quality. The concepts and techniques presented here are not an exhaustive discussion of BCA, but rather are a summary of the most important features of an analysis. The techniques outlined here will generate correct analyses. Most of the presentation should be accessible to anyone with a good understanding of economics, although some topics use indifference curve analysis or some basic calculus.

The great advantage of BCA is that it provides an objective framework around which discussion, correction and amendment can take place. Its greatest risk is that hard numbers will tend to drive out soft. Care must be taken that unquantified or roughly quantified effects be given their proper weight. In doing this it is useful as well as politically realistic to regard BCA as an aid to discussion and to decision and not as the decision itself.

BCA should not be a mysterious process. Stated quite simply, it is the calculation of values for all the inputs into and outputs from a project and then the subtraction of the first from the second. At times some intricate procedures might be used to determine the value of a good for which a price is not readily available, but the core concepts of BCA are fairly simple.

The reader should recognize that BCA is not the only means of evaluating projects, and that it may be acceptable to evaluate a project on a basis other than the value of its net benefits. Projects may be approved for political expediency even when a rational assessment of the net benefits would suggest rejection. There may be important values that are not quantified or quantifiable in BCA, meaning that projects might be valuable even when they do not strictly pass a BCA. The results of a BCA do, however, tend to shift the burden of proof to those who wish to make a decision contrary

1

to the BCA. For this reason, politicians are often opposed to BCA, feeling correctly that such analyses may constrain their choices. This is of course not always a bad thing. At the very least, though, BCA allows an explicit cost to be attached to projects that do not pass BCA or to projects whose goals are larger than those encompassed by BCA.

1.2   WHAT BCA IS

Benefit–cost analysis is one technique of analyzing proposed or previously enacted projects to determine whether doing them is in the public interest, or to choose between two or more mutually exclusive projects. BCA assigns a monetary value to each input into and each output resulting from a project. The values of the inputs and outputs are then compared. In the most basic sense, if the value of the benefits is greater than the value of the costs, the project is deemed worthwhile and should be executed.

Projects identified as worthwhile by BCA are likely to generate outputs that are more valuable than the inputs used. In the case of mutually exclusive projects, BCA will identify the project that will generate the greatest net benefit. BCA may also be used to assess the sensitivity of project outcomes to risk and uncertainty.

Although the idea is simple, the execution of a good BCA can be difficult. Simply determining what to include as a cost or a benefit can require careful thought and may be subject to difference of opinion. While some inputs and outputs will have well-known and stable prices, others may experience price changes as a result of the project. Still other inputs and outputs may not be traded in markets at all, necessitating other valuation methods.

BCA presumes that goods have values to people that can be measured or mapped into monetary values. This is necessary for comparing inputs and outputs and determining whether or not a project is economically desirable. While there are appropriate techniques for attaching monetary values to most goods, others are more difficult to value. For example, clean air and good health are clearly valuable, but it is a challenge to precisely determine the benefits of a program that would yield cleaner air and better health at some cost. However, there are certainly ranges of costs over which a program to reduce air pollution would be worthwhile and over which it would not be worthwhile.

It should be recognized that decisions regarding projects will not and should not be made simply on the basis of BCA. Political and social considerations not included in a BCA may be at least as important as economic benefits in deciding whether or not a project is done. Especially in public decision making, resources are often allocated for reasons other than allocative efficiency, and such issues of justice and fairness may supercede even large net benefits. At the very least, it might be hoped that a good BCA can sway an otherwise undecided person or help in the choice between multiple projects with similar political and social implications.

1.3   STEPS IN BCA

Benefit–cost analysis may be thought of as an operation in which there are a number of distinct steps. Not all analyses will require all of these steps. A short-lived project may require no discounting of future benefits. A project that has been conducted many times may involve little risk or uncertainty. In most cases, however, to clearly consider any project or choose between projects, the following steps should be taken:

1. *Clarify issues of standing*   At the start of an analysis, it should be stated for whom the study is being done and whose costs and benefits will be included. In addressing these issues and calculating benefits or costs to different people or groups it is important to be clear and consistent.
2. *Identify the alternatives*   An analysis needs to be clear about which project or projects are under consideration and whether they are mutually exclusive and should seek to include relevant alternatives. The option of doing nothing is often used as a benchmark, but this may be only one basis of comparison. For example, in the discussion of the Tellico Dam, the Tennessee Valley Authority failed to compare the dam with the alternative of using the free-flowing river to run a turbine (Zerbe and Dively, 1994). Such failures of imagination are not uncommon. Altering the size and duration of the project may be relevant alternatives. For example, a vaccination program that fails a BCA nationally may pass a BCA if analyzed only in a region with a high incidence of the associated disease.
3. *Set out assumptions*   Assumptions are necessarily part of an analysis and some will be better than others. It may be necessary to use assumptions for a wide variety of factors including quantities of goods, costs, market conditions, durations or interest rates. In a responsible analysis, these assumptions will be explicit and attributed to reliable sources when possible. If a range of assumed values is offered then this range should be explicit.

4. *List the impacts of each alternative project*   The potential impacts of each considered project should be listed as completely as possible. This should be done both for the project or projects explicitly under consideration as well as for the status quo or do-nothing alternative.

    It is important that impacts be quantified where possible. Proper evaluation of a project requires knowing what quantities of inputs and outputs will be involved. When quantification is impossible, the impact should at least be mentioned. For example, a project that will limit individuals' personal freedom should mention this fact, even if no attempt will be made to value personal freedom.

5. *Assign values to these impacts*   Appropriate monetary values should be attached to each of the impacts when possible.

6. *Deal with unquantified impacts*   Any impacts that have not been assigned values should be clearly listed so that they may be considered against the explicitly valued costs and benefits.

    One approach to non-quantified benefits is to calculate how large they would need to be to reverse the BCA results. Often a judgment can be made to the effect that their magnitude is likely or unlikely to be large enough to reverse the decision. By explicitly considering such effects in this way, the analyst can take his/her analysis beyond hard numbers.

    For example, in considering a project that will limit personal freedom, the other costs and benefits may be used to calculate the net benefits of the project, excluding any considerations of personal freedom. It might then be left to the reader to determine whether he/she believes that the loss of personal freedom resulting from the project is justified by the other net benefits.

7. *Discount future values to obtain present values*   For most projects it is necessary to discount costs and benefits occurring at different times. This is usually done using exponential discounting to calculate present values of all future costs and benefits. The choice of an interest rate for this can be difficult, but many organizations that conduct analyses have standard rates to use in their analyses.

8. *Identify and account for uncertainty*   Perhaps the failure to deal with risk or uncertainty is the most common shortcoming in BCA. Many aspects of a project may be subject to uncertainty and these sources of uncertainty should be identified as completely as possible. Examples include construction cost estimates that can vary widely, unpredictable weather that may make outdoor activities more difficult, or varying population growth that can increase or decrease the use of facilities.

    Some attempt should be made to recognize the uncertainty or risk involved in the project. This may be as simple as offering a sensitivity analysis that calculates the value of the project under different outcomes or as complex as a real options analysis that attempts to calculate an explicit value in light of the risk.

9. *Compare benefits and costs*   Having calculated (or at least listed) the costs and benefits, they should be compared to determine whether the project might have a positive net present value (NPV). If multiple projects are being considered, the project with the highest NPV will usually be chosen.

10. *Conduct a post-project analysis*   When possible, a follow-up analysis after completion of the project should be conducted. A post-project analysis can offer direction for the project's managers, determine the quality of the pre-project analysis, serve as a forecast of the *ex post* benefit and help improve future analyses and projects. Ideally a pre-project analysis should provide structure for the post-project analysis.

1.4   ASSIGNING MONETARY VALUES

BCA uses monetary values to compare goods. The values attached to inputs and outputs represent their relative importance in the analysis. If the total value of the outputs is greater than the total value of the inputs, the project is considered desirable because the total importance to society of the outputs is greater than the total importance of the inputs. Although it is necessary for making comparisons, assigning monetary values to inputs and outputs is often controversial and should be done with care and some sensitivity.

Many inputs and outputs will be goods that are regularly traded in markets at well-known and predictable prices. Inputs such as labor, concrete, steel, computers and gasoline or outputs such as electricity can usually be valued at their market prices with adjustments in some special circumstances.

Other inputs and outputs are not directly traded and are more difficult to value. Examples include commuting time saved by a highway project, the value of irrigation services resulting from a dam project, and improved public health from upgraded sewers and water treatment. Values for these goods must be estimated through indirect, complicated and somewhat subjective calculations. The most expedient course of action is usually to find previous studies estimating values for these goods and to use these values in an analysis.

This book offers a list of resources for finding market and non-market values for a wide variety of goods, and guidelines for dealing with multiple, potentially wide-ranging values in your analysis.

1.5   TIME STRUCTURE OF COSTS AND BENEFITS

Most projects are executed over some period of time. In doing a BCA you should determine when the various costs and benefits will occur and what the final time horizon for the analysis, if not the project, should be.

For example, a highway may be built over three years and then used in perpetuity with some necessary maintenance every five years. The construction and maintenance costs will occur at regular intervals while benefits to drivers will be continuous and could increase over time if the population of a region increases. Although the highway could last forever, it may be an administrative guideline to consider only the first twenty years when evaluating the project.

It is generally recognized that benefits and costs occurring in the future are of less value than benefits and costs today.[1] For this reason, it is an accepted practice to discount future costs and benefits using some interest rate and exponential discounting. The most difficult decision usually encountered in this process is deciding on a proper interest rate to use, although many agencies will specify a rate or rates to be used in their analyses. This book will demonstrate the mechanics of discounting and provide a range of interest rates used or advocated by various groups and agencies.

1.6   SENSITIVITY ANALYSIS

There will often be a wide range of proposed numbers attached to any project. Estimates of the amounts of materials and labor required, prices for these inputs, the number of final users, what value to attach to their use and an appropriate rate to use in discounting future costs and benefits may all be subject either to error or to disagreement. The most responsible response to having ranges of estimated or suggested values is to offer calculations based on various scenarios and to discuss the effect that different numbers have in a sensitivity analysis. That is, you should clearly state the effect of changes in various values on the final assessment of the project. For example, if construction costs are 10 percent over the estimate, how will the net benefit of the project change? If a higher interest rate is used to discount future costs and benefits, will the project still be desirable? If the value attached to a project's health benefits are at the low end rather than

---

[1]   There are well-supported disagreements with this idea. Many argue that discounting is inappropriate under some circumstances, and there is a technical suggestion for what rates should be for very long-lived projects of say 100 years or so. See Portney and Weyant (1999).

the high end of the range of estimates, how does the value of the project change?

One common approach is to calculate best-case, worst-case and inter-mediate scenarios. That is, an analyst would first calculate the NPV of a project using the estimates that maximize its calculated value, then the values that minimize its value, and finally some middle values. This will give policy makers an idea of the degree of uncertainty surrounding the project and how important that uncertainty might be.

1.7 RESOURCES

The greatest practical problem in actually doing a BCA may be finding appropriate values for a project's inputs and outputs. Project planners should have some idea of the quantities of inputs that will be used and outputs that will be generated, but how should they be valued?

This book will provide you with a variety of resources and references that provide prices and other values for inputs and outputs, suggested interest rates to use in discounting, and elasticities of demand and supply. We will also offer guidelines for valuing goods not typically traded in markets.

While the list of resources is surely not exhaustive, at the very least it will give the reader a start in finding values needed either to analyze a project or to critically evaluate an existing study.

1.8 THE STRUCTURE OF THIS BOOK

The contents of this book proceed roughly in the order they would be needed in carrying out an analysis.

Chapter 2 discusses some of the legal and theoretical foundations of BCA. Chapter 3 discusses the issue of standing, or whose values will be included in the analysis. This will affect how various payments are treated in an analysis, but more importantly it will determine which costs and benefits will be included.

Most inputs and outputs are traded in markets and can be valued using these market prices and basic supply and demand analysis. Chapter 4 discusses the theory of welfare changes resulting from projects. Chapters 5 and 6 describe methods of valuing inputs and outputs that are traded in markets at well-known prices.

Many goods are not traded in markets and must be valued through other methods. Chapter 7 describes techniques involving shadow values and the contingent valuation method.

Chapter 8 looks at the ways the area of general equilibrium analysis can be applied to BCA and the extent to which its application can affect the results of an analysis.

Once inputs and outputs have been valued, there are a few additional steps in preparing an analysis. Chapter 9 presents the mechanics of discounting and offers some guidance on choosing appropriate interest rates to use in discounting future costs and benefits. Chapter 10 discusses sensitivity and risk analysis, a particularly important consideration when, as is usually the case, there is uncertainty about costs or benefits.

Chapter 11 describes two case studies, illustrating the application of these techniques to real-world questions. The first case study looks at the costs and benefits of a federal policy granting exemptions from fuel taxes to blends of gasoline that include ethanol. The second looks at the costs and benefits of banning the use of cellular phones while driving.

Finally, Chapter 12 offers resources that readers of this book might find useful when either preparing or reviewing analyses including sources for prices, interest rates, elasticity estimates and market quantities.

1.9   TERMS OF ART

As with any discipline there are terms of art whose understanding is necessary to pursuit of the subject. So it is with benefit–cost analysis. This chapter defines fundamental terms. In some cases, more elaborate definitions are given later.

1. *Willingness to pay (WTP)*   The amount that one or more persons are willing to pay for a good.
2. *Willingness to accept (WTA)*   The amount one of more persons is willing to accept for a good.
3. *Benefits*   The sum of the WTPs for changes that are seen as gains and of the WTAs for changes that are seen as restoration of losses.
4. *Costs*   The sum of the WTAs for changes that are seen as losses and of the WTPs for changes that are seen as forgone gains.
5. *Standing*   The right to have one's values counted in a benefit–cost analysis.
6. *Net present value (NPV)*   The amount that needs to be invested at a rate r to yield some future amount. The NPV of a future sum, F, received at time t is: $NPV = F/(1+r)^t$.
7. *Discount rate*   The rate at which future sums are to be discounted to find the NPV.
8. *Shadow price*   The estimated putative price of an unpriced good.

9. *Annuity* A stream of uniform payments.
10. *Kaldor–Hicks (KH)* The usual criteria for benefit–cost analysis. It requires that benefits exceed costs and that a project satisfy a potential compensation test.
11. *Potential compensation test (PCT)* A test of whether a project is worthwhile that requires that winners from a project be able to *hypothetically* compensate the losers. An alternative test (Scitovsky) would require that the losers not be able to bribe the winners.
12. *Aggregate measure (AM)* The same as Kaldor–Hicks except that all sentiments for which there is a WTP are included. Thus, unlike KH, AM includes moral sentiments.
13. *Kaldor–Hicks–Moral (KHM)* Similar to AM but with additional assumptions.

REFERENCES

Portney, Paul R. and John G. Weyant (1999), *Discounting and Intergenerational Equity*, Washington, DC: Resources for the Future.
Zerbe, Richard O., Jr. and Dwight D. Dively (1994), *Benefit–Cost Analysis in Theory and Practice*, New York: Harper Collins College Publishers.

2. Legal and philosophical foundations for benefit–cost analysis

2.1 BENEFIT–COST ANALYSIS AND ITS CRITICS

Benefit–cost analysis (BCA) or cost–benefit analysis[1] (CBA) is a methodological framework first developed in the 1930s that is used in public policy decision making, particularly at the federal level. It has been a staple of public policy analysis for some sixty years.[2] Economists claim that further application of BCA could save billions of dollars annually. The BCA approach also forms the core of a substantial portion of normative thinking about the law associated with law and economics, usually under the rubric of wealth maximization.

The methodology is widely, and repetitively, criticized on foundational grounds. The criticisms concern moral and ethical limitations and, to a much lesser extent, technical ones. A common view is thus that BCA is a flawed science that deprives citizens of the opportunity to participate in democratic processes that bear on the allocation of public resources. Economists and other practitioners actually doing BCAs generally ignore these criticisms. There are three reasons for this. One is that the critics fail to offer viable substitutes, except for rather sketchy references to political discussion. The critics do not compare the results of BCA with those of alternate approaches, so they are unable to answer the question of whether BCA is better than alternatives. Second, they fail to address the issue of whether BCA is useful and, if it is, how it might be improved. Defects found by the critics are generally uncontaminated by actual BCAs so that it is unclear whether, as a matter of fact, these defects exist. Not surprisingly then, practitioners find little to learn from the criticisms. Without determining relative usefulness, how is it possible to argue persuasively against the use of BCA? Third, practitioners are divided, internally and externally, about what BCA is. Critics make one set of assumptions about the nature

---

1 Benefit–cost is more closely associated with the economic approach and cost–benefit closer to the engineering approach.
2 It is not widely used at the municipal level, according to a recent survey by David Layton and Richard Zerbe (2004).

of BCA and the practitioners another. Indeed even among the critics and the practitioners there is no uniformity of concept. The issue of the validity of these criticisms is thus unresolved, and indeed irresolvable within the existing framework, because there is no general agreement about what BCA is, or what it might be.

The criticisms rest on a limited and narrow concept of BCA, but one that derives from its historical origins. The critics see BCA as a sort of mechanical algorithm that falsely claims to provide the answer to the question of what people want. Many see BCA as missing important values such as integrity and equity, as rooted also in a narrow utilitarianism, and as using private values where public values are relevant. It is said further that BCA does not make the necessary exclusions, such that it includes bad values like envy and malice. Critics see BCA as an attempt to combine incommensurables in a single metric so that the answer it provides is without meaning. Others find that it loses legitimacy as it favors the preferences of the rich and is defective or not deserving of our approbation, because it does not consider issues of income distribution or fairness. In so far as it ignores transactions costs it is seen as flawed. A few critics see the Scitovsky (1941) reversal paradox as rendering BCA useless. (The Scitovsky reversal paradox arises when analysis recommends a move from position A to position B and, having arrived at position B, to then recommend a move back to A.)

The responsibility for the failure to provide a clear definition for BCA lies with economists. As the inventors, users and, in general, the proponents of BCA, economists have responsibility for explaining the foundations of their methodology. This they have failed to do. What, for example, is the relation of benefits and costs to legal rights? Is 'bad utility' to be counted? Are moral sentiments to be counted? Is the benefit–cost analyst's role one of providing information to a decision-making process or the answer to a public policy question?

It is unnecessary to hold to the narrow concept of BCA depicted by the critics. There is a more expansive version that is fairly immune to these criticisms. Here we present two archetypal versions of BCA, representing the narrow, older mainstream version (generally referred to as Kaldor–Hicks, or KH) and a different, modified version that emerges from commentary and practice of recent years. The latter version is called Kaldor–Hicks–Moral or KHM. KHM is more clearly grounded in legal rights than is KH, more closely represents preferences, is more realistic about the role for BCA and is more acceptable because it obviates most of the foundational criticisms of BCA. In short, the use of KHM is more likely than KH to come closer to satisfying a Pareto superior test in that its broad use leads to gains for most members of society.

2.2   A HISTORY OF THE KALDOR–HICKS CRITERION

The Pareto Criterion

Vilfredo Pareto (1896) introduced a welfare criterion, the Pareto optimum, which became a foundational concept in welfare theory. A Pareto optimum is a state of affairs such that no one can be made better off without making someone else worse off.[3] A change in the economy is said to represent a Pareto improvement, or to be Pareto superior, if at least one person is made better off as a result of the change and no person is made worse off. The Pareto criterion is similar to a voting role that requires unanimity. The attraction of the Pareto notion of efficiency is that it seems to eliminate interpersonal comparisons of welfare. Its obvious limitation is that it is not very policy relevant; few policies have no losers.[4] This limitation resulted in a search for a more applicable measure of welfare that continues to this day and of which this chapter is a part. The major substitute for the Pareto criterion came to be the potential Pareto criterion or the Kaldor–Hicks criterion.

The Kaldor–Hicks Criterion

Nicholas Kaldor built on the foundation provided by Pareto. The Kaldor–Hicks criterion (KH) is the standard criterion for BCA. It arose out of discussions among prominent British economists during the late 1930s in discussions about repealing the Corn Laws. Before that time it was generally assumed that each individual had an equal capacity for enjoyment, and that gains and losses among different individuals could be directly compared. However, Robbins (1932, 1938) pointed out that interpersonal comparisons of utility cannot rest on a scientific foundation because utility

---

[3]   In its strong form, Pareto efficiency states that state A is preferred to state B when state A is ranked higher than state B for one person and all other persons rank A at least as high as B. If the utility (well-being) of each individual is higher in state A, then state A is preferred according to the weak form of Pareto efficiency.

[4]   We challenge the reader to recommend one in the absence of explicit compensation for losers. Even a voluntary sale of a good by one person to another is probably not Pareto efficient, because even though both the seller and the buyer are better off as a product of the sale, other members of the community may suffer, at least marginally, because the sale might drive the market price up (harming consumers) or down (harming suppliers). Of course, the probable harm to potential buyers and sellers is low, approaching zero, but any potential harm defeats Pareto efficiency.

cannot be measured, and that the justification for such comparisons is more ethical than scientific.[5] By the late 1930s, leading British economists, including the future Nobel Prize winner Sir John Hicks (1939), were raising questions about such policy prescriptions because they were seen to rest on interpersonal comparisons of utility. Economists responded by developing a welfare measure they believed would avoid interpersonal comparisons and that was more broadly applicable than Pareto efficiency.

Nicholas Kaldor (1939) provided a solution while acknowledging Robbins's point about the inability to make interpersonal utility comparisons on any scientific basis; he suggested it could be made irrelevant. He adopted a variant of the Pareto criterion called the potential Pareto criterion. Kaldor (1939, pp. 549–50) suggested that where a policy led to an increase in aggregate real income it was desirable because:

> [T]he economist's case for the policy is quite unaffected by the question of the comparability of individual satisfaction, since in all such cases it is possible to make everybody better off than before, or at any rate to make some people better off without making anybody worse off.

That is, a project is desirable if the money measure of gains exceeds a money measure of losses. Kaldor goes on to note (p. 550) that whether such compensation should take place 'is a political question on which the economist, qua economist, could hardly pronounce an opinion'.[6] Hicks, perhaps the most prominent economist of that time, accepted the Kaldor approach. The approach then became known as the Kaldor–Hicks criterion. The KH criterion is the usual BCA criterion.

The Scitovsky Criterion

A few years after the creation of KH, Scitovsky (1941) introduced a parallel, but slightly different, criterion that states that a project is desirable if the losers are unable in the original state of the world to bribe the potential winners not to undertake the project. Both of these criteria are referred to as potential compensation tests (PCTs). (The KH test is associated with the compensating variation measure of welfare change and the Scitovsky

---

5   Robbins (1938, p. 635) believed it politically expedient to treat all people as if they had the same marginal utility of income but was concerned that this be seen to rest on an ethical not a scientific principle. In fact, he says, '*But I do not believe that, in most cases, political calculations which do not treat them [men] as if they were equal are morally revolting*' (ibid., emphasis added).

6   It was thought that politicians or non-economists should make judgments and decisions about income distribution effects.

criterion with the equivalent variation measure. Scitovsky suggested that both criteria be used.) Shortly after this Hicks showed that the Kaldor and Scitovsky criteria are related to measures of willingness to pay (WTP) or to accept payment (WTA) for a good.

2.3   VIEWS DEFINING THE CHARACTERISTICS OF BCA

The K–H Criterion (the Mainstream View)

The modern version of KH is the mainstream view of BCA. It may be reasonably characterized by the following assumptions: (1) the use of the WTP for gains and the WTA for losses; (2) a reliance on PCTs so that a project is KH efficient only when it passes a PCT; (3) an emphasis on efficiency that is separated from equity; (4) an assumption of equal and constant marginal utility of income so that each person is treated equally, in the sense that a dollar is assumed to have the same value to each person; (5) a recognition and inclusion of non-pecuniary effects; (6) the omission of values represented by moral sentiments; (7) a reliance on externalities and market failure to determine where BCA might be useful in making corrections; (8) an assumption that transactions costs are zero; (9) the treatment of BCA as a mechanism to provide the answer rather than an approach to proving information as part of an ongoing discussion; and (10) the inclusion of wealth maximization as congruent with mainstream BCA.

Unfortunately, KH has been judged a failure with respect to its initial aims. Chipman and Moore (1978), in their trenchant survey of post-1939 welfare economics, conclude that 'judged in relation to its basic objective of enabling economists to make welfare prescriptions without having to make value judgments and, in particular interpersonal comparisons of utility, the New Welfare Economics must be considered a failure' (1978, p. 548).

KHM: A New View

A survey of benefit–cost and theoretical literature reveals an implicit view that differs from KH. This alternative has been called KHM.[7] This view builds on KH. The characteristics of KHM are the following. First, KHM uses WTP for gains and WTA for losses. This is similar to KH but more explicit on this point. Second, KHM uses WTP and WTA from the legal

---

7   And also KHZ, see Zerbe (2001).

status quo, inherently acknowledging existing property rights. Third, KHM excludes gains or losses that are legally illegitimate or that violate well-accepted moral principles. One example of this is that KHM would attach zero value to goods in the hands of a thief and would view the return of these goods to their rightful owner as a benefit rather than merely a transfer. Fourth, KHM recognizes and includes non-pecuniary effects, and in this way is identical to KH. Fifth, KHM uses an efficiency test that is passed when and only when the aggregate benefits exceed aggregate losses rejecting use of the PCT. In this way, KHM is very materially different from KH. Sixth, KHM includes all goods, including moral sentiments, as economic goods as long as there is a WTP from them. (This is also materially different from KH.) Seventh, KHM makes an assumption of equal marginal utility of income so that each person is treated the same, identical to KH. Eighth, KHM does not rely on market failure or externalities to justify the use of BCA, and in this way is different from KH. Ninth, KHM includes transactions costs of operating a project, which is different from KH. Finally, KHM includes an understanding that the role of BCA is to provide information to the decision-making process and not to provide the answer, an understanding that is different from the mainstream view.

This new view shares with KH the use of WTP and WTA but grounds their use in the legal–psychological framework. As with KH, it gives each person the same weight and like KH also includes non-pecuniary effects. Unlike KH, it includes all goods for which there is a WTP, including equity goods and those represented by moral sentiments. Unlike KH, it excludes values that are illegal or widely considered immoral. Unlike KH, it makes no use of PCTs. And, unlike KH it does not rely on market failure to indicate where BCA will be best used. Most importantly, it rests on a different concept of the role of BCA as one of providing information and not of providing the answer, unlike KH.

2.4 CRITICISMS OF KH AND BCA

The criticisms of BCA are extensive and frequent. (For a more extended discussion, see Zerbe, 2005.) They are directed primarily at the KH version.[8] Criticisms are made on technical, political, and moral grounds. Technical criticisms include the absence of any scientific method of aggregating preferences, Scitovsky reversals (again, in which analysis recommends a move from A to B and, having arrived at B, a move back to A),

---

[8] The newer version that we present here is too new to have generated sufficient interest or criticism as of yet.

failure to pass a PCT, a bias in favor of the status quo, and the failure to include transactions costs of achieving a new state of the world. Political criticisms include the fact that BCA is not voting and that private values are used when social values would be more appropriate. Moral criticisms include that values are weighted by income, that equity and fairness and moral values in general are ignored and that BCA fails to exclude bad or morally repugnant values. These criticisms are summarized in Table 2.1.

The Absence of any 'Scientific' Method of Aggregating Preferences

This is not a real criticism. Rather, it is just a fact of nature. Neither BCA nor economics assumes that utility can be measured in a cardinal sense. There can be no utility ranking of people. BCA suggests a social algorithm for aggregating preferences based on the willingness to pay (or accept payment) for them. The moral status of this algorithm rests on its acceptability. This acceptability rests in turn on the acceptability of existing rights and the price system, that is, in property rights in general, which serve to ground BCA. The moral basis of these rights rests on the capacity to increase the well-being of all or most of society. Similarly, the acceptability of BCA rests on the likelihood that the application of the algorithm will over time increase the well-being of all persons. The connection with legal rights is made explicit in KHM.

The Grounding of BCA in Legal Rights

Economic theory takes for granted, far more extensively than either economists or the critics explicitly recognize, the normative force of established rights and obligations. For some time it has been recognized that the policy and welfare implications of any substantive economic analysis depend upon the legitimacy of the property rights that underlie the relevant supply and demand functions. Heyne (1988) notes that, because this legitimacy depends on existing law, the foundations of economics may be said to rest in the law. It is fair to say, however, that economists have not always, or even usually, been clear on this point.

The conventional assumption has been that the WTP and WTA measures will usually lead to similar valuations – under conventional assumptions economists expect that the difference between them will be small in most cases (see Willig, 1976).

KHM is explicit about this connection, which is usually shadowy. Benefits and costs are to be measured as changes from the status quo. Gains from the status quo are measured by the WTP, losses by the WTA. The status quo position is determined by expectations and these expectations

Table 2.1   Criticism of KH and BCA

Criticism	Basis for criticism
1. The absence of any 'scientific' method of aggregating preferences	Utility cannot be measured so we cannot, in general, say if total happiness has increased if a project increases the wealth of some more than it decreases the wealth of others
2. The results of a BCA will reflect the existing pattern of wealth	As a result the results will be unfair
3. BCA rests on market values	Market values are inferior and degrade the value of moral sentiments
4. Status quo bias	Using KH it is possible to suggest a move from A to B but then, having arrived at B to suggest a move back to A, and so on endlessly
5. BCA does not consider the income distribution	Thus it ignores important values
6. Moral vales are neglected	Thus it ignores important values
7. Failure to pass the PCT	Use of KH may not guarantee that a compensation test is passed
8. BCA does not exclude bad utility	Thus it is said to be a deficient moral standard that fails to condemn rape or slavery
9. Failure to consider transactions costs	The efficiency of an operation is judged by comparing it to an alternative that operates without transactions costs
10. BCA is not voting	Voting and political discussion are held to be superior to BCA
11. The use of private values when public values are appropriate	The choices an individual makes as a public citizen may differ from those he/she makes as a private person
12. Scitovsky reversals	KH assumes the existing pattern of rights
13. BCA may result in a neglect of non-quantitative values	Thus it may miss important values
14. The role of BCA: Discussion is better than BCA	Public decisions should be decided in public forums, not by BCA

are defined primarily by legal rights. From a legal perspective, the use of the WTA to measure losses and the WTP to measure gains rests on a normative decision to recognize ownership. Gains and losses are to be measured from a psychological reference point, which stems from beliefs about ownership. Legal rights largely determine one's beliefs about ownership. The WTP measure assumes that one does not have psychological or legal ownership of the good, and asks how much one would pay to obtain it. The WTA measure assumes that one owns the good, and asks how much one would accept to sell it.

One's sense of psychological ownership will usually conform to one's knowledge of legal ownership. Most people feel that they have a moral right to what they legally own, and do not feel that they have the moral right to something they do not own. For most cases, then, the law will determine whether the WTP or WTA will be used even if the economic standard is psychological ownership. The common assumption is that a choice based on assigned legal entitlements will usually be correct, but it is correct because of the correspondence between the legal and psychological states; it is not correct as a matter of principle, and it is incorrect in important cases. The psychological reference point is, however, not just that of the individual but of society generally, so that in so far as the law embodies the general understanding the law should govern. Because the underlying basis is the general psychological reference point, however, where this differs from the law, it furnishes a guide for further development as indeed it has done with the development of common law.

Measurement of Benefits and Costs

Part of the moral justification of BCA lies in its grounding in legal rights. How is this applied in practice? Benefits and costs are measured, respectively, by the WTP and by the WTA with KHM as with KH.[9] The WTP reflects the amount that someone who does not have a good would be willing to pay to buy it; it is the maximum amount of money one would give up to buy some good or service, or would pay to avoid harm.[10] The WTA reflects the amount that someone who has the good would accept to sell it; it is the

---

[9] Zerbe and Dively (1994).

[10] These are non-technical definitions and, as such, are not wholly accurate. The compensating variation (CV) is the sum of money that can be taken away or given to leave one as well off as one was *before* the economic change. The equivalent variation (EV) is money taken or given that leaves one as well off as *after* the economic change. See Zerbe and Dively (1994, Ch. 5), for a derivation of these concepts in terms of indifference curves.

minimum amount of money one would accept to forgo some good, or to
bear some harm. The benefits from a project may be either gains (WTP) or
losses restored (WTA). The costs of a project may be either a loss (WTA) or
a gain forgone (WTP). Both the benefits and the costs are the sum of the
appropriate WTP and WTA measures. Thus, the relation of benefits and
costs to the WTP and the WTA may be measured in the following manner:

Benefits   The sum of the WTPs for changes that are seen as gains and of the
WTAs for changes that are seen as restoration of losses.

Costs   The sum of the WTAs for changes that are seen as losses and of the
WTPs for changes that are seen as forgone gains.

The measurements are summarized in Table 2.2.[11] Note that whether a
change is a benefit or cost is a different question from whether it is a gain

Table 2.2   *The measurement of benefits and costs in terms of gains
and losses*

	Gain	Loss
Benefits	Consumers	Consumers
	WTP – the sum of CVs for a positive change – is finite	WTA – the sum of EVs for a positive change – could be infinite
	Producers	Producers
	WTP – the sum of EVs for a positive change – is finite	WTA – the sum of CVs for a positive change – could be infinite.
	Gain forgone	Loss restored
Costs	Consumers	Consumers
	WTP – the sum of EVs for a negative change – is finite	WTA – the sum of CVs for a negative change – could be infinite
	Producers	Producers
	WTP – the sum of CVs for a negative change – is finite	WTA – the sum of EVs for a negative change – is finite

[11]   The difference between benefits and costs is simply their sign: positive for
benefits and negative for costs. Thus, without loss of accuracy, costs can be
counted as negative benefits and benefits can be counted as negative costs.

or a loss. The point here is that benefits are not measured exclusively by the WTP, or costs exclusively by the WTA. Benefits are measured by the WTA, where benefits include losses restored, and costs are measured by the WTP, where they include gains forgone. The rationale for this arrangement lies in the individual's psychology.

The justification for adopting these methods of measurement is that they correspond with the psychological sense of gains and losses, which will also generally accord with legal rights.

The Effect of Wealth on Willingness to Pay or Accept

Wealth will in general generate higher values for the WTP or the WTA. Just as people with more income or wealth can purchase more goods, so also will the values for projects reflect the incomes of the individuals affected. In any BCA, wealth will play a role in the outcome. This is seen as a major problem by some critics, yet the recognition of the existing pattern of legal wealth is simply consistent with the KHM recognition of existing legal rights. The objection is at base not to BCA but to the existing pattern of rights. KHM provides a mechanism for changing this pattern by the recognition of sentiments toward greater equity.

Consider a project to locate a municipal incinerator in one of two neighborhoods, one rich and one poor. Neither neighborhood wants it. The amount required to hypothetically compensate the persons in the richer neighborhood will usually be considerably more than for the poorer neighborhood. That is, the WTA payment to put up with the incinerator by the rich will be greater than the WTA payment by the poor. In addition, the land for the incinerator will generally be cheaper in the poorer neighborhood. Thus the benefit–cost criterion will usually lead to location of a NIMBY ('not in my backyard') in a poorer rather than a richer neighborhood. The result can be changed, however, by changing existing rights. For example, suppose that each neighborhood had a right to reject the incinerator. The authority would then have to purchase the right from the neighborhood so that there would be actual rather than hypothetical compensation. The result would likely still be the location of the NIMBY in the poorer neighborhood but the poorer neighborhood would be better off; it would in fact now be somewhat richer.

Just as people with more income or wealth can purchase more goods, so also will the values for projects reflect the incomes of the individuals affected. That is, the values are income dependent. This fact is a result of the more fundamental property of Kaldor–Hicks – that it takes existing rights as given.

Market Values

Because BCA rests on market values, its values are said to be degraded by putting a price on them, as if the value of life could or should be monetized or that one would, for example, put a monetary value on friendship or preventing the abuse of one's children. In general, critics of BCA object to what they see as the limitations of market values, which are embedded in normative economic analysis; in this view, economics is concerned only with market values.[12]

The purpose of BCA analysis is not to monetize values, but rather to provide a ranking of choices expressed in monetary terms. In the language of BCA, the market is a *metaphor* for a mechanism for determining value. Market values, in the language of the metaphor, need not represent 'mere commodities' but instead represent choices. Choices, of course, exist outside a commodity-type market. Goods that are not purchased with money may nevertheless be ranked in monetary terms.

The distinction is crucial. For instance, the value that I place on a friendship is not one that is or that I wish was determined in a commodity market. When I harm my friend by canceling a lunch appointment at the last minute in order to attend a lecture of particular interest (Sunstein, 1997, pp. 73–4),[13] I do not compensate or offer to compensate my friend by offering a sum of money. Yet I might perform other acts – perhaps acts with a monetary value – which are consistent with friendship, to show its value to me. I might offer to drive him when he needs a lift; I might give him a present; I might agree to participate in an activity he enjoys. So when I talk about the value of friendship and its value in the 'market for friendship', I am merely calling attention to the fact that friendship has a value. More important, in missing the lunch to attend the lecture, I am making a choice, and the role of BCA is to reflect that choice. The value of friendship, in principle, has been neither missed nor undervalued by BCA.

---

12   The criticism is elegantly expressed by Lumley (1997, p. 72): '[I]f a single discount rate is applied to environmental resources, the implications of non-monetary aspects of those resources are often ignored for these intangible factors are the ends to which money is not a means'.

13   Sunstein (1997, p. 81) notes: '[W]e may believe that goods are comparable without believing that they are commensurable'. I would say further that the use of monetary figures to rank preferences can be done even where the choices are not made with respect to a monetized frame of reference. We do not think of friendships in terms of money, but we make trade-offs with respect to them. The problem of the effect on future generations of using the discount rate and the problem of estimating losses are endemic to any decision-making process that uses information.

The legitimate concern is whether or not presenting values in monetary terms, as BCA does, distorts their discussion. There is no evidence that it does but this remains a possibility.

Status Quo Bias

The KH criterion assumes the rights and duties extant in the status quo. This has been said to be an undesirable bias. It can lead to a situation in which starting from point A, no move to B is justified. Yet starting from B, no move to A is justified. This is shown in Table 2.3, in which Person 1 is the winner in a move from A to B, but Person 2 is the winner in a move from B to A.

KH for a move from A to B will be the difference between the winner's (Person 1) WTP for the move, $100, and the loser's (Person 2) WTA for the move, $105, or −$5. The move does not satisfy the KH test and the status quo, A, is favored over the move to B. Now starting from position B, KH would give us the difference between the winner's (this is now Person 2) WTP of $90 and the loser's (this is now Person 1) WTA of $120, or −$30. As before, the status quo is favored. Thus position A is best if we start with A and position B is best if we start with B. Thus the outcome is determined by the status quo.

Critics of BCA call this effect a status quo bias, and see it in a pejorative light. We think that a criterion that recognizes existing rights is desirable and certainly the only sort the public will accept. Who would want anything different? The status quo bias simply recognizes existing rights. This seems a desirable characteristic in any criterion that will actually be used and will actually be useful.

For example, for many years the Pacific Lumber Company has been trying to cut the last privately owned stand of ancient redwoods from the Headwaters Grove in Northern California. The value of these trees as timber is $300 million. Environmental groups have thwarted the company's efforts for many years. If we start with the state of the world as one in which

Table 2.3   The status quo effect

Persons	WTP	WTA
Person 1	100	120
Person 2	−90	−105
KH for a move from A to B	$100−$105=−$5	
KH for a move from B to A	$90−$120=−$30	

the lumber company has the legal right to cut, then it is doubtful that the environmental groups would have the WTP to buy them off. That is, the environmental groups might not be able to pay the $300 million required. However, from the success of the environmental groups the legal right to cut is not so clear. Suppose that the environmental groups are found to have the right to preserve the Grove. It is doubtful, and certainly at least possible, that they would sell this right to the lumber company for anything like the value of timber. Thus the legal right would determine the outcome. This hardly seems undesirable.

BCA Does Not Consider Income Distribution

No criticism of the KH criteria is more widespread than that they neglect distributional effects (Zerbe, 1991). The views of the former Solicitor General of the United States, Charles Fried (1978, p. 93), are representative. He sees the economic analysis of rights as using a concept of efficiency that is removed from distributional questions. He believes that economic analysis does not consider whether the distribution is fair or just. He then concludes from this that the fact that a given outcome is efficient does not give it 'any privileged claim to our approbation' (p. 94). The view that efficiency is unconcerned with distributional issues, or with fairness, is widespread in both law and economics (Zerbe, 1998).

Economists often hold that distributional effects are irrelevant for their analysis, that it is not part of their job to consider distributional effects. This view of BCA is, of course, consistent with the origins of KH. More often economists have maintained that both efficiency and distribution are relevant but that they are best considered separately. The defense for KH is that it is only meant to measure efficiency and that distributional effects can be considered separately and addressed in other ways.

Economists have not, however, been entirely bound by KH in considering distributional effects. There have been many suggestions for giving weight to distributional effects. Most of these involve assigning weights to people on the basis of their income (see Zerbe and Dively, 1994, Ch. 13). None of these approaches has gained great acceptance, presumably because there is no agreement on what the weights should be. Whatever value this criticism has for KH, it has none for KHM for this approach explicitly considers income and equity.

KH Neglects Moral Values: A Definition of Moral Sentiments

The KH criterion has existed for more than sixty years without directly facing the issue of whether moral sentiments should be included in normative economic analysis.[14] By moral sentiments we mean those involving concern for other beings. Moral sentiments include also immoral sentiments such as might arise when one wishes harm to others, or is envious.[15]

One may care about others from one's own perspective as when a parent requires a child to eat spinach when the child would rather not. This is paternalistic altruism. One may have an existence value for goods unrelated to their use or to goods based on their use or appreciation by others that can reflect either paternalistic or non-paternalistic altruism or both. According to Johansson (1992a), it is far from unusual that non-use values such as bequest values and benevolence toward friends and relatives are claimed to account for 50 to 75 percent of the total WTP for an environmental project. In economic terms we say that moral sentiments exist when there is a WTP for them.

The criticism of KH's neglect of income distribution effects is part of a more general class of criticism of its neglect of moral values. The usual argument goes that BCA is derived from utilitarianism and, as such, is missing important values such as integrity, the importance of standing on principle, and keeping promises. For example, Williams (Williams and Smart, 1973) considers the case of George:

> George, who has taken his Ph.D. in chemistry, finds it extremely difficult to get a job. An older chemist who knows about the situation says that he can get George a decently paid job in a certain laboratory, which pursues research into chemical and biological warfare. George says that he cannot accept this, because he is opposed to chemical and biological warfare. The older man replies that George's refusal is not going to make the job or the laboratory go away; what is more, he happens to know that if George refuses to take the job, it will certainly go to a contemporary of George's who is not inhibited by any such scruples, and who is likely, if appointed, to push along the research with greater zeal than George would. What should George do?

Williams argues that under a utilitarian analysis, George must accept the job, because it improves the position of his family, and advances the work more slowly (a desirable aim). The critics see BCA as an expression

---

14 This is due in part to historical reasons, in part to normal inertia associated with any academic discipline, and in part because existence values are a relatively new idea.

15 One may care about others as a result of kinship, empathy, envy or hatred or as a matter of justice. Charity is an expression of moral sentiment. One may care about others from their perspective (one cares about their utility function) and this is called non-paternalistic altruism.

of utilitarianism and so they see the values they claim as missing in utilitarianism as missing in BCA.

This line of attack is not valid as BCA does not rest on utilitarianism of this sort. Rather BCA is a pragmatic approach whose justification must lie in its usefulness; economists understand this and as a result have paid little attention to this sort of criticism. Nevertheless, as we have seen, the KH version of BCA is missing important values, equity concerns and, at least arguably, moral values in general.[16]

Yet these missing values are explicitly considered in KHM. Moreover their inclusion can yield a different and superior result to that of KH. Both the sign and magnitude of the difference between benefits and costs using KHM can differ from KH. If moral sentiments are regarded as pertinent to human welfare then the KHM results will be superior to those of KH. And surely such values are pertinent to human welfare.

There is dispute among economists about the desirability of including moral values. Thus at this time KHM is not wholly accepted. Five arguments have been advanced against inclusion of moral sentiments in BCA. It is said that their inclusion may result in: (i) the acceptance of projects that fail to pass a PCT, (ii) the irrelevancy and/or double counting of benefits, (iii) different weights being assigned to different individuals, (iv) the inclusion of purely redistributive policies, and (v) the inclusion of undesirable sectarian sentiments.

The first criticism is true but applies only in uninteresting cases where moral sentiments are weak and the number of people with such sentiments is small (Zerbe et al., 2006). The second criticism has been shown to be incorrect (Zerbe, 2002; Zerbe et al., 2006). The third is a matter of semantics. It seems to be more accurate to say simply that a dollar is viewed the same no matter who receives it in terms of the recipient's welfare. Others, altruists, may gain but this is just from the purchase of a good, moral satisfaction. The fourth criticism is true by definition but we would regard this as a virtue, not a defect. The fifth is not a valid criticism of KHM as the concept of standing vitiates this criticism.

Surely the language of BCA is not the right language to use in determining the right thing to do in situations involving issues of fundamental values. Critics are no doubt right that BCA is of little aid in the tasks by which community values are formed or in deciding issues of fundamental

---

16 For example, in the Tennessee Valley Authority (TVA) analysis of the Tellico Dam, the value of sacred burial grounds to the Cherokee was ignored. This might, however, be more properly regarded as a failure, if it is a failure (and we think it is), of the legal system to specify rights in accord with reasonable psychological expectations (Zerbe and Dively, 1994).

values. Nevertheless the point is almost wholly irrelevant. Who would think that BCA was the best or only tool for this task?[17] When a BCA approach is applied to a question of fundamental values the typical result is that the legal starting point determines the outcome. That is, no answer can be given without specifying the right that is the subject of the question.

BCA is dependent on community values. If these values are thought immoral or deficient, the BCA will also be deficient. Why would it be otherwise? What would be worse is for the analyst to substitute his or her own values, giving or taking away standing without mandate. BCA rests on societal values and this is both its strength and a possible weakness.

Failure to Pass a Potential Compensation Test (PCT)

This is a criticism of KHM not of KH. Milgrom (1993) argues that non-paternalistic moral sentiments should not be included in BCA because it may lead to violations of the PCT. He considers a project that costs $160 and affects two people, U and A. Individual U bears no costs of the project and has a gain of $100. Individual A's gain from the project is $50 + 0.5 times U's net surplus. Thus A has a gross gain of $100 at a cost of $160 for a net loss of $60. The project passes a cost–benefit test if altruism is included, but fails if altruism is excluded. (The net benefits are $200 − $160 = $40 and $150 − $160 = −$10, respectively.) Less evident is that the project fails the PCT: each dollar that U gives A in compensation provides a net benefit to A of only $0.50, so even transferring U's entire $100 gain cannot overcome A's initial net loss of $60. Milgrom concludes that altruism and other moral sentiments should not be included in BCAs.

This is a theoretical possibility but not a practical one. As long as the sum of moral sentiments across all altruists is greater than one, the PCT will be passed. The student should reconsider Milgrom's example, letting the aggregate moral sentiment be greater than one. The student will find it impossible to construct a failure to pass the PCT.

Why Include the PCT? A Difference Between KH and KHM

An important difference between KH and KHM is that the former requires the PCT but the latter does not. The PCT has no claim to our moral sentiments. The fact that a project passes the PCT does not mean that losers can actually be compensated. Actual compensation is not costless, so actual compensation can take place only if the net gains are sufficient to cover

---

17   Maybe Richard Posner, but Posner is neither a proficient user of BCA nor a careful analyst of its use.

both the compensation of losers and the cost of making the compensation. Thus PCT cannot claim the virtue of providing for actual compensation when desired. Moreover, this sort of information about compensation is valuable only if we value moral sentiments.

Moreover, there is good reason to abandon the PCT. Returning to the previous example: suppose A's benefit from the project is $40 + 1.5$ times U's net surplus. Then A has costs of $160 and benefits of $40 + (1.5)($100) = 190. So this would pass a PCT because there is no need for compensation. Excluding altruism, though, the project still does not pass KH. Thus KH can reject a project that passes the PCT. In this example, KH rejects the project even though it is a Pareto improvement because both A and U gain. Following the PCT therefore leads us afoul of what may be the most fundamental principle of BCA: never pass up an opportunity to make a Pareto improvement.

The moral basis of KH lies powerfully in the argument that its use will increase wealth and will likely result in all, or at least most, groups gaining over time from its application as long as losers in one period become winners in the next. This justification, however, applies more strongly to KHM with its inclusion of moral sentiments than to KH. One common argument against KH is that it is dependent on income so that the losers are more likely to be the poor, and that having lost, they are ever more likely to lose in subsequent rounds. This is less likely under KHM as long as there are moral sentiments in favor of avoiding income losses by the poor. In sum, the PCT does not convey useful information about whether a project is desirable beyond the requirement that net benefits be positive.

If we are going to consider distributional effects as is required under the aggregate measure (AM), then the justification for mere hypothetical compensation does not arise. The argument for dropping the PCT is that it does not work for us. The justification for BCA is that its use will tend to increase the well-being of all groups over time as long as the increase in wealth which its uses produces is spread over all.

The Failure to Exclude Bad Values

This criticism is best addressed by the concept of standing introduced earlier. The fifth criticism rests on noting that it would be necessary to include negative moral sentiments such as hatred and envy as well as good moral sentiments. This is true but the analyst should not be in the position of suggesting what are bad and good values unless the legal guidelines are clear. Gains consistent with values that are either illegal or immoral (theft being an example of the former and, perhaps, sadism as an example of the latter) would represent benefits to which the beneficiary has no property right and, thus, are of zero value. As an example, if a person takes pleasure in the knowledge that a hate crime has occurred, this pleasure should have no value attached to it because the hate crime represents an infringement on another's rights and is, in some sense, comparable to theft.

Now it is true that BCA will embody bad values as well as good. But it will not embody all bad values. Just as legal rights determine whether one has standing so that a thief has no standing to have his value of the stolen goods count in BCA, so also will reasonably clear public sentiment about value determine whether envy or malice or such sentiments count. Sen (1982, pp. 7–9) has written of the example of Ali, modified here as follows:

> Ali is a successful shopkeeper who has built up a good business in London since emigrating from East Africa. He is hated by a group of racists, and a particular gang of them, the bashers, would like to beat him up. In fact the WTP of the bashers, because there are so many of them, exceeds the WTA of Ali.

Yet allowing the bashing of Ali does not pass KHM as the bashers have no standing to have their desire to bash counted; it is against the law. In the context of BCA itself, the law can be taken as the results of a prior BCA that justifies making assault and battery illegal. Were we to consider the question of whether battery should be illegal, in a BCA framework the sentiments of the bashers should count. It is not unreasonable to extend this sort of clear case to instances in which envy or malice or similar values are ignored because there is a social decision that they should be, that is, to ignore such values would itself pass KHM. The fact is that we have never encountered an instance in which values of envy or malice were counted in a BCA.

Illegitimate Preferences

Including moral sentiments in KHM potentially allows the possibility of including bad sentiments. The issue is not, in fact, confined to moral sentiments but to bad acts or goods generally, and thus is also an issue for KH. This issue, sometimes referred to as the issue of bad utility, is discussed extensively in the philosophic and legal literature. (For example, see Posner, 1981, and Sen, 1982.) Critics are concerned that BCA will count 'bad utility' along with good.

Martha Nussbaum (2000) makes the general point: WTP does not make the necessary exclusionary moves, for example, omitting preferences based on ignorance or hate preferences deformed by malice, envy, resentment or fear, and preferences that reflect adaptation to a bad state of affairs. This claim is that BCA ignores legal and moral rights, but as we have seen any well-grounded BCA must make the exclusionary moves; these moves rely on existing rights as embodied by the legal system, which shows that certain values have no standing.

KHM does make the necessary exclusionary moves (Zerbe (1998, 2001). It cannot, however, do this on its own. The values calculated in BCA necessarily and by definition rely on the sentiments of society so that they are dependent on the prior determination of rights particularly as embodied in law. Zerbe (1998, p. 419) notes that 'values in BCA rest in large measure on law'.

The policy literature has since 1986 included the concept of 'standing' that determines whether one's values are to count in an economic analysis. On this basis Zerbe (1991, 2001) has argued that the thief's valuation of his stolen goods ought not to count, on the basis that theft is illegal. By extension one can reject values of envy or malice. Neither the analyst nor the philosopher should substitute his/her own values or those of Quiggin (1991) and Nussbaum, for example, for those of society more generally in undertaking a BCA whose values purport to reasonably represent those of society. BCA cannot do what philosophy has not, namely rest on a set of widely accepted ethical principles that stand apart from social sentiments. Such a set of principles is needed but does not yet exist.

At the most basic level the assignment of gains and losses depends on rights. The decision to use the WTP rather than the WTA or vice versa rests on legal rights. When one gains a right to a good one did not previously own, this gain is measured by the WTP. When, however, one gives up a right this is properly measured by the WTA, so that legal ownership determines the starting point of analysis. That is, valuation depends on rights. This understanding clarifies the following problem of the thief.[18]

Derek sues Amartya for stealing his book. He asks for the return of the book and costs. Derek is poor and Amartya is rich. Derek loves the book but Amartya cares only a little for it. Derek would have sold the book to Amartya for $2 had he had it. Amartya values it at $3. A benefit–cost analyst hired by Amartya testifies at trial that the value of the book is greater for Amartya than for Derek in the sense that Amartya's willingness to pay exceeds Derek's willingness to accept. So, the BCA suggests that wealth is maximized if the book goes to Amartya. The court finds, however, that Amartya did, in fact, steal the book, and awards the book to Derek, the BCA notwithstanding.

KHM does not, however, award the book to Derek. Consider a real world analog to the Derek–Amartya problem. A major national utility collected payments one month in advance. When customers discontinued service, the company kept the credit balances unless explicitly requested by

---

[18] Zerbe (1998).

the customer to return them. The result was that the company retained
several million dollars in this way. The company agreed to stop this practice. The issue that arose was whether the company should be required to
return the existing credit balances. Any BCA approach (ignoring any
deterrence effects) that gives the thief's valuation of the stolen goods standing will result in the conclusion that the company should keep the funds
because there are transactions costs incurred in their return.

The KHM answer to both the Derek–Amaryta problem and the FTC's
(Federal Trade Commission) problem is that the thief can have no claim to
the funds or to the book; the value of stolen goods in the hands of the thief
is zero. Such a conclusion is derived from the legal status of theft.

Benefit–Cost Analysis Ignores Transactions Costs

The criticism here is that economists often compare a project in the real
world against what is economically efficient, while the efficient scheme is an
ideal that could not be reached because the actual costs of its operation are
not fully considered. This is a criticism applied to economic theory in many
instances. It does not apply, however, to a properly done BCA. The requirement to consider such costs is more explicit for KHM.

BCA Is Not Voting

The argument here is that voting is superior to BCA as it gives an equal
weight to all voters. However, it is very doubtful that voting is always superior. First, many people do not vote and these tend to be the poorer and
less educated. Second, elections can be greatly influenced by money. Third,
voting does not allow an aggregation of preferences as does BCA. I may
care greatly that the Headwaters Grove not be cut and be willing to pay a lot
to prevent it. My neighbor cares little either way but has a slight preference
for cutting the Grove and using the timber. We each have one vote and
count equally so that the intensity of sentiments is lost in voting where it
might not be in BCA. BCA can be useful in its own right; it does not claim
to be voting. The two methods approach decisions in very different ways
and one should not be seen as a substitute for the other.

The Use of Private Values When Public Values Are Appropriate

Several philosophers have devoted significant effort to distinguishing our
preferences as consumers from our preferences as citizens. For example, out
of need we might allow our child to work, but may generally be in favor of
child labor laws. What makes these philosophers critics of BCA is that they

go on to assume or to show in specific instances that BCA measures values only as privately appropriated goods. For example, the use of wage premiums for dangerous jobs to measure the value of life has been criticized on the grounds that these premiums also reflect the risks people feel obliged to assume in order to discharge their responsibilities and not just their own value of life. (See Anderson, 1993.)

This criticism cannot be a criticism in principle but one of practice. BCA attempts to measure the value of changes in the state of the world. These criticisms are useful in pointing out additional care that may need to be taken if gathering or interpreting data.

Scitovsky Reversals

Scitovsky showed that it is possible to use KH to recommend a move from a state of the world A to a new one B and then, having arrived at B, to recommend a move back from B to A. The example in Table 2.4 illustrates this. The KH value of the move from A to B is the WTP for Person 1, who would be a gainer, and the WTA for Person 2, who would be a loser. This would be $100 − $95 or $5. For a move back from B to A the signs get reversed, as do the winners and losers. The KH value of a move back from B to A would be WTP for Person 2 minus the WTA for Person 1. Because the move is from B back to A, Person 2 gains and the WTP is positive. Similarly the WTA for Person 1 will be negative, so the KH value is $90−$80 or $20. Thus we have a situation in which KH suggests a move from A to B and then back again ad infinitum. This has been held, for example, by Jules Coleman (1980), to destroy the usefulness of KH.

It does not, however. Reversibility cannot occur unless the move to the new state of the world is an inferior good for at least one person. For a normal good, WTA > WTP by definition. Notice that for Person 1, the move from A to B involves a WTA less than the WTP. This means that the move is like an inferior good for Person 1. The student can demonstrate to his or her own satisfaction that no such move is possible unless inferiority is involved. Thus this result is more of a curiosity than a meaningful criticism. Moreover, the existence of inferior goods is not enough to cause reversal; it is a necessary but not a sufficient condition.

Table 2.4 Scitovsky reversals

Value of a move from A to B	WTP	WTA
Person 1	$100	$80
Person 2	−$90	−$95

The Neglect of Non-quantitative Values

A realistic criticism noted by a number of commentators is that BCA tends
to bring undue focus on values that are quantified and thus on those that
are most easily quantified. That is, in using BCA, hard numbers tend to drive
out soft. This problem justifies efforts to ameliorate it through the presentation of BCA results to give due weight to factors that are not explicitly
valued. Complete listing of factors not explicitly valued in an analysis allows
a reader to reach his/her own conclusion about a project's desirability.

The Role of BCA

Under KH, economists often assume that the BCA furnishes the answer.
The KHM approach sees BCA as furnishing information for the decision-
making process. This understanding that the role of BCA is to provide information to the decision-making process immediately obviates many and
probably most of the criticisms of it. Some see BCA as foreclosing deliber-
ate and intelligent deliberation. But if the BCA is seen simply as providing
relevant information then it does not foreclose deliberation. In our experience it encourages it. It does this by proving a framework for discussion that
allows data to be challenged, allows new data to be provided, and increases
the transparency of the process. Our experience is that BCA helps to subvert
blatant special interest regulations or decisions. A very great advantage is
that it provides a framework for questioning and refutation. Instances of
agency bias in preparing BCAs are widespread, but these biases will be
expressed in other more opaque ways in the absence of BCA. The advantage of BCAs is that they can be questioned and changed. Example 2A
shows the difference between a KH and a KHM evaluation of two projects.

EXAMPLE 2A   TWO SCHOOL PROJECTS

The two projects, A and B, have already been completed. You have
been asked to perform an after-the-fact evaluation of these projects to provide data for future projects. Project A involved building
a new school in a poor neighborhood. Project B involved placing a
new school in an affluent neighborhood. It is known that in both
building projects some fraud occurred and that there were fraudu-
lent gains (gains to the thief). It is also known that certain members
of the affluent community believed that Project A would materially
benefit members of the poor neighborhood and were willing to pay
to locate the school there, even though the affluent members were

not members of that community and would receive no direct benefit. The table shows the gains and losses of the three parties: the users of the school, the altruists who care about Project A but not about Project B, and the perpetuator of fraud who stole funds from both projects. For Project A the assumption is that the gains of the altruists are 1.2 times the gains to the users minus costs to the altruists of $230, who are assumed here to bear part of the cost of the school.

	A		B		A'		B'	
	KHM	KH	KHM	KH	KHM	KH	KHM	KH
Net gains to users	200	200	260	260	250	250	310	310
Net gains to altruists	10	−230	−230	−230	70	−230	−230	−230
Net gains from theft to thief	Not counted	50	0	60	0	0	0	0
Total net gains	210	20	30	90	320	20	80	80

Using KHM, Project A (building the school in the poorer neighborhood) has the greatest net value. In arriving at this value the altruistic sentiment is counted. In arriving at this result, KHM ignores the value to the thief, while this is counted by KH. In this example, it might be argued that in future projects, if theft could be prevented, this value would then accrue to the users. In this case the value to users would be $250 for Project A, shown as Project A', and, under KHM, would be $70 to altruists so that the total net value would be $320. This sentiment is ignored under KH. The result is that under KH, Project B appears to have the greatest value. Under KH, Project A would have the same value whether or not theft could be prevented. In evaluating Project B, the KH net value is unchanged, while the KHM value would increase by $60 for a total of $110.

The KHM criterion gives a better representative of actual preferences by taking into account the altruistic preferences, and by counting society's preferences regarding theft. For example, suppose that the fraud has been discovered and the issue is whether the money is to be returned. If the value of the stolen money to the theft is counted, return could never be justified under KH because the costs of return would always produce a negative net value. Under KHM, the return is justified as long as the return costs are less than the value to the legitimate recipients.

The Choice of a Foundation for BCA

We have presented two archetypes of BCA. Both are consistent with existing literature. The KH version closely represents what a majority of economists have in mind when they refer to BCA. The KHM version is a newer development and has attracted proponents in recent years. The understanding of what is meant by BCA is changing, however slowly and controversially, from the mainstream view to what we have called the KHM view. For example, the importance of defining gains and losses from a status quo position is now recognized by many, if not yet most, economists. The concept of standing, as one used to make proper exclusions that reflect broad public sentiments, has found its way into textbooks and is increasingly cited in the literature. The critics of BCA have made gains transforming its role to that of providing information to a decision-making process rather than one of providing the answer itself. Those doing practical BCA have shown that they cannot ignore transactions costs. Finally, increasing attention has been paid to moral sentiments.

The tension between the concept of BCA as a market-based analysis that attempts to mimic the market and the practice of ignoring distributional effects is clear. For a BCA to disagree with the workings of free enterprise in such a situation is truly astounding.

The best example of the transformation process is found in the economics literature dealing with moral sentiments. The recent interest in moral sentiments has been driven by interest in donations to charity, funding of public goods and environmental valuation. Economists have been interested in the fact that private donations to public goods occur when free riding is expected instead. For many economists it has become important to understand the role of social and cultural factors like altruism and 'warm glow'. Similarly, in environmental economics recognition of the importance of non-use values is intrinsically bound with issues of moral sentiments. This is particularly the case with existence values. Respondents to surveys and to experiments show a willingness to pay for the existence of environmental amenities that will be used by people other than the respondents themselves.

It seems certain that the trend toward the inclusion of moral sentiments in welfare analysis, including BCA, will continue. They are simply too important; and if they are being examined in the experimental literature, they will, in time, come to be examined also in the policy and benefit–cost literature. The technical objections are already proving to be unimportant.

Table 2.5 summarizes the criticisms and the replies offered, respectively, by KH and KHM.

Table 2.5   Criticisms of and responses by KH and KHM

Criticism	KH response	KHM response
1. The absence of any 'scientific' method of aggregating preferences	The fact that utility cannot be measured is a fact of nature. This is not a criticism	The issue is whether a rule that in general approves of projects that increase aggregate wealth, and that rests on existing rights, is useful and broadly acceptable
2. The results of BCA reflect the pattern of existing wealth	This is true, but the criticism, if any, should be directed at the pattern of wealth, not at BCA	This is true, but the criticism, if any, should be directed at the pattern of wealth, not at BCA
3. BCA rests on market values	This is true but is not bad	These values simply reflect existing rights
4. Status quo bias	True, but not a defect	True, but arising from a respect for rights and is thus not a defect
5. BCA does not consider the income distribution	True, this is a defect in KH	Not a true criticism of KHM
6. Moral values are neglected	True, this is a defect in KH	Untrue, this is not the case with KHM
7. Failure to pass the PCT	True, but only in trivial cases	True in trival cases, but irrelevant as the PCT has no moral claim
8. BCA does not exclude bad utility	True, but why should it?	True, but why should it?
9. Failure to consider transactions costs	Sometimes true	Not true
10. BCA is not voting	BCA is not a substitute for voting but a complement	BCA is not a substitute for voting but a complement
11. The use of private values when public values are appropriate	Not a true criticism in principle. Whatever values used should be as inclusive as possible to include public and private	Not a true criticism in principle. Whatever values used should be as inclusive as possible to include public and private
12. Scitovsky reversals	These are seen as a problem	Scitovsky reversals apply only when the WTA for one person is greater than the WTP for the good or project in question. This can only

Table 2.5   (continued)

Criticism	KH response	KHM response
		occur when the good or project involves inferior goods. Since inferior goods are uncommon such reversals will be uncommon. Even if there are inferior goods reversal may not occur because inferiority is a necessary but not sufficient condition for reversal
13. BCA may result in a neglect of non-quantitative values	True, but these values can always be included verbally	True, but these values can always be included verbally
14. The role of BCA: discussion is better than BCA	Public decisions should be decided in public forums, not by BCA	Public decisions should be decided in public forums, not by BCA
15. A project that passes KH may fail to pass the PCT	This is seen as a problem for KH	Traditionally the PCT is defined as a situation in which a hypothetical transfer could compensate the losers. This does not apply to KHM, as it abandons the PCT. This failure can only happen (1) if there are inferior goods involved or (2) if there are weak moral sentiments involved. Thus here again this is unlikely. The historical purpose of the PCT was to separate equity considerations from economic analysis. Thus, a better defense lies in considering moral sentiments, including those concerned with equity, directly in which case there is no need for the PCT
16. Equity effects and fairness effects are not considered	This is seen as a deflect for KH	This is true of KH though some BCAs attempt to consider such effects. It is not true of KHM

2.5 CONCLUSION

BCA is not meant to be a recipe for all seasons. It is not the appropriate language for the most fundamental and important decisions. We do not
discuss the great moral decisions or questions of our time solely, if at all,
in benefit–cost terms. BCA takes rights as given and is meant to mimic the
market in most respects. Its virtue is that it is practical, useful, generally
acceptable, notwithstanding the extensive academic criticism, and it is
generally recognized as useful. It is not meant to furnish the decision, but
rather to furnish a framework for discussion and for analysis, and to
provide information relevant to a decision. When its legitimate claims are
understand to be modest, most of the criticisms of it disappear. The
remaining criticisms of its failure to consider equity and, arguably, moral
sentiments can be addressed by modifications of KH suggested here.

REFERENCES

Anderson, Elizabeth (1993), *Value in Ethics and Economics*, Cambridge, MA:
Harvard University Press.
Chipman, John and James C. Moore (1978), 'The new welfare economics,
1939–1974', *International Economic Review*, **19** (3): 547–83.
Coleman, Jules (1980), 'Efficiency, utility, and wealth maximization', *Hofstra Law
Review*, **8** (3): 509–51.
Fried, Charles (1978), *Right and Wrong*, Cambridge, MA: Harvard University
Press.
Heyne, Paul (1988), 'The foundations of law and economics', *Research in Law and
Economics*, **11**: 53–71.
Hicks, J.R. (1939), 'The foundations of welfare economics', *Economic Journal*,
49: 696.
Johansson, Per-Olov (1992a), 'Altruism in cost–benefit analysis', *Environmental and
Resource Economics*, **2**: 605–13.
Johansson, Per-Olov (1992b), *Cost–Benefit Analysis of Environmental Change*,
Cambridge, New York: Cambridge University Press.
Kaldor, Nicholas (1939), 'Welfare propositions in economics and inter-personal
comparisons of utility', *Economic Journal*, **49**: 549.
Layton, David and Richard Zerbe (2004), 'Municipal use of benefit–cost analysis',
working paper, University of Washington.
Lumley, Sarah (1997), 'The environment and the ethics of discounting: an empir-
ical analysis', *Ecological Economics*, **20**: 71–82.
Milgrom, Paul (1993), 'Is sympathy an economic value? Philosophy, economics, and
the contingent valuation method', in Jerry A. Hausman (ed.), *Contingent
Valuation: A Critical Assessment. Contributions to Economic Analysis*, Amsterdam,
London and Tokyo: North-Holland, distributed in the United States and Canada
by Elsevier Science, New York, pp. 417–35.
Nussbaum, Martha (2000), 'The costs of tragedy: some moral limits of cost–benefit
analysis', *Journal of Legal Studies*, **29**, 1005, 1032.

Pareto, Vilfredo (1896), *Cours d'Économie Politique*, vol. II, Lausanne: F. Rouge.

Posner, Richard (1981), *The Economics of Justice*, Cambridge, MA: Harvard University Press.

Quiggin, J. (1991),'Does existence value exist', working paper, Department of Agricultural and Resource Economics, University of Maryland.

Robbins, Lionel (1932), *An Essay on the Nature and Significance of Economic Science*, London: Macmillan.

Robbins, Lionel (1938), 'Interpersonal comparisons of utility: a comment', *Economic Journal*, **48**: 635.

Scitovszky, Tibor de (1941), 'A note on welfare propositions in economics', *Review of Economics and Statistics*, **9**: 77–88. (Note: this author hereafter wrote as Tibor Scitovsky.)

Sen, Amartya (1982), 'Rights and agency', *Philosophy and Public Affairs*, **11** (1): 1–20.

Sunstein, Cass (1997), *Free Markets and Social Justice*, Oxford and New York: Oxford University Press.

Williams, Bernard and J.J.C. Smart (1973), *Utilitarianism: For and Against*, Cambridge: Cambridge University Press.

Willig, Robert (1976), 'Consumer surplus without apology', *American Economic Review*, **66** (4): 589–97.

Zerbe, Richard O., Jr. (1991), 'Comment: does benefit–cost analysis stand alone? Rights and standing', *Journal of Policy Analysis and Management*, **10** (1): 96–105.

Zerbe, Richard O., Jr. (1998), 'Is cost–benefit analysis legal? Three rules', *Journal of Policy Analysis and Management*, **17** (3): 419–56.

Zerbe, Richard O., Jr. (2001), *Efficiency in Law and Economics*, Cheltenham, UK and Northampton, MA, USA: Edward Elgar.

Zerbe, Richard O., Jr. (2002), 'Can law and economics stand the purchase of moral satisfaction?', *Research in Law and Economics*, **20**: 135–72.

Zerbe, Richard O., Jr. (2005), 'The legal foundations of benefit–cost analysis', working paper, University of Washington, Evans School of Public Affairs.

Zerbe, Richard O., Jr. and Dwight Dively (1994), *Benefit–Cost Analysis in Theory and Practice*, New York: Harper Collins.

Zerbe, Richard O. Jr., Yoram Bauman and Aaron Finkle (2006), 'An aggregate measure for benefit–cost analysis, *Ecological Economics*, (forthcoming).

EXERCISES

Questions

1. The state wishes to use its power of eminent domain to take some land for public use. One of the owners of part of the land is an 87-year-old woman who doesn't wish to sell for the price that an outside consultant has determined is the market price. Should the city exercise its right of eminent domain and take the land for this price? Why or why not?
2. Suppose she doesn't want to sell at any price (her WTA is infinite). Should the city reconsider? Why or why not?
3. How do you know if her price is infinite or what her true price is?
4. In this particular instance there is considerable public sentiment to leave the woman where she is and to not take the land at this time. Should this sentiment be considered in a BCA? Why or why not?

3. Standing in benefit–cost analysis

3.1 INTRODUCTION

The first step in doing a benefit–cost analysis is to decide who has standing. That is, who has the right to have his/her benefits and costs included in the analysis? Standing determines the perspective from which the analysis is being done and can have a tremendous effect on calculations of benefits and costs.

Standing is a recent concept as traditional theory assumes everyone has standing. To include the values of all affected is, however, neither practical nor desirable. Some people are affected slightly and the costs of capturing these effects are not worthwhile. In some cases, however, the law is an aid to capturing widespread effects cheaply. Thus the value of goods in the hands of a thief may reasonably be given a value of zero since the illegality of theft creates a presumption that the value of discouraging thievery is worthwhile. That is, thieves have no standing with respect to their valuation of stolen goods.

In addition, every analysis is done from a perspective and this perspective by definition excludes some of those affected. Analyses performed by the federal government often exclude effects on foreign citizens. Similarly, those performed by state or local governments may exclude effects that arise outside their jurisdictions. Purely private analyses will focus only on the results for the private parties.

Practical issues of standing are essentially political and in particular jurisdictional. Most benefit–cost analyses are done from a national perspective so that in effect foreigners do not have standing. But the same issue arises on a more local level. As a practical matter imagine a project being done by a department of a city government. If a BCA is done from the perspective of that department, it may be only the members or interests of that department that have standing and only the department's costs and revenues might matter. If, instead, a BCA is done from the perspective of the entire city, the residents of that city and the city government would have standing. Ideally, standing would be global or universal, so that the interests of people in the city, in neighboring cities and elsewhere would be included, but this is often either impractical or inconsistent with the interests of the analyst.

The point of view from which the BCA is done (or who has standing) should be clear and consistently applied throughout the study. For example, imagine that a town is considering building a hospital that will put a neighboring town's hospital out of business. If the residents of the neighboring town have standing, their benefit from having access to a new hospital should be included along with their cost of the loss of an older but closer hospital. An unscrupulous analyst might be tempted to include one of these but not the other.

This chapter will address the issue of standing first in a traditional sense, looking at the implications of expanding or contracting the group of people who have standing. We will then consider distributional considerations in BCA as a particular form of question of standing. Finally, we will extend the distributional model to include future generations and the issue of granting standing to people not yet born who will enjoy the benefits or suffer the consequences of projects done prior to their existence.

3.2 STANDING AND TRANSFERS

One of the most important implications of standing is how transfers between people or organizations are handled. Transfers of money, goods or services from people with standing to other people with standing should not be included as either costs or benefits in the analysis on the grounds that the benefits to one group are just offset by the costs to the other. Transfers from people without standing to those with standing should be included as benefits while transfers from people with standing to those without standing should be treated as costs as Example 3A suggests.

EXAMPLE 3A   STANDING AND WATER TREATMENT ON THE DANUBE

The Danube River originates in Germany and runs through Austria, Slovakia, Hungary, Croatia, Serbia, Bulgaria and Romania before emptying into the Black Sea. If the Austrian government is considering building a water treatment plant that will improve water quality in the Danube, they may grant standing only to Austrians and ignore the benefits to people in other countries along the river's course. This will make the benefits of the resulting improved water quality smaller and may doom a project that would be worthwhile if standing were global.

Imagine that the Hungarian government wants to see the treatment plant built and offers $100 million to Austria to assist with construction costs. From a global perspective, this payment is a transfer and is neither a cost nor a benefit of the project. However, if a BCA is done in which only Austrians have standing, the $100 million would be counted as a benefit of the project. If a BCA is done from the Hungarian point of view, the $100 million would be a cost of the project.

Standing is often improperly applied in analysis of economic development projects intended to help impoverished areas. The money for such projects may be taken from taxes collected elsewhere and used, perhaps, to hire residents of the area. If this tax money is paid to local residents as wages, the wages may be incorrectly counted as benefits of the project. However, as long as taxpayers have standing, the wage payments are transfers instead of benefits or costs.[1] These transfers may be desirable for other reasons, but these reasons should be made clear in the analysis. For example, consider the following cases (Examples 3B and 3C) of logging and mass transit:

EXAMPLE 3B   VALUING LABOR IN RESTORING LOGGING ROADS

A project is proposed to reforest logging roads in an area to prevent erosion and improve water quality in streams. Due to recent reductions in logging, the area in which this project will be done has high unemployment rates. A representative from the area says that the wages paid to local people who work on the project are benefits and should be counted as such. Is he/she correct?

The answer depends on the perspective adopted for the analysis and the project's funding source. If the analysis is done from a local perspective and the funds for it are coming either from state or from federal taxpayers, the wages paid are a benefit. If the analysis is done from the perspective of the state and funding is provided by state taxpayers, then the wages paid are simply a transfer and should not be included as a benefit, unless they are also included as an offsetting cost. If the analysis is done from the

---

[1] The proper treatment of the cost of labor in the project is its opportunity cost, a concept considered later in this book.

perspective of the state and the federal government would provide funds for the project, then the wages paid are a transfer from federal taxpayers (who lack standing) to state residents and should be counted as a benefit.

A separate issue here is the value of the labor used in the work. If the people working on the project would have been unemployed, it may be tempting to assign a value of zero to their labor. This ignores the value of household services they might have provided and the value of their leisure, though in areas of high unemployment the marginal value of leisure might be zero.

EXAMPLE 3C   MASS TRANSIT OPTIONS

A city is considering two options for expanding mass transit. One option is to expand the bus service, the other is to install a light rail system. For various reasons the options are mutually exclusive; only one of the two projects can be done. Reliable BCAs have been done for the two options and it is found that expanding the bus service will generate net benefits of $40 billion while installing and operating light rail will generate net benefits of $35 billion. Due to a federal light rail program, the city can get a $10 billion grant for the construction of light rail, but not for an expanded bus service. Which project should be done?

Standing plays an important part here. If the analysis adopts national standing, the $10 billion to be contributed by the federal government would simply be a transfer and have no impact on the net benefits of the project. From the point of view of the city, however, the $10 billion is a benefit of choosing light rail and will increase that project's net benefits to $45 billion, making it preferable to build the light rail system despite the fact that, from a national perspective, an expanded bus service is preferable.

3.3   INCLUSION OF COSTS AND BENEFITS

Standing determines which costs and benefits will be included in an analysis. At the simplest level, damages suffered by and benefits accruing to people with standing are included. This distinction may be subtler, however, depending on the exact point of view of the study.

Imagine that a city department of parks and recreation is considering construction and operation of a golf course. The costs are fairly well known, but they are trying to decide what to include as the benefits. An analysis done with universal standing would attempt to measure the value that all golfers would attach to having one additional course in the area, perhaps in terms of reduced congestion on the course, greater variety and greater convenience. An analysis from the city's point of view would try to estimate as benefits the additional enjoyment that the city's resident golfers would gain from the course's creation plus the revenues earned from non-resident golfers. An analysis strictly from the point of view of the department of parks and recreation would look only at the revenues that the course would generate and might ignore the value of any benefits in excess of the price paid by golfers using the course. Each of these approaches would generate different results, but any of them might be correct given the described conditions of standing as shown in Example 3D.

EXAMPLE 3D   STANDING AND THE BENEFITS OF BICYCLE HELMETS

In an analysis of the benefits and costs of bicycle helmets, Ginsberg and Silverberg (1994) estimate the value of injuries and deaths that would be prevented by mandatory helmet use. In their valuation, however, they include only the cost of treatment (for injuries) and lost economic production. No value is given to the value that a person might put on his/her own life or injury. The result is that the value used for lives saved is unusually small. What is included is the value of economic services provided by that person to others (measured through per capita GDP) and the cost to society of caring for them if they are injured.

The justification for ignoring the value people put on their own lives is that this value has already been included in the individual decision to wear or not wear a helmet. The analyst is interested in the extra value from mandating helmet use. However, there will be value placed on the individual's life by others who care for him or her. It is, for example, well known that parents care more for their children than their children care for them. Many users of bikes have living parents so that the analysis denies standing for the group that cares about bike riders. The only reason to deny standing to the parents of bike riders and others who have a special concern is that their paternalistic sentiments are not in accord with individual liberties. The authors do not discuss this issue so their analysis can be challenged on the basis of their denial of standing to parents and others.

Should BCA count the value of envy or malice equally with other values? Should the utility of the rapist or a sadist count along with the suffering of the victim? Or should it count the value of goods to a thief if the question arises of returning the goods? The analyst cannot and should not interject his or her own values into the analysis. Yet it does not seem morally defensible to include utility from bad acts in a normative analysis. And indeed benefit–cost has been criticized as failing on moral grounds for failing to distinguish bad from good utility. Can these two positions be reconciled?

Standing provides a vehicle. If we are to count all values, then we count not only bad utility but also the disutility that comes not only from the objects of the hatred or malice, envy or sadism but also from the value of the repugnance that society at large has for the bad acts. The distinction between bad and good acts lies not with the analyst but with the laws and norms of the society. These laws may be taken to represent the outcome of a survey that counts all utility, bad and good, equally. The fact that murder or theft is illegal may be taken to mean that the utility from their commission is on the whole negative. This may be taken to deny standing to the value of goods to the thief or the utility that a murderer gains from murder. Consider Example 3E based on a real life situation.

EXAMPLE 3E   THEFT

A utility company requires that its customers pay one month in advance for its services. In many cases when a customer quits the service there is a credit balance owed to the customer. The company will pay back the credit balance if the customer requests it but does not if the customer does not request payment. In this manner the company has accumulated several millions of dollars. The government discovers the practice and brings suit; the company agrees to stop the practice. The issue is now whether or not the company should be required to return the overcharges. The economist hired by the company argues that the return of money fails a benefit–cost test. The loss to the company of the return would be $3 million plus the cost of return; the gain to the customers would just be $3 million.

The cost of return, mailing, cutting the check, finding the addresses and so on is about 10 percent of the total return, or $300,000. The return then fails a benefit–cost test with a loss of $300,000. The problem is that the $3 million is represented as just a transfer. The economist for the government, who has read this book, argues that the thief has no standing to have his gains counted. The benefit is then just the $3 million gain for consumers minus the resource cost of the transfer of $300,000 so that net benefits are $2.7 million.

3.4   ECONOMIC IMPACT ANALYSES

A variant of BCA is *economic impact analysis*, which attempts to estimate all of the economic effects a major project or facility will have on an area or a region. The primary difference between an impact analysis and a BCA is that the former makes no proper claim to count benefits and costs but looks rather at gross impacts. The economic impact is often defined as the sum of the revenues of the facility, the expenditures of the facility, resulting tax revenues and the additional revenues enjoyed by associated businesses. These studies are often used to argue that projects should be carried out for the sake of local or regional economic development, even if they will not generate positive net benefits in any traditional BCA sense.

For example, a new concert venue in a section of a city will likely attract a large number of people to the area several dozen times each year, creating jobs and generating revenue both for the venue itself and for nearby restaurants and bars. These revenues will almost certainly be taxed, so there will be additional income for local governments. The economic impact of the concert venue might include ticket revenues, wages paid to venue employees, the increase in revenues for local bars, restaurants and other businesses, and the tax collected on all of these transactions. All of these amounts might be included as benefits of the venue in the impact analysis.

They would not all be included as benefits in the BCA. The BCA would consider the costs of staging performances and the opportunity cost of the labor employed at the concert venue. The actual benefit to local business owners will be not the increase in their revenues, but the increase in their profits, which is the measure that would be used in a benefit–cost analysis.

The differences between an impact analysis and a BCA can be viewed, *inter alia*, as a difference in standing. An economic impact analysis often restricts standing to those businesses located in a particular and fairly limited area. Treating revenues to the facility as a benefit suggests that attendees have no standing in the analysis. This problem is recognized in more sophisticated impact analyses and is handled by looking only at the impact of 'new money', money that would not otherwise be spent in the relevant area. Even here, however, the impacts are not benefits and costs.

Of course a BCA can be restricted in scope but it is recognized that a proper BCA would acknowledge that attendance at concerts replaces other entertainment expenditures and that the additional visits that people make to bars and restaurants in conjunction with concert attendance are probably offset by reductions in visits to bars and restaurants elsewhere. Put another way, businesses near the concert venue will simply take business away from businesses in other neighborhoods. Expanding the analysis to grant standing to all businesses in a city or in a region may reveal little net impact of a new facility, even though the local economic impact might be huge.

3.5   RELATIVE STANDING AND DISTRIBUTIONAL ISSUES

Thus far, we have considered only inclusion or exclusion in discussing standing. Those people who have standing in an analysis all have the same relative importance, a situation consistent with the *potential Pareto* or *Kaldor–Hicks* (KH) criterion, which states that a project is desirable if its winners could potentially compensate its losers from their gains. Expressed in a slightly different way, the criterion is that a project is desirable if its benefits are greater than its costs, regardless of the distribution of each.

A number of attempts have been made to incorporate distributional considerations into BCA. There is, however, no agreed-upon approach. The ideal is that different people may be assigned different degrees of standing in a study, and costs or benefits may mean more if imposed on one person than on another. The relative levels of importance assigned to different people are called *distributional weights*.

One of the most common reasons for assigning people different levels of relative standing is income distribution. That is, a program's benefits may mean more if they go to poor people than if they go to rich people. A program with negative net benefits may be desirable if the costs are imposed on the rich and the benefits accrue to the poor. A program with positive net benefits may be undesirable if most of the costs are borne by poor people while the gains accrue to the rich.

As an example, consider programs whose only effect is income redistribution. Any sort of program for the redistribution of income involves some costs. As a result, the money taken into the program from the general populace will be greater than what is eventually distributed to the program's recipients. The costs will almost certainly be greater than the benefits. If, however, the contributors to the program have relatively high incomes and the recipients have relatively low incomes, the program may be desirable. If this sort of program is desirable, it suggests that we might attach greater distributional weights to the poor than to the rich. The question is how should the weights be determined?

There are a number of practical approaches that modify the KH criterion to include distributional considerations in BCA. The first, suggested by McKean (1958), includes in the list of costs and benefits the groups that will most likely bear costs and enjoy benefits. In this case, the analyst need not make any decision about how different people will be weighted, but can rather leave it up to the reader to decide. For example, if federal gasoline taxes were to be increased with the goal of reducing fuel consumption and improving air quality, the burden of this tax increase would fall heavily on residents of rural areas who drive disproportionately long distances, but the benefits would accrue to urban dwellers who generally experience lower air quality. An analyst preparing a report on the prospect of increased gasoline taxes could simply state this without assigning relative weights to rural and urban dwellers. How the two groups should be weighted in evaluating the project could be left to the reader of the report.

A second technique that could be used is to attach explicit weights to different groups affected by the project. Each group's gains or losses could be calculated; these gains or losses would be multiplied by the group's distributional weight and these would be added together to generate a weighted net benefit. Consider the example, shown in Table 3.1, of a project that will impose net costs on residents of neighborhood A and have net benefits for residents of neighborhood B. The residents of A are wealthier than the residents of B and, as such, have smaller distributional weights attached to them.[2]

Table 3.1   Attaching distributional weights

Neighborhood	Net benefits	Distributional weight 1	Weighted net benefit	Distributional weight 2	Weighted net benefit
A	−100	1	−100	1	−100
B	+80	1.2	+96	1.4	+112
	−20		−4		+12

[2] Of course, the residents of neighborhood A may have a diminished distributional weight for any of a variety of reasons that are left to the reader's imagination.

Under the KH criterion, the project is undesirable because the net benefits are negative. Increasing the relative weight attached to residents of neighborhood B by 20 percent still results in a negative assessment of the project, but increasing their weight by 40 percent results in a positive assessment. The difficult parts of explicit distributional weighting are first determining how costs and benefits will be distributed among different segments of the population and then choosing distributional weights on which people can agree. Example 3F tells of an example that became controversial.

EXAMPLE 3F   DISTRIBUTIONAL WEIGHTS AT THE OMB

An excellent example of the use of distributional weights and the difficulty they can cause comes from guidelines used by the Office of Management and Budget (OMB) regarding the relative value attached to younger and older people whose lives might be saved by improvements in air quality.[3] Lives of some older people were valued less than the lives of younger people. This was actually a result of basing the analysis on the years of life saved, but the effect was identical to that of assigning different distributional weights: a benefit (a life saved) accruing to a member of one group was valued differently from the same benefit accruing to a member of another group.

Two effects are important to note. The first is that if two programs saved the same number of lives at the same cost, the program that saved a higher proportion of younger people's lives would be preferred. The second, and perhaps more important effect is that explicitly assigning distributional weights can be extremely controversial.

A third technique eliminates at least some of the difficulties of assigning distributional weights. If costs and benefits can be divided between two groups, and a net benefit for each group can be calculated, it is possible to calculate an *internal weight* for the project.[4] An internal weight is a

---

[3]   'Placing Lower Value on Senior Lives Stirs Anger', *Los Angeles Times*, April 30, 2003.
[4]   This technique is suggested in Boardman et al. (2000, p. 467). For an example where this procedure is used, see the discussion by Zerbe and Knott (2004) of the Canadian merger of superior Propane with ICG Propane.

distributional weight assigned to the more disadvantaged group that will make the project's weighted net benefits equal to zero. The reader is then free to decide whether the necessary weighting is reasonable or unreasonable. In the above example, the internal weight is calculated as:

$$NB_A + (IW \times NB_B) = 0$$
$$-100 + (IW \times 80) = 0$$
$$IW = 1.25.$$

If the reader considers this a reasonable relative weighting, the project is desirable. If the reader feels that this assigns too much weight to the residents of neighborhood B, the project should, in the reader's opinion, be rejected.

None of these approaches is very satisfactory as there is no agreement about what the weights should be. Indeed it is possible to take a project with a negative value, add income transfers from the rich to the poor to it until the greater weight given the poor turns it into a good project. The objection to this is that the project may in fact be an inefficient way to transfer money. To account for this, Arnold Harberger (1978) has suggested that no weight be given beyond that determined by the cheapest method of transferring money directly. This is a better approach.

Building on the Harberger approach, it is possible to use a weights approach that is consistent with the way sentiments for other goods are valued. The only general method of incorporating weights that is consistent with the original formulation of BCA is to value some people according to the willingness to pay by others for their welfare. This approach is developed by Zerbe in a series of articles.[5] Thus moral sentiments toward others would be given standing. This approach has been called the aggregate measure or AM. Such an approach helps to solve a number of benefit–cost problems.

3.6   STANDING, DISTRIBUTION AND FUTURE GENERATIONS

A particularly challenging issue related to standing is that of the costs and benefits borne or enjoyed by future generations as the result of projects with long-lasting implications. Standard inter-temporal discounting, discussed elsewhere in this text, tends to greatly discount costs and benefits that occur far in the future.[6]

---

[5]   See for example Zerbe and Knott (2004).
[6]   For example, $1 discounted at the relatively low interest rate of 1 percent has a present value of only $0.007 after 500 years.

The effect of such discounting is seen by some as essentially denying standing to future generations merely because they did not have the good fortune to be born sooner. Of course if present investments yield benefits in the future, then future generations will benefit. A reasonable way to give a sort of standing to future generations is to imagine that future generations are treated just as future extensions of the current generation. That is, imagine that lives are infinite and consider what decision would be made. If the discount rate is correctly chosen, this is what BCA does.

What about the case, however, in which present generations reap the benefits but future generations bear the costs? Moreover, to deny oneself future benefits in order to enjoy present ones is not the same as denying future benefits to those who cannot enjoy present ones. Even if programs that imposed costs on future generations carried with them the provision of compensatory transfers, very few financial (or even governmental institutions) have had reliable existences stretching into multiple centuries, so the cost of transferring money directly to adversely affected future generations may be prohibitively high.

For this reason, ethical arguments for using low or zero discount rates for long-term projects are widespread. Recently these arguments have gained policy currency. The Office of Management and Budget's (OMB) 2003 Final Report for benefit–cost analysis suggests using lower discount rates for long-term projects based on ethical reasons.[7] The Final Report claims that 'special ethical considerations arise when comparing benefits and costs across generations' (OMB, 2003, p. 152). It notes arguments that it is 'ethically impermissible to discount the utility of future generation' (ibid.). The Final Report provision reflects the long-standing arguments of critics that discounting benefits and costs borne by future generations is immoral since we should regard future generations as equally important as our own (for example, Schultze et al., 1981; Pearce and Turner, 1989; Parfit 1992, 1994).

The most fundamental failure to give standing in issues affecting future generations is, however, the failure to give standing the moral sentiments of the present generation about future ones. Consider Example 3G.

---

[7] The normal term structure of interest rates is upward sloping, suggesting that discount rates for long-term projects should be greater than for short-term projects. That is, longer-term market rates are higher than shorter-term rates. This is because the lender must bear the risk of a change in rates over time and the probability of a change increases with time. Recently Weitzman (2000) showed that rates for longer-term projects should be lower than for shorter-term ones. This result does not contradict the existing upward term structure, as it is based not on bearing the risk of a rate change over time but rather on the uncertainty about what is the true rate.

EXAMPLE 3G   NUCLEAR WASTE

A nuclear project is being considered that produces benefits of about $65 billion at a cost of about $35 billion but, in addition, produces a toxic time bomb that will cause enormous environmental costs some time in the far future.[8] (We remove questions of uncertainty of the discount rate from this example.) Suppose that current waste-disposal technology will contain this waste for 500 years after which it escapes its sarcophagus but will remain toxic for 10,000 years. The estimated cost of the future environmental damage in constant, year 2000 dollars will be about $32 trillion, about twice the size of the current US GDP. The present value of these damages discounted at a 3 percent real social rate of time preference (SRTP), assuming the waste escapes at the first opportunity 500 years from now, is about $12 million. This amount is not insignificant, but it is far far less than the damage that will occur in 500 years and far too small to affect the results of the benefit–cost analysis. Discounting these damages then results in the project going forward as the benefits are determined to exceed the costs by almost $30 billion.

It is said that the nuclear waste project would be unfair to future generations and on this basis it is argued that the use of discount rates is immoral. A commonly proposed solution to the problem of unethical harm to future generations is to use low, or even negative, discount rates (for example, Schultze et al., 1981) or not to use discount rates at all (Parfit, 1994). This sort of argument is a moral plea about what our sentiments should be toward future generations, but not an effective statement about what or whether discount rates should be used or even about the relevant actual moral sentiments. The proposed solution of using no or low discount rates is *ad hoc* and, if generally applied, will lead to other ethical problems – for example, the adoption of projects that give less benefit to both present and future generations.[9]

---

[8]   Cases in which this sort of issue have arisen include *Baltimore Gas & Electric v. Natural Resources Defense Council, Inc.* 462 US 87 (1983); and *Pacific Gas and Electric Co et al. v. State Energy Resources Conservation and Development Commission*, 461 US 190 (1991). See also 123 US 45 (1999).

[9]   Infra, footnote 3.

In Table 3.2, a standard KH benefit–cost approach to the hypothetical nuclear waste example is compared to AM under four different scenarios: in scenario 1, neither compensation nor mitigation occur; in scenario 2, compensation occurs; in scenario 3, mitigation occurs since

Table 3.2   *A comparison of KH and AM*, present values of gains and losses*

Benefits and costs	[1]	[2]	[3]	[4]
	No compensation or mitigation occurs (PV bn)	Compensation occurs (PV bn)	Mitigation occurs; compensation is not feasible (PV bn)	Neither compensation nor mitigation are feasible (PV bn)
Ordinary benefits	65	65	65	65
Ordinary costs	35	35	35	35
Harm to future generations	0.012	0.012	[0.012]	0.012
Administrative costs of actual compensation	[4]	7	Infinite	Infinite
Mitigation costs	[5]	[5]	4	100
Moral harm to present generation	35	[35]	[35]	35
KH NPV	29.988	22.988	26	29.988
AM NPV	−5.012	22.988	26	−5.012
Conclusion	Neither compensation nor mitigation appear worthwhile under KH as moral harm is ignored	Compensation eliminates moral harm	Mitigation eliminates moral harm	Moral harm renders project undesirable under AM

Note: *Figures in brackets are costs not included in the given scenario. Note that not all figures are relevant to KH and that mitigation and compensation are substitutes so that one or the other but not both are included in the AM calculation.

Critics of BCA suggest that the values individuals hold as private persons are used in BCA, but that these differ from those they hold for public decision making (Sagoff, 1988; Anderson, 1993). This criticism, however, works better as a caution to measure the actual values than of BCA methodology (Zerbe, 2001).

the administrative costs of compensation are too expensive; and lastly, in scenario 4, neither occur. Compensation as determined by the current generation for harm done to the future generation is $7 billion and mitigation costs are $4 billion. An example of mitigation might be to create a more secure holding container or shipment into space. The results are expressed by the net present value, NPV.

The highest NPV value of $30 billion for KH occurs when there is neither mitigation nor compensation; yet, this occurs because KH ignores the values of compensation and mitigation. Mitigation is ignored as long as its value is less than the present value of future harm caused by a failure to mitigate. The moral harm to the current generation is ignored under KH. Compensation is also ignored as this is a distributional effect not considered by KH. The KH test considers hypothetical rather than actual compensation. Implicit in this hypothetical test is the assumption that the amount of hypothetical compensation is simply the present value of future harm, since if this amount is invested at the assumed interest rate, it will grow to the amount of future harm. Hypothetical compensation determines whether the winners could, in principle, compensate the losers, ignoring the costs of actual compensation. Yet if compensation is actually to be provided, the amount required will be greater than this and in many cases much greater. The administrative costs of providing compensation can be quite large and, in the case of the far future, even infinite as shown in Scenario 4 of Table 3.2. The ability to even provide the required long-lived institutions at almost any cost has been found to be improbable (Leshine and McCurdy, 2001). The administrative costs must be included in examining the costs of actual compensation.[10]

Mitigation or compensation can eliminate moral harm. But this does not enter the KH calculus. The NPV under KH is the same whether or not compensation and mitigation are more or less costly than the moral harm they could eliminate.[11] Thus KH misses values and information. It ignores moral harm and it ignores the cost of actual compensation.

---

[10] Even if compensation could be provided, the decision to compensate may be made by others than those that suffer moral harm. That is, for goods supplied by the public, there is a distinction between those who would purchase moral satisfaction and those who make the decision to purchase it. The transactions costs of actually persuading the decision makers to compensate may be prohibitive, especially since any attempt at agreement may suffer from a free-rider problem. Thus compensation may not be provided even if it is less costly than the moral harm that compensation could eliminate.

[11] It is not the amount of compensation actually required for those injured that is directly relevant here. Rather, it is the amount of compensation the current generation thinks is correct. This is information that is likely to be obtainable as it

The analysis of the nuclear waste example is quite different under AM as the NPV for a scenario without mitigation or compensation is negative. The calculated NPV when neither mitigation nor compensation is chosen is a negative 5.012 billion under AM instead of the nearly 30 billion under KH. This is because moral sentiments are included as required by AM that are not included under KH. When compensation or mitigation occurs, the moral harm is eliminated and the KH and AM values are the same since the missing values are now included. The AM approach shows that the cheaper of mitigation and compensation is desirable as long as they are less than the moral harm to the current generation. When neither mitigation nor compensation is feasible, the project is rejected under AM, though not under KH, as the inclusion of moral harm shows a negative NPV. The AM approach is superior as it gives a truer and fuller accounting.

The most probable scenario is one in which mitigation but not compensation is feasible. The inclusion of the value of moral sentiments to reduce harm to future generations could provide a justification for such moral mitigation.

Under AM we can give standing to the moral sentiments of the current generation towards future generations. AM allows us to compare compensation, mitigation and no action correctly. It avoids projects that appear worthwhile but impose moral harm greater than their value. It allows a solution to the ethical dilemma of the discount rate problem that acknowledges ethical concerns as valid and seeks an ethical solution, while acknowledging the values that commend use of a discount rate. The economic efficiency of the project will then depend on the sentiments of the present generation. For example, the present generation may feel future generations should be free of problems caused by the current generation. Evidence from Easterling (1992) and from Svenson and Karlsson (1989) suggests that, at least as regards nuclear waste disposal, individuals tend to place a high weight on future consequences. On the other hand, the present generation may find that compensation for environmental harm is unwarranted, given their belief that future generations will be wealthier than the present one.[12]

---

is possible through a contingent valuation survey to determine, at least in principle, the WTP or WTA of 'others' who have moral sentiments about the project.

[12] The assumption of declining marginal utility of income with increasing income applies to distributional effects in general, as well as to short-term rates, and not just to long-term discount rates. If there is a declining marginal utility of income then the benefits accruing to the wealthy should receive less weight. The 2003 Final Report cannot, without being inconsistent, recognize such decline for one purpose and not for another.

These considerations do not affect the approach here though they may affect relevant values. Taking into account the effect of declining marginal utility of

The highest NPV of $30 billion for KH occurs when there is neither miti-
gation nor compensation. Mitigation is ignored as long as its value is less
than the present value of future harm caused by a failure to mitigate. Since
this is the case, the scenarios in which mitigation occurs are rejected by
KH. Compensation is ignored as this is a distributional effect not considered by KH. The KH test considers hypothetical rather than actual compensation. Implicit in this hypothetical test is the assumption that the
amount of hypothetical compensation is simply the present value of future
harm, since if this amount is invested at the assumed interest rate, it will
grow to the amount of future harm. Hypothetical compensation determines
whether the winners could, in principle, compensate the losers, ignoring the
costs of actual compensation. Yet if compensation is actually to be provided, the amount required will be greater than this and in many cases much
greater. The administrative costs of providing compensation can be quite
large and, in the case of the far future, even infinite as shown in Scenario 4.
The ability to even provide the required long-lived institutions at almost any
cost has been found to be improbable (Leshine and McCurdy, 2001).

The AM approach takes into account the current generation's willingness to pay to reduce harm to the future generation. The NPV for a scenario without mitigation or compensation is negative. The calculated NPV
when neither mitigation nor compensation is chosen is a negative 5.012
billion under AM instead of the positive nearly 30 billion under KH. This
is because moral sentiments are included as required by AM that are not
included under KH. When compensation or mitigation occurs, the moral
harm is eliminated and the KH and AM values are the same since the
missing values are now included. The AM approach shows that the cheaper
of mitigation and compensation is desirable as long as it is less than the
moral harm to the current generation. When neither mitigation nor compensation is feasible the project is rejected under AM, though not under
KH, as the inclusion of moral harm shows a negative NPV.

The AM approach is superior as it gives a truer and fuller accounting.
Under AM we can give standing to moral sentiments about future generations. AM allows us to compare compensation, mitigation and no action
correctly. It avoids projects that appear worthwhile but impose moral harm
greater than their value. It allows a solution to the ethical dilemma of the
discount rate problem that acknowledges ethical concerns as valid and

income with wealth can be done directly through valuations of benefits and
costs rather than by changes in the discount rate. The magnitude of moral sentiments about compensation or mitigation as expressed by WTP amounts might
be affected by the way benefits and costs are calculated, but such sentiments will
still exist and should be taken into account as far as possible.

seeks an ethical solution, while acknowledging the values that commend use of a discount rate.

3.7   SUMMARY

One of the first decisions that needs to be made in doing a BCA is who shall have standing. This decision will affect the factors included as costs and benefits and which, if any, will be regarded as mere transfers. Exactly who has standing should be stated clearly and adhered to consistently through-out the study.

Within the group of people to be included in the study, it may be desirable to exercise some sort of distributional weightings, for reasons of politics, social goals or economic redistribution. While the unweighted costs and benefits should be reported, these distributional weightings, or at least a breakdown of who will suffer costs and who will enjoy benefits, may enhance the analysis and allow the reader to determine whether distributional considerations may make a good project bad or vice versa.

A particularly challenging issue in BCA is the treatment of far-future costs and benefits affecting future generations. Thinking of this as a question of standing and applying the concept of moral sentiments to the welfare of future generations offers some insight into dealing with this problem.

REFERENCES

Anderson, Elizabeth (1993), *Value in Ethics and Economics,* Cambridge, MA: Harvard University Press.

Boardman, Anthony E., David H. Greenberg, Aidan R. Vining and David L. Weimer (2000), *Cost–Benefit Analysis: Concepts and Practice,* Englewood Cliffs, NJ: Prentice-Hall.

Easterling, Douglas (1992),'Fair rules for siting a high-level nuclear waste repository', *Journal of Policy Analysis and Management*, 111(3): 442–75.

Ginsberg, Gary M. and Don S. Silverberg (1994), 'A cost–benefit analysis of legislation for bicycle safety helmets in Israel', *American Journal of Public Health*, **84**, 653–6.

Harberger, Arnold (1978), 'On the use of distributional weights in social cost–benefit analysis', *Journal of Political Economy*, **86**: 87–120.

Leshine, Tom and Howard McCurdy (2001), 'The limitations of institutional controls in a high reliability organization: U.S. nuclear legacy waste site management', working paper, University of Washington.

Mauskopf, J.A., C.J. Bradley and M.J. French (1991), 'Benefit–Cost analysis of hepatitis B vaccine program for occupationally exposed workers', *Journal of Occupational Medicine*, **33** (6): 691–8.

McKean, Roland N. (1958), *Efficiency in Government Through Systems Analysis*, New York: Wiley.

Office of Management and Budget (OMB) (2003), 'Informing Regulatory Decisions: 2003 Report to Congress on the Costs and Benefits of Federal Regulations', Washington, DC, September.

Parfit, Derek (1992), 'An attack on the social discount rate', in Claudia Mills (ed.), *Values and Public Policy*, Fort Worth: Harcourt Brace Javanovich.

Parfit, Derek (1994), 'The social discount rate', in R.E. Goodwin (ed.), *Politics of the Environment*, Aldershot, UK and Brookfield, USA: Edward Elgar.

Pearce, David and R. Kerry Turner (1989), *Economics of Natural Resources and the Environment*, Baltimore: Johns Hopkins Press.

Sagoff, Mark (1988), *The Economy of the Earth: Philosophy, Law, and the Environment*, Cambridge: Cambridge University Press.

Schultze, William D., D.S. Brookshire and T. Sandler (1981), 'The social rate of discount for nuclear waste storage: economics of ethics', *Natural Resources Journal*, **21**: 811–32.

Svenson, Ola and G. Karlsson (1989), 'Decision making, time horizons and risk in the very long term perspective', *Risk Analysis*, **9**: 385–98.

Weitzman, M. (2000), 'Gamma discounting', *American Economic Review*, **91**: 260–71.

Zerbe, Richard O. (2001), *Economic Efficiency in Law and Economics*, Cheltenham, UK and Northampton, MA, USA: Edward Elgar.

Zerbe, Richard O. and Sunny Knott (2004), 'An economic justification for a price standard in merger policy: the merger of Superior Propane and ICG Propane', *Research in Law and Economics*, **21**: 409–44.

EXERCISES

Questions

1. Vaccinations against diseases such as the flu and some forms of hepatitis are often not covered by health insurance, despite the fact that analysis of the benefits and costs of the vaccination clearly demonstrates that they are worthwhile.[13] Explain why standing might matter in insurers' decision not to cover these vaccinations.
2. A project will have impacts on two groups of people. Group B has greater political clout and has used this fact to create rules mandating that analyses of projects affecting them assign them a distributional weight that is 20 percent greater than the weight assigned to the general population. Assess the indicated project based on the potential Pareto or Kaldor–Hicks criterion and on the mandated distributional weight. What internal weight will give the project a net benefit of zero?

Group	Aggregate net benefits
A	−$300m
B	+$280m

3. A local airport authority has decided to construct an additional runway. The construction will involve a large amount of steel reinforcing bars that will help strengthen the runway. A domestic steel company has quoted the authority a price for the bars that is higher than the price quoted by a foreign company. However, there is a tariff imposed by the federal government on steel imports that would make the foreign steel more expensive. Explain how the question of standing affects the decision about which company to buy the steel from.

Answers

1. An insurer is likely to make a decision about paying for a vaccination based on the likely expenses they will have to incur for medical care if an individual contracts the disease. To the insurer, the benefit of the

---

[13] An excellent example of a paper presenting such analysis is Mauskopf, J.A., C.J. Bradley and M.J. French (1991), 'Benefit–cost analysis of hepatitis B vaccine program for occupationally exposed workers', *Journal of Occupational Medicine*, **33** (6): 691–8.

vaccination is simply the avoided medical bills. However, to the individual there are additional, and possibly much greater benefits from being vaccinated and avoiding an illness. In addition to medical bills, being sick results in such things as discomfort and suffering and lost time at work. These costs of illness are not included from the insurer's perspective, but are included when the individual makes a decision about being vaccinated.

Interestingly, if the costs of illness are sufficiently divided (the insurer pays all of the medical bills while the individual bears all non-monetary costs) it may be that neither the insurer nor the individual would find a vaccination worthwhile, even though it might be if their costs of illness were combined.

2. To assess the project under the potential Pareto or Kaldor–Hicks criterion, add the net benefits associated with the two groups to get −$20 million. Under this criterion, the project is not desirable.

To assess the project under the mandated system of distributional weights, assign a weight of 1.0 to group A and 1.2 to group B. This generates weighted net benefits to group B of $336 million. Because this is larger than the costs to group A, the project is desirable under the mandated weighting system. It may be that any weight could be assigned to group A as long as the weight assigned to group B is 20 percent greater.

Finally, the internal weight that generates zero net benefit is calculated as

$$NB_A + (IW \times NB_B) = 0$$
$$-300 + (IW \times 280) = 0$$
$$IW = 1.071.$$

So any system that assigned a weight to group B that was more than 7.1 percent greater than the weight attached to group A would make the project seem desirable.

3. The issue here is whether or not the federal government (or the federal taxpayers) have standing. If the federal government has standing, then the tariff paid on the imported steel is neither a cost nor a benefit, but simply a transfer. In this case, the foreign steel is cheaper and should be purchased. The more likely case is that the steel purchase decision is made from the point of view of the airport authority without including either the federal government or federal taxpayers. In this case, the tariff is a cost of purchasing foreign steel and the decision would likely be made to purchase domestic steel. It is somewhat ironic that granting the federal government standing leads to the purchase of foreign steel.

4.   Analyzing welfare changes

4.1   INTRODUCTION

At the heart of BCA is the question of whether or not a project makes people better off. Projects alter the combination of goods that people consume, reducing quantities of some things and increasing quantities of others. While our goal is to make statements about an entire community and whether it is made better off as a result of a project, we must start the analysis at the level of an individual and ask whether a project makes one person better off.

This chapter starts with a theoretical discussion of changes in individual utility, how a project might make an individual better off or worse off and how these changes might be valued. From there, we will discuss what should be done to evaluate projects in situations with many people where there is perfect information about individuals' preferences and projects' effects. Finally, we will move from these somewhat abstract ideas of individual utility and social welfare toward more realistic approaches to determining whether or not projects are economically desirable.

The concepts discussed in this chapter form a basis for the practical techniques described in Chapters 5 and 6. More importantly, these concepts should help the reader to determine when straightforward application of the more practical techniques in benefit–cost analysis is appropriate and when it is likely to yield incorrect results.

4.2   ANALYSIS OF INDIVIDUAL UTILITY CHANGES

The proper assessment of a project in BCA is based on its effects on a group of people. However, because group well-being, or social welfare, is dependent on individual utility, our discussion begins with the effects of a project on an individual.

The real effects of a project are the resulting changes in consumption. If a project uses a good as an input, there may be less of this good available for people to consume. If a project produces a good as an output, there may be more for people to consume. In either case, private individuals' consumption decisions are likely to change as a result of the project.

We can analyze a project's impact on an individual using indifference curves. If, for example, a person consumes more of one good and the same quantity of all others, his/her utility will increase, which simply means that he/she will be better off as a result of the project. If, on the other hand, a person consumes less of one good and the same quantity of all others, his/her utility will decrease. The more common case is that a person will consume more of some goods and less of others as a result of a project, making the effect on utility ambiguous. That is, such a project may increase, decrease or leave unchanged a person's utility level.

We will consider first the situation where a project has no impact on market prices and then the situation in which a project affects prices for either its inputs or its outputs.

The effects of a change in consumption on an individual's utility are illustrated in Figure 4.1. Moving from A to B, an increase in the quantity of Good Y puts the individual on a higher indifference curve, indicating that they are better off. Moving from A to C, a decrease in the quantity of Good Y makes the person worse off. If a project increases consumption of one good and decreases consumption of another, the effect on utility or well-being is ambiguous. Increased consumption of Good X and decreased consumption of Good Y may result in the individual being better off (movement from A to E) or worse off (movement from A to D) depending on the specific changes and the individual's preferences.

The economic measure of well-being, utility, is ordinal rather than cardinal. This means that there is no numerical value that allows for measurement of how much better or worse off a person is as a result of a change in consumption. The only thing that can be said is whether a person was made better off (utility increased) or worse off (utility decreased) as a result of the change.

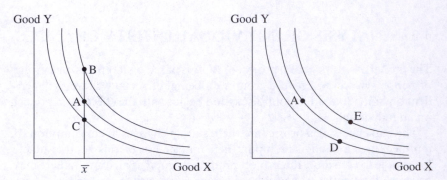

Figure 4.1   Change in consumption on an individual's utility

4.3   PROJECT EFFECTS WHEN PRICES DO NOT CHANGE

Consider a project that consumes some goods (inputs) and creates others (outputs) without affecting market prices. This would happen if the project were sufficiently small relative to the market that it resulted in no discernible price change. If this is the case, it is appropriate to simply consider the impact on an individual's consumption assuming no price change. Changes in consumption will impact a person's well-being or utility and a dollar value may be attached to the change based on the change in the value of the goods consumed.

For example, imagine a program that distributes surplus cheese. If cheese sells in markets at $4/pound and the program distributes five pounds to a person, it is reasonably valued at $20[1] if the recipient is indifferent between receiving the cheese and receiving the cash equivalent and if the program does not result in a change in the price of cheese relative to other goods. Put another way, $20 might be an appropriate value for the cheese distributed if the person would have consumed the same quantity of cheese had they simply been given $20 in cash. This is the situation illustrated in Figure 4.2.

It is possible that some programs directly distribute goods that people either would not have consumed or would have consumed in relatively small quantities. If recipients cannot resell what they receive, it may be inappropriate to value the project output at the market price. More specifically, if the project gives large quantities of goods to people, the market value is only appropriate if the recipients, given the equivalent value in cash, would have spent it all on those same goods.

In terms of the previous example, imagine that instead of being given five pounds of cheese, the program recipient was given five hundred pounds of cheese that, for various reasons, could not be resold. Assuming recipients would not otherwise consume that much cheese, the correct value for this benefit is probably less than the cash equivalent of $2000.[2]

As another example, consider a public housing project[3] that provides housing equivalent to privately supplied housing that is valued at $1500/month. It might be tempting to attach a value of $1500/month to the project's units.

However, this will only be appropriate if the resident, if given $1500 per month, would spend it all on housing. If the same person were given

---

[1]   Five pounds of cheese at $4/pound.
[2]   Again, 500 pounds at $4/pound.
[3]   This example is based on Olsen and Barton (1983).

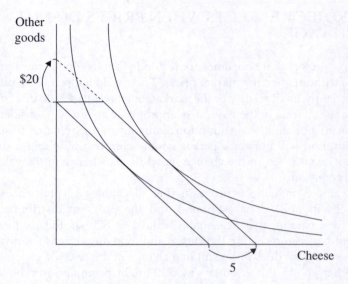

Figure 4.2   Distribution of non-money goods

$1500/month and spent only a portion of it on housing, the proper value to attach to the housing would be smaller. How much smaller depends on some fairly technical assumptions about individuals' preferences, but it is certainly true that the value is less than $1500.

The standard and productive approach to valuing a benefit is to imagine what a beneficiary would be willing to pay if he/she were to purchase it. In the above examples, this would be what recipients would be willing to pay for five pounds of cheese, one hundred pounds of cheese or an apartment that rents on the market for $1500. This is the willingness to pay (WTP) value of the project's benefit. The inherent assumption here is that the beneficiary has no pre-existing right to the benefit, so the value should be based on pre-project conditions.

Alternatively, it might be assumed that the beneficiary has a pre-existing right to the benefit and if the project were not done he/she would be entitled to compensation. Under this assumption, the value of the benefit is the level of compensation necessary to make his/her utility level equivalent to what it would have been had the project been done. This is the willingness to accept (WTA) value of the project's benefit and its value should be based on post-project conditions.

In general, the WTP value of a benefit will be less than its WTA value. However, in situations where prices do not change, they will be identical and equal to the price. These points are illustrated in Examples 4A and 4B.

EXAMPLE 4A   PUBLIC HOUSING

Imagine that a public housing project will provide 100 units of housing to a person. To keep things relatively simple, assume that housing is defined so that a unit of housing has a market price of $1. All other goods (a composite of all the other things the person consumes) are similarly priced at $1/unit.

How should the 100 units of public housing be valued?

Simply valuing them at $1/unit (for a total value of $100) may be incorrect. Consider the figure below, showing the effect of the housing project on a person's budget. Giving the person 100 units of housing moves the budget line out, increasing the maximum quantity of housing they can consume, but does not affect the maximum quantity of other goods.

If the indifference curve is not tangent to a point in the downward-sloping portion of the budget line, the person will wind up choosing to consume at the corner point of their budget constraint.

The person will be on an indifference curve that could have been attained through a smaller cash grant.

As shown in the figure overleaf, the person could have achieved the same level of utility with a smaller cash grant of, say, $80. So, the proper value to attach to the units of public housing is $80.

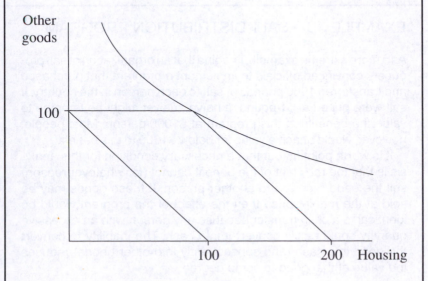

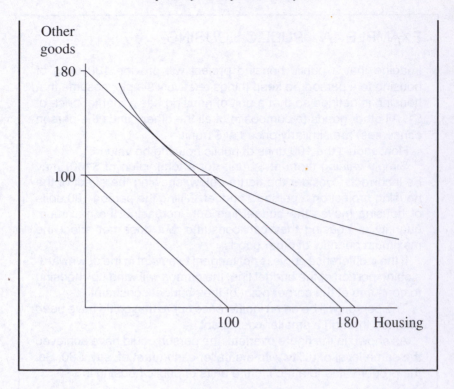

EXAMPLE 4B   SALT DISTRIBUTION PROGRAM

As a more extreme example, imagine that an organization of salt producers convinced officials to implement a program that purchased
and transferred 1000 pounds of salt to each person in the country. If
salt were priced at $1/pound, a naïve analyst might be tempted to
value the benefits of this program at $1000/person. Most people,
however, would attach a value far below $1000 to this benefit.

It is worth pointing out that a necessary condition for this analysis is that the recipient of the benefit cannot (for whatever reason)
sell the good received to another person. If these goods may be
sold at the market price then the effect of the program would be
identical to a cash transfer because any person with an excessive
quantity could easily convert it into cash. The inability to convert
the good into cash (and subsequently into other goods) reduces
the value of that good to some degree.

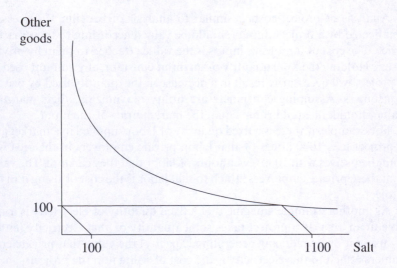

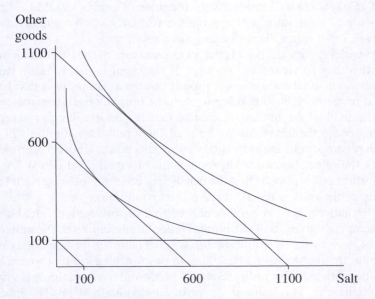

This figure illustrates the valuation of the salt program. Giving a person 1000 units of salt is really worth only $500 if it cannot be resold. If, however, the salt can be resold at the market price of $1/pound, the program is equivalent to giving them $1000 in cash, minus the cost of selling the salt, and they wind up on the higher indifference curve.

Analysis of project costs is similar to analysis of benefits. If prices are unaffected by a project, inputs should be valued according to their market price. The cost of a project's inputs is the value attached to them by private users. Holding the total quantity of an input constant, any amount used by a project will necessarily result in a decrease in the quantity used by private consumers. Assuming consumers are utility maximizing, their marginal value should, in equilibrium, equal the market price of the input.

For example, if there is a fixed quantity of labor supplied in a market and a project uses 1000 hours of that labor, private employers in the area will find themselves with 1000 fewer hours of labor that they can hire. The value that these private employers attach to that labor is the cost of using it in the project.

As another example, imagine that a fixed quantity of electricity is available in an area. If a project takes some quantity of that electricity (either by using it or by reducing generating capacity) the value that private consumers attach to this electricity is the cost of using it in the project.

If markets are well functioning,[4] the price of inputs should be a good measure of their value. If the project is relatively small compared to the market, input prices may not change as a result.

As with benefits, the price is the correct measure of the value of an input, but this may be viewed in two ways. If the input is simply taken from a private individual for use in the project but the assumption is that he/she has a property right to that input, then the project's operators must offer that individual an amount of money that he/she is willing to accept in exchange for the use of his/her units of the input. This amount will adequately compensate the individual for the units taken. Under these assumptions, the value attached to the input is the private individual's WTA. The important assumption is that the beneficiary has a pre-existing right to the input, so the value is based on pre-project conditions.

Alternatively, the assumption may be that the private individual has no inherent right to units of the input. Under this assumption, the individual might have to pay to purchase the good. There will be some maximum amount that he/she would be willing to pay for the good that would leave him/her with the same utility level as if he/she did not have the opportunity to purchase it. This value is the private individual's WTP. The inherent assumption here is that the beneficiary has no pre-existing right to the input, so the value is based on post-project conditions.[5]

---

4   Meaning that there are no externalities, no firms with significant market power, no taxes and so on.

5   The phrase 'post-project conditions' implies that you should imagine that the project has already been done and the analyst is asking, hypothetically, what the

As before, while it is generally true that the WTP value of an input will be less than its WTA value, in situations where prices do not change these values will usually be identical and equal to the market price.

One exception to this rule might be made for goods that are in some way unique. Two important examples are real estate and goods involving some sentimental value. A home that is taken for a project may have some fair market value that an appraiser could estimate, but if the land is in some way unique or the resident of that home is greatly attached to it, the resident's WTP or WTA value may be well in excess of the appraised value. In these situations, the fair market value should be regarded as a lower bound on the value of the good.

Evaluation of a project's effects becomes more complicated when there is the possibility that prices will change as a result of a project.

4.4 PROJECT EFFECTS WHEN PRICES DO CHANGE: COMPENSATING AND EQUIVALENT VARIATIONS

Most often, project inputs and outputs are traded in markets. That is, the agency doing a project purchases inputs and distributes outputs through markets. Alternatively, a program might require that private individuals make purchases in markets.[6] This may result in price changes, especially if the project is relatively large relative to the size of the market. Changes in consumption resulting from a project may occur as a result of price changes rather than direct appropriation or distribution of inputs or outputs.

A number of projects serve as examples. Ethanol, a gasoline substitute made from corn, is produced as a result of several government programs and is sold in regular gasoline markets. Electricity from federal dam projects is sold in regional electricity markets. If outputs of these projects are sufficiently large relative to the size of the relevant markets, they will result in price changes. Production and sale of ethanol might reduce fuel prices, leading to increased consumption. Sale of electricity from federally funded dams will reduce electricity prices, again leading to increased consumption. Lower prices will benefit consumers of these goods, both because of the cost savings on units they would have purchased anyway and because of the value they attach to the additional units they consume. Alternatively, a law requiring a large number of people to begin wearing bicycle helmets might

---

private individual in that position would be willing to pay to purchase back his/her units of the input.

6   One example is a program that would require cyclists to wear helmets.

sufficiently increase demand for helmets that the price would rise. The resulting increase in prices will hurt other helmet consumers.

The value to a consumer of a price change is equal to either their WTP for the price change (either to effect a decrease or to avoid an increase) or their WTA in exchange for the price change (in compensation for a decrease that does not happen or for an increase that does). Indifference curve analysis lends some insight into these concepts.

Consider first the benefit that a consumer gets from a price decrease. An initial attempt at valuing the price change would be to simply multiply the change in price by the quantity of the good originally consumed. However, this would ignore the fact that there may be additional consumption of that good and/or other goods.

If the initial price of a good is $20/unit and a typical consumer purchases 100 units, the value of a decrease in price to $18/unit might be valued at $200, but this would be an imperfect approximation. This valuation fails to take into account the value of any additional consumption that might result.

The proper valuation of such a price change is done through analysis of indifference curves. For purposes of this example, imagine that a government project will result in a reduction in the price of wine. The price decrease and resulting change in the consumption of wine and other goods is shown in Figure 4.3.

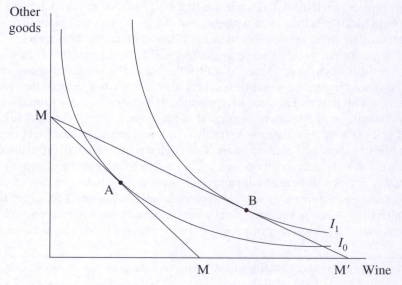

Figure 4.3   The effect of a price decrease

The decrease in the price of wine rotates the budget line from MM to MM'. This results in the consumer moving from point A to point B, consuming more wine and less of other goods.

There are two approaches to valuing this price change: equivalent variation (EV) and compensating variation (CV). Each approach looks at the value of a change in the price of wine in terms of units of other goods. The difference between the two approaches is that one uses prices prior to the effect of the program while the other uses prices after the effect of the program.

To simplify this analysis, assume that Other Goods are priced at $1/unit. Thus, one unit of Other Goods is the same as $1 spent on Other Goods.

The equivalent variation is the consumer's WTA in exchange for forgoing a decrease in the price of wine. That is, it is the amount in terms of other goods that this consumer would have to be given in order to make him/her as well off without the price change as he/she would have been had it occurred. The prices used to calculate this value are those that were in effect prior to the project. As illustrated below, the decrease in the price of wine moves the consumer from indifference curve I_0 to I_1. The value attached to this move, in terms of other goods at the initial price ratio, is N–M. This is the equivalent variation. (See Figure 4.4.)

The compensating variation is the consumer's WTP for a decrease in the price of wine. This is the maximum amount the consumer would be

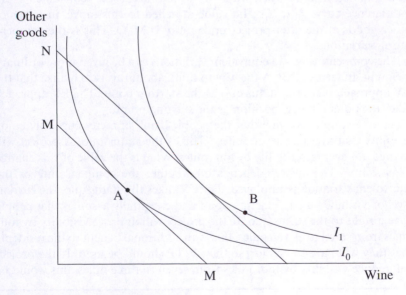

Figure 4.4 The equivalent variation

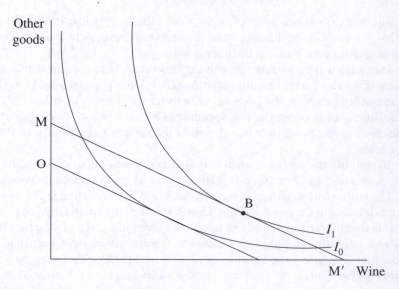

Figure 4.5   The compensating variation

willing to pay to make the price change happen. The prices used to calculate this value are those in effect after the project. As shown in Figure
4.5, the decrease in the price of wine moves the consumer from
indifference curve I_0 to I_1. The value attached to this move, in terms of
other goods at the after-project price ratio, is M–O. This is the compensating variation.

The compensating and equivalent variations can be given more ordinary
meaning. In terms of BCA the way to think about this is to realize that the
CV approach takes the status quo as the starting point. The EV approach
takes the potential new position as the starting point.

As an example, imagine that the people living in a city currently enjoy
visibility that averages seven miles.[7] This is the status quo. A project will
change this average visibility by four miles. What is the value of this change
in visibility? The answer depends on whether the compensating or the
equivalent variation is employed. The CV takes the status quo, the current
level of visibility, as the starting point and essentially assumes that people
have a right to the status quo. If the project will improve visibility by four
miles from seven to eleven miles, this is an additional benefit to the residents
that they will have to pay for, so their WTP should be used. If the project
will reduce visibility by four miles from seven to three miles, this would be

---

[7]   The authors are grateful to an anonymous reviewer for suggesting this example.

something that is taken from the residents for which they should demand compensation, so their WTA should be used. On the other hand, the EV takes the potential new situation as the starting point and assumes the people have a right to that. If the project will improve visibility to eleven miles, EV assumes that people have a right to eleven miles and will demand compensation if it is not enacted, so WTA should be used to value the increase in visibility. If the project will reduce visibility to three miles, EV assumes that people have the right to only three miles and must pay for seven miles, so their WTP should be used.

Return for a moment to the project that would cause a decrease in the price of wine. The CV assumes that the consumer does not have the right to the price decrease and must purchase the price decrease at some cost. The EV assumes that the consumer has the right to a decrease in the price of wine and must be paid to give up this right. For a gain from the status quo (such as a decrease in the price of wine) the WTP is the CV measure of the welfare gain while the WTA is the EV. The CV is the measure normally used in BCA.

In terms of the visibility example, using CV means that a visibility of seven miles is what people have a right to. An improvement to eleven miles must be paid for and is evaluated using WTP. A reduction to three miles requires compensation for the residents and is evaluated using WTA.

Now, consider a project that would raise the price of wine. The CV assumes that the consumer has a right to the status quo, the current low price of wine, and must be compensated if the price rises. The necessary level of compensation is the WTA. The EV assumes that the consumer has no right to the status quo and no right to prevent the price increase. In order to prevent the price increase, the consumer would offer an amount up to his/her WTP. For a loss from the status quo (such as would result from an increase in the price of wine) the WTA is the compensating measure of the loss.

To summarize, the compensating variation is typically used in BCA. In the case of gains, this is WTP. In the case of losses, this is WTA. So, in BCA it is generally the case that gains or benefits are valued using WTP and losses or costs are valued using WTA, both of which are consistent with use of CVs.

These ideas are summarized in Tables 4.1 and 4.2. If, as a result of a project, the price of a good increases, consumers of this good suffer a loss. If you assume that these consumers have a right to the lower (pre-project) price, then this should be valued using WTA. If, as a result of a project, the price of a good decreases, consumers of this good will enjoy a benefit. If you assume that these consumers do not have a right to the lower (post-project) price, then this should be valued according to WTP. The proper use

Table 4.1   Property rights affect gains and losses

	Price increase, consumer loss	Price decrease, consumer gain
Consumer has a property right	WTA, CV, higher value	WTA, EV, higher value
Consumer does not have a property right	WTP, EV, lower value	WTP, CV, lower value

Table 4.2   Change in rights affects gains and losses

Gain from status quo	WTP (CV) Lower value
Loss from status quo	WTA (CV) Higher value
Net gain	WTP−WTA

of WTP for benefits and WTA for losses is shown in Table 4.2. It should be noted that the use of CVs is conservative in that it includes the lower value for a project's benefits and the higher value for its costs.

Thus the distinction between the EV and the CV has its basis in ownership and thus in legal concepts of rights. The realization of this leads to the rule that BCA is not independent of the law. Because valuations are not independent of property rights, analysis of projects using BCA must consider property rights. As an extreme example, consider that theft of a bicycle is merely a transfer from one person to another. However, legal rights attach a positive value to that bicycle in the hands of the rightful owner and zero value to that bicycle in the hands of the thief, leading to the happy conclusion that theft reduces social welfare and is socially undesirable.

To apply EV and CV in an example, consider the case of electricity generated by federally funded dams in the United States. When these dams were originally built, it may have been the case that a person who would eventually buy the resulting electricity had no inherent legal right to it. As such, the relevant valuation question was, 'What is that person willing to pay to get this electricity?'. This is the compensating variation. Once the dam is built and generating electricity, the consumer may be seen as having some right to it, perhaps as a result of precedent. If a proposal is made to sell this electricity to residents of a foreign country, the cost of this would be the amount of compensation that consumers would require to make them as well off had the electricity not been sent abroad, their willingness to accept. This is the equivalent variation.

For an individual both the CV and EV are referred to as exact utility indicators. This means that either the CV or the EV (depending on assignment of property rights) will properly order the choices for an individual. If the CV for one project's benefit is $100 and the CV for another's is $150, the second will be preferred to the first.

So, in theory, the correct value to attach to a project that impacts private consumption through price changes is to calculate the equivalent and/or compensating variations for each good and for each person affected by the project. Such calculations are challenging even when done for only one person, so we will eventually discuss more practical approaches.

For now, let us move from consideration of the effects of a project on the well-being of an individual to the effects on the well-being of a group.

4.5   SOCIAL WELFARE AND NET BENEFITS

The situation is far different when multiple individuals are considered. In the previous section, we considered the gains or losses of one person. To assess the impact of a project on a group, the gains or losses to each person in the group must be somehow combined. This may be done in a variety of ways.

One way to combine individuals' gains and losses is the *Pareto criterion*, which says that if a project makes at least one person better off and leaves no one worse off, then that project is desirable. If a project makes even one person worse off, the project is deemed undesirable. In effect, the Pareto criterion applies infinitely large weight to any loss, no matter how small, while applying a finite weight to any gain. It is a rare (and perhaps non-existent) project that makes all those affected better off, or at the very least leaves no one worse off. A project that makes at least one person better off while leaving no one worse off would satisfy the Pareto criterion, and would be economically desirable, but this standard is unrealistic.

Normally, a project will make some people better off and some people worse off. The challenge is apparent: how can the welfare changes of these people be compared? We will approach this problem by treating utility as if it were measurable and then move toward something more practical.

Analysis of Utility Functions

Utility, the economic measure of individual well-being, cannot be compared between people because it cannot be measured and because the measures of utility resulting from utility functions are ordinal rather than cardinal, meaning that they allow only different sets of goods to be ranked. If, however, utility were measurable and comparable between people, we might be able to devise a rule for approving or rejecting projects based on their effect on the combined utility of the people who have standing. Such a decision rule is called a social welfare criterion. To develop the social welfare criterion supporting BCA, we begin as if utility were measurable and determine what assumptions are necessary to create a practical rule.

In mathematical terms, social welfare is a function of the utility levels of the N people in a society:

$$W = W[U_1, U_2, \ldots, U_N].$$

The partial derivative of social welfare with respect to the utility of any individual i, ($\partial W / \partial U_i$), indicates how important that person is in the social welfare function.

Most projects generate net gains for some people and net losses for others. A social welfare function describes how the gains and losses should be compared. If the changes in the utility levels of all of a society's members were known, the marginal effect of a project on social welfare would be given by:

$$dW = \sum_{i=1}^{N} \frac{\partial W}{\partial U_i} \cdot dU_i,$$

where dU_i is the change in utility for person i.

Social welfare is a subjective concept. In theory, the social welfare function describes the overall well-being of a society as a function of the utility levels of its members, but the exact mathematical relationship and the relative importance of different people (young and old people, law-abiding citizens and criminals) are open to great differences of opinion.

Ideally, the goal of any public project should be to increase social welfare. As a result, the proper criterion by which any project should be judged is whether it increases the value of the social welfare function.[8] Unfortunately, this is operationally impossible. Explicit social welfare functions do not exist. Even if there were a unanimously agreed-upon social welfare function, individual utility functions are not easily observable and changes in utility cannot be measured. So, assessing projects according to their effects on individual utility and social welfare is impossible. With some modifications, however, the social welfare criterion can be made more practical.

---

[8]   Meaning that it increases social welfare or, put another way, improves the well-being of the society.

We begin by assuming utility maximization. If individuals are utility maximizing (the primary economic assumption) then a useful relationship exists between marginal utility and net benefits. A person maximizing utility subject to a budget constraint solves the problem:

$$\max_{x} U(\mathbf{X}) \quad \text{s.t.} \ \mathbf{P'X} = Y,$$

where:

X is a vector of quantities of goods;
$U(\mathbf{X})$ is the individual's utility function;
P is a vector of prices; and
Y is the individual's income.

In the simplest case, this problem may be solved by using the Lagrangian:

$$U(\mathbf{X}) + \lambda[Y - \mathbf{P'X}],$$

which has the first-order conditions:

$$\frac{\partial U}{\partial x_i} = \lambda \mathbf{P}_i.$$

In this situation, λ is interpreted as the marginal utility of income.

If an individual is utility maximizing and experiences a change in the quantities of goods consumed, the total change in utility resulting from this change is the sum of the effects of the changes on utility:

$$dU = \sum \frac{\partial U}{\partial x_i} dx_i = \sum \lambda \mathbf{P}_i dx_i = \lambda \sum \mathbf{P}_i dx_i.$$

So, the change in utility resulting from a change in a person's consumption bundle is equal to their marginal utility of income, λ, multiplied by the sum of the product of the prices and quantities of the consumption change. However, for any person, $\Sigma \mathbf{P}_i dx_i$ is the value of the net benefits of the project, so, for any person:

$$dU = \lambda * \text{NB}.$$

We get the result that the change in social welfare may be described as:

$$dW = \sum_{i=1}^{N} \frac{\partial W}{\partial U_i} \lambda_i \text{NB}_i,$$

where:

$\partial W / \partial U_i$ is the marginal effect on social welfare of an increase in person i's utility

λ_i is person i's marginal utility of income

NB_i is the money measure (either CV or EV) of the value of the net benefits accruing to person i.

While we can estimate the NB_i values for changes in consumption that would result from a project, we cannot measure a person's marginal utility of income in a manner that allows comparison with others. That is, we cannot say on the basis of measurements that an additional dollar to Mr. X is worth less than an additional dollar to Ms. Y. What could be compared, however, is how we think the well-being or utility of a person is affected by receiving an additional dollar and how important that person is to social welfare.

In the above formula, the change in social welfare, dW, is a weighted sum of the net benefits of each person. The weight attached to each individual's net benefit is the product of a term describing their relative importance to the society, $\partial W / \partial U_i$ and their marginal utility of income, λ_i. Combined, these two terms comprise the relative value that society attaches to a unit increase in that person's income. This is also the value that society attaches to that person receiving a dollar of net benefit from a project.

The term, $\partial W / \partial U_i$, is the relative importance of person i in the social welfare function. In other words, this is how much society cares about person i. In a totally egalitarian society, this term might be the same for everyone, each person would be equally important to social welfare. Alternatively, there might be different values for different people, reflecting the idea that society cares more about some people than others. Children might be valued more highly, either because they are less able to care for themselves or because they represent the society's future. Doctors, firefighters and teachers might be valued more highly as a result of their public service. Criminals, on the other hand, might be valued less than law-abiding citizens.

So, in general, determining whether a project increases social welfare does not depend upon knowing exactly how each person's utility changes as a result of a project. If you know the social welfare function, you will know how each person's utility affects social welfare, $\partial W / \partial U_i$. You may have some assumptions regarding each person's marginal utility of income, λ_i. Lacking these separate components, you may have a basis for valuing the combined effect of a change in a person's income on social welfare, $(\partial W / \partial U_i)\lambda_i$. Given values for $(\partial W / \partial U_i)\lambda_i$, you need only know the net benefits enjoyed by each person, NB_i, to determine the impact of a project on social welfare. Of course most projects affect numbers of people sufficiently large to make even this simplified version of social welfare practically impossible to implement. The next subsection will discuss several assumptions that are necessary for practical BCA.

Some Special Simplifying Assumptions

Were they practical, the methods discussed in the previous subsection would allow an analyst to determine the impact of a project on social welfare and, as a result, correctly assess whether or not a project is desirable. Unfortunately, even the simplified version of the social welfare criterion presented above will, in most cases, require more information and subjective valuation than is likely to be possible. Even reaching agreement about what social weights to apply to different people would be a hopeless task.

The BCA solution is to use the same weight for all. The social weight of each person is the same. That is, $\partial W / \partial U_i = 1$ for all individuals. This leaves us with the simplified equation for the change in social welfare:

$$dW = \sum_{i=1}^{N} \lambda_i \cdot \mathrm{NB}_i.$$

This states that the change in social welfare is equal to the sum of each person's marginal utility of income multiplied by his/her net benefit.

This simplifying assumption deserves some discussion. First, the assumption that all people are of equal importance to society is egalitarian. Second, this assumption helps assure that projects that increase total wealth will be labeled desirable because the creation of wealth matters more than to whom a project grants that wealth. Finally, if in fact there are some people who matter more to society than others, programs of direct wealth transfers may be used to assist those more valuable people more efficiently than will projects that take some other form.

The term λ_i is person i's marginal utility of income. A common assumption in economics is diminishing marginal utility of income, the idea that the increased utility resulting from a small increase in income falls as income rises. This assumption is consistent with risk-avoiding behavior such as purchasing insurance and diversifying investments. More intuitively, it is consistent with the idea that an extra $1000 in income may be seen as being more important to a person when he/she is desperately poor than when he/she is comfortably wealthy. So, for any one person, the marginal utility of income falls as income rises.

While interpersonal utility comparisons cannot be made, many people would argue that a given increase in income makes more of a difference in the life of a desperately poor person. If people are assumed more or less alike in terms of their capacity for enjoyment then an extra dollar of income should mean more to a poorer person than it does to a richer person. If this is the case, λ_i will be larger for poorer people and smaller for richer people and a person with lower income will be of greater importance in the social welfare function. The implication that, other things being the same, benefits or costs accruing to poorer people should be seen as more important than benefits or costs accruing to richer people has led to a number of proposals for a type of BCA in which different weights are attached to people of different income.[9] This is not, however, the standard approach.

The problem is, just as with the social weight given to individuals, agreement about marginal utility of income for individuals has not been forthcoming. So again the standard approach is to proceed as if the marginal utility of income is the same for all. This gives us the following equation for the change in social welfare resulting from a project:

$$dW = \sum_{i=1}^{N} \text{NB}_i.$$

In this simplified version, social welfare increases as long as the sum of each person's net benefits, the total net benefits of the project, is positive. More simply, a project is economically desirable if it has positive net benefits.

This formulation is known as the Kaldor–Hicks criterion (KH). KH was proposed by Kaldor (1939), adopted by Hicks (1939) and may be stated as: 'A project is acceptable when the winners could hypothetically compensate the losers from the project' (Kaldor, 1939, pp. 549–50). A simplified, though not identical version of this statement is that a project is acceptable when the benefits to the winners are greater than the losses to the losers or, alternatively, that the sum of individuals' net benefits are positive.[10]

This test is what most economists mean when they speak practically of economic efficiency. The criterion is also known as a potential compensation test (PCT) as the winners could potentially compensate the losers. The original justification for this test was to separate efficiency considerations from equity considerations as the former but not the latter were held to be the proper domain of economists.

---

9 Examples include Feldstein (1974) and Willig and Bailey (1981).
10 The differences between these statements of the KH criterion become important when people are altruistic because altruism complicates the ideal of hypothetical compensation.

4.6 A DISCUSSION OF THE KALDOR–HICKS CRITERION

The test as proposed by Kaldor assumes the status quo as the starting point. In a move[11] from the current state of the world to a new state of the world, KH measures the gains and losses from moving. Gains are measured by WTP, losses by WTA and the value of the move is the sum of these compensating variations. The CVs take the original level of utility as the starting point. The winner has no inherent right to the gains he/she will enjoy from the project and must pay for them, hence the WTP. The loser has an inherent right to avoid the losses associated with the project and must be compensated for them, hence the WTA. KH is the standard BCA criterion. It incorporates the CV measure of a welfare change.

Imagine a project affecting two people, moving them from one state of the world, A, to another state of the world, B. Person 1 benefits from the project while Person 2 suffers from it as shown in Table 4.3a. KH adds the WTP for the winners to the WTA for the losers. That is, gains are measured by the WTP and losses by the WTA. Thus the KH measure of the value of moving from A to B is $100 − $95 or $5.

Note that it would also be possible, though inconsistent with KH, to measure the welfare change by the sum of the EVs. This would be the WTA for gains and the WTP for losses. For the above example this would be $120 − $75 or $45.

Suppose we used KH to measure the reverse change, from state of the world B to state of the world A, as shown in Table 4.3b. Person 1 would

Table 4.3a   The value of a move from A to B

	WTP	WTA
Person 1 – winner	CV = $100	EV = $120
Person 2 – loser	EV = −$75	CV = −$95

Table 4.3b   The value of a move from B to A

	WTP	WTA
Person 1 – loser	EV = −$100	CV = −$120
Person 2 – winner	CV = $75	EV = $95

---

[11]   A move resulting, perhaps, from a public project.

then be the loser and person 2 the winner. Person 2's gains would be measured by WTP for this move and would be + $75. Person 1's losses would be measured by WTA and would be $120.[12] The KH for a move from B to A would be $75 − $120 or − $45. This is the negative of the EV measure of the value of the move from A to B. That is, the absolute value of the KH (based on CV) measure of the value of a move from B to A is the same as the absolute value of the EV measure of the move from A to B.

For a normal good the absolute value of a person's WTA will be equal to or greater than their WTP. This is because WTA is measured from a higher welfare position than the WTP. Using WTA assumes that an individual has the right to refuse a loss, suggesting greater initial wealth. In addition, WTP is constrained by the person's income while the WTA is not.

The decision regarding a move is dependent on the initial state of the world. If you imagine two states of the world, C and D, KH could imply both the undesirability of a move from C to D and the undesirability of a move from D to C. The starting point would determine the result. This is not a problem. Our recommendation is to use the status quo as the starting point. Such an approach is consistent with the extant set of legal rights. In some cases legal rights and thus the starting point might be wholly unclear. In this case the granting of the right can be regarded as a benefit to the party receiving the right and the WTP used so that the right could be sold at auction under a KH rule.[13] Consider the real life example in Example 4C.

EXAMPLE 4C   ANCIENT REDWOODS IN HEADWATERS GROVE[14]

Headwaters Grove in Northern California is the last major privately owned stand of ancient redwood trees. The value of the trees as timber is estimated to be between $100 million and $500 million. For about ten years the Pacific Lumber Company has been trying to cut the trees, filing logging plans with the California Forestry Board. The company's efforts have been thwarted by environmental groups who have thus far been successful in preventing the logging, suggesting that whatever the legal property rights over the land might be, the economic property rights seem to lie with the environmental groups.

This is a case in which the cost of cutting the trees, as repre-

---

[12] The treatment in this chapter is in parts similar to that of Zerbe and Dively (1994).

[13] For an elaboration of this, see Zerbe (2001).

[14] This example is taken from Zerbe (2001).

sented by the environmental groups WTA is in excess of the lumber company's WTP. Indeed, if this were not the case, the lumber company might be able to offer the involved environmental groups compensation (either in terms of cash or property rights or easements on other land) in exchange for their ceasing opposition to logging Headwaters Grove.

If, instead, the logging company held the right to cut the trees, the relevant project for analysis might be to cancel logging. In this case, the benefits (preservation of the trees) would be valued according to environmental groups' WTP while the costs, the lost timber value of $100 million to $500 million, would be valued according to WTA. In this situation, it might be that WTA exceeds WTP and the trees would be logged. The outcome would be reversed because the initial state of the world and the relevant property rights would have changed.

4.7 CONSUMER AND PRODUCER SURPLUS

The WTP or WTA associated with a program, as measured by the compensating and equivalent variations, are the correct measure of welfare changes. These measures can be difficult to calculate as they require analysis of compensated or Hicksian demand curves along which utility is held constant. Observation of the actions of consumers yields ordinary or Marshallian demand curves, along which income is held constant, though it is usually possible, with some difficulty, to calculate Hicksian demand curves from Marshallian demand curves. Fortunately, observation of the behavior of consumers based on ordinary demand curves yields values that are usually good approximations for compensating and equivalent variations. These measures are consumer surplus and producer surplus.

Consumer Surplus

Consumer surplus is the gains from trade accruing to consumers in a market, roughly analogous to producers' profits. In its simplest sense, it is equal to the difference between consumers' maximum WTP for some quantity of the good and their total expenditure for that quantity. Put another way, the total value that consumers attach to some quantity of a good is equal to their total expenditure plus their consumer surplus. This is illustrated in Figure 4.6. Consumer surplus is generally a good approximation

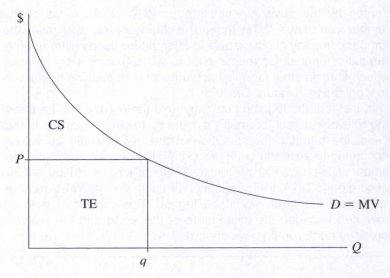

Figure 4.6   Consumer surplus

to compensating or equivalent variation in the sense that the additional consumer surplus generated by a price decrease is equal to either the compensating or equivalent variation, with some qualifications.

More specifically, correctly expressing the relationship between consumer surplus and the compensating and equivalent variations depends on specification of the Hicksian demand curve, or a demand curve along which utility remains constant. This makes this measure a bit difficult to estimate because the demand relationships most often observed are Marshallian demand curves, along which income, rather than utility, is held constant. As the price of the good rises or falls, utility decreases or increases. The implied Hicksian demand curves are, as a result, shifted in or out while the Marshallian demand curve remains stable. Figure 4.7 illustrates this for a consumer of a good whose price falls from P_0 to P_1, raising his/her utility level from U_0 to U_1. These give rise to two Hicksian demand curves, H_0 and H_1, but only one Marshallian demand curve, D.

The consumer surplus gained when the price falls from P_0 to P_1 (or lost when it rises from P_1 to P_0) is the additional area under the demand curve resulting from the price change, but which of the three demand curves (H_0, H_1 or D) to use in calculating this depends on the situation.

The CV for this price change is given by the area A. This would be the appropriate value to attach to the change in the price of this good if the price were to fall from P_0 to P_1 or if the consumer did not have some initial

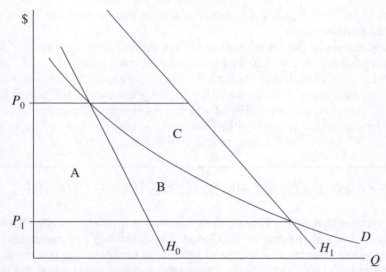

Figure 4.7   EV, CV and consumer surplus

right to the lower price. This amount is relatively small because the lack of a right to the lower price makes the consumer worse off, leaving him/her with a lower level of utility consistent with the Hicksian curve at the lower utility level, H_0.

The EV for this price change is given by the area A + B + C. This would be the appropriate value to attach to this price change if the price were to rise from P_1 to P_0 or if the consumer has some right to the lower price. This amount is relatively large because the consumer's implicit right to the lower price makes him/her better off, endowing him/her with a higher level of utility consistent with the Hicksian curve at the higher utility level, H_1.

As discussed above, estimated or observed demand curves are most often Marshallian demand curves, such as *D*. The consumer surplus calculated from such an observed demand curve would be equal to the area A + B, and in general would never be exactly the correct value.

Fortunately, consumer surplus as measured by the Marshallian demand curve, *D*, is likely to be close to the appropriate value in each case. Willig (1976) demonstrated that under ordinary conditions consumer surplus as given by the Marshallian demand curve is a good approximation to either the compensating or equivalent variation, and that the error of the approximation will likely be much smaller than the errors inherent in the estimation of the demand curve.

Less fortunately, since Willig's work, evidence suggests the divergence between the compensating and equivalent variations can be much larger

A primer for benefit–cost analysis

than he believed. In these situations consumer surplus may not be such a good approximation.

Operationally, if a project will result in a price change for a good, if the initial price and quantity are known and if the post-project price and quantity can be estimated, then the area A + B may be approximated with some degree of accuracy. This should be a reasonable measure of the gain or loss to private consumers regardless of whether the compensating or equivalent variation would be theoretically more correct as long as these variations are not too far apart. An illustration is shown in Example 4D.

EXAMPLE 4D   AGRICULTURAL PRICE CHANGES

Imagine that one million tons of broccoli are produced and sold each year at a price of $2000/ton. Consider two programs with opposite impacts of the cost of producing broccoli: one will lower the price to $1800/ton and increase the quantity sold by 200 thousand tons while the other will raise the price to $2200/ton and reduce the quantity sold by 200 thousand tons.

We calculate the area of the changes in consumer surplus from each program, assuming linear demand curves:

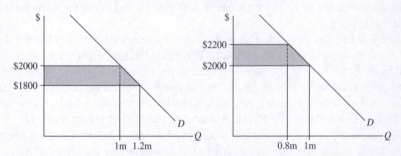

In the case of the price decrease, the calculated change in consumer surplus is $200/unit multiplied by 1.1 million units, or $220 million. However, because this is a price decrease, the CV is the correct measure of the gain, so the value of $220 million may, perhaps, be thought of as an upper bound.

In the case of the price increase, the calculated change in consumer surplus is $200/unit multiplied by 0.9 million units, or $180 million. However, because this is a price increase, the EV is the correct measure of the loss, so the value of $180 may be thought of as a lower bound.

Producer Surplus

Producer surplus is the gains from trade accruing to the producers or suppliers in a market. It is the difference between their revenue and their variable costs of production. Put another way, producer surplus is equal to economic profit not including any fixed costs, or is the difference between total revenue and variable costs, as illustrated in Figure 4.8.

Because suppliers are generally considered to be profit maximizing, much of the complexity surrounding consumer decisions and the associated changes in welfare may be avoided. Initial allocation of property rights (having the right to the status quo, for example) should not affect a firm's profit-maximizing level of output.

While producer surplus is never reported and probably rarely calculated, changes in profits will usually be a good approximation to changes in producer surplus as long as there are no large changes in the quantity of fixed inputs used.

For example, if a project produces a large quantity of an output, driving down the price received by private producers of the good, producers' loss would be the reduction in producer surplus (ΔPS) shown in Figure 4.9. While this change in producer surplus would never be reported, as long as there were not major changes in the firm's fixed inputs (the number of plants they operate, for example) then the change in profit, which would be

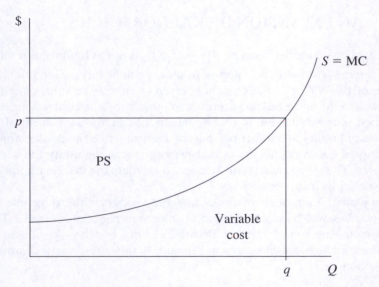

Figure 4.8   Producer surplus

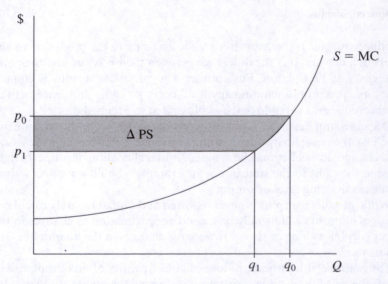

Figure 4.9　Producer surplus

reported if the firm is publicly held, should closely approximate the change in producer surplus.

4.8　AN EXPANSION OF KALDOR–HICKS

The expression for net benefits, $dW = \sum_{i=1}^{N} \mathrm{NB}_i$ is not as limiting as it might first appear. The worth of a person to society can be included in NB in the form of the WTP by others for that person's welfare. The value placed on the welfare of or on benefits accruing to other people is clearly a measure of their social value, that is, of $\partial W/\partial U_i$. In making the assessment of the increase in utility to another person, the assessor will estimate the value of additional goods or income to that person, that is the utility the person receives. Thus the assessor will attempt to estimate the marginal utility of income for the other person.

To write this out mathematically, imagine a society with two people and two goods in which Person 1 has moral sentiments regarding Person 2. That is, Person 1 has some interest in Person 2's utility. For the sake of simplicity, Person 2 has no such interest in Person 1. In this case, social welfare may be written as:

$$W = W\{U_1[x_{11}, x_{12}, U_2(x_{21}, x_{22})], U_2(x_{21}, x_{22})\}$$

where x_{ij} is the consumption by person i of good j. A program affecting consumption of Person 2 only would have the following impact on social welfare:

$$\Delta W = \frac{\partial W}{\partial U_1}\frac{\partial U_1}{\partial U_2}\left(\frac{\partial U_2}{\partial x_{21}}\Delta x_{21} + \frac{\partial U_2}{\partial x_{22}}\Delta x_{22}\right) + \frac{\partial W}{\partial U_2}\left(\frac{\partial U_2}{\partial x_{21}}\Delta x_{21} + \frac{\partial U_2}{\partial x_{22}}\Delta x_{22}\right)$$

which, if Person 2 is utility maximizing is equal to:

$$\Delta W = \frac{\partial W}{\partial U_1}\frac{\partial U_1}{\partial U_2}(\lambda_2 NB_2) + \frac{\partial W}{\partial U_2}(\lambda_2 NB_2)$$

$$\Delta W = \lambda_2 NB_2\left(\frac{\partial W}{\partial U_2} + \frac{\partial W}{\partial U_1}\frac{\partial U_1}{\partial U_2}\right).$$

So, assuming that Person 1's sentiments toward Person 2 are positive ($\partial U_1/\partial U_2 > 0$) and that Person 1 is positively regarded by society ($\partial W/\partial U_1 > 0$), the recognition of Person 1's moral sentiments as an economic good with a WTP allows for Person 2 to have some augmented social weight within the context of Kaldor–Hicks.

This expanded concept of KH is similar to the original, but is expanded to include the idea that all goods for which there is a WTP are economic goods. Thus moral sentiments regarding the welfare of others would be included among the goods to be valued. This issue is explored further in the propane merger (Example 4E).

EXAMPLE 4E   THE PROPANE MERGER

Superior Propane and ICG Propane provide retail sales and distribution services to residential and commercial propane customers. They have historically competed against each other in a number of overlapping geographic and product markets, and they are the only two companies that supply propane to end-users throughout Canada. In 1997, Superior had 130 branches and ICG had 110 branches and satellite locations across Canada. On December 7, 1998, Superior acquired all outstanding shares of ICG (the merger) but the implementation of the merger was delayed pending the Canadian Competition Tribunal's initial decision.

Equity Concerns of the Merger

The merger raised several flags to the Competition Tribunal due to the relatively low incomes of the customers and the essential character of the good. Superior and ICG Propane tend to serve businesses and individuals that reside in rural areas. These businesses are usually small and often use propane for essential purposes like cooking and heating. Residential customers are older on average, nearly a third are retired, and generally have less education. Households use propane for a variety of purposes including heating, cooking, and running a hot water heater. Farmers use propane to dry damp grain. A smaller fraction of customers use propane solely for unessential or less essential amenities such as heating a swimming pool or operating a fireplace. Residential consumers of propane also tend to earn lower levels of income with approximately 63 percent earning less than the Canadian median income. The relatively high cost of switching to different fuels makes it difficult to change to new fuel sources. Substituting natural gas could be a cheaper option for those with access, but often this fuel is not available. Electricity often costs more per BTU than propane and switching to electricity would involve buying new appliances and some rewiring of the house. Switching from propane to heating oil costs over $4000 (Canadian) and the use of heating oil has other costs including bad odor and higher levels of indoor and outdoor environmental pollution.

Estimated Benefits and Costs of the Merger

The merger's effects as estimated by the Tribunal are shown in the figure opposite. Following the Tribunal, we assume the marginal and average cost curves are flat so that it is a constant-cost industry. The assumptions of competition and flat marginal and average cost curves imply that producer surplus did not exist before the merger. Price before the merger is determined by the intersection of demand and supply at P_1. Gains in efficiency from the merger will reduce costs from AC_1 to AC_2 and, after the merger, the price will be determined by the monopolist and will be above costs at, say, P_2. The merger will create producer surplus both because of the reduction in costs and because of the gain in monopoly pricing power. Since price is expected to increase, as shown in the figure, consumer surplus will fall. The loss of consumer surplus will consist of the deadweight loss (DWL), which is lost to everyone,

and the income transfer (a welfare neutral transfer), which was initially consumer surplus and now becomes producer surplus. That
is, both the DWL and the income transfer were consumer surplus
before the merger. After the merger, the producer surplus will
be the efficiency gains plus the income transfer. These will also
represent economic profits. Since the wealth transfer is a gain to
producers and a loss to consumers, traditional economic analysis
regards this as an offsetting transfer with no net welfare effect. The
DWL represents surplus lost to society because the monopolist
can raise the price above the supply curve (above average and
marginal costs). The economic welfare effects of the merger will
then be found by comparing the DWL with the efficiency gain and
this is shown as follows:

$$\Delta W = (\Delta CS + \Delta PS).$$

Since ΔCS $= - (DWL + Wealth\ Transfer)$
and ΔPS $= + (Efficiency\ Gain + Wealth\ Transfer)$,
then ΔW $= - (DWL + Wealth\ \ Transfer) + (Efficiency\ \ Gain +$
             $Wealth\ Transfer)$,
or ΔW $= - DWL + Efficiency\ Gain.$

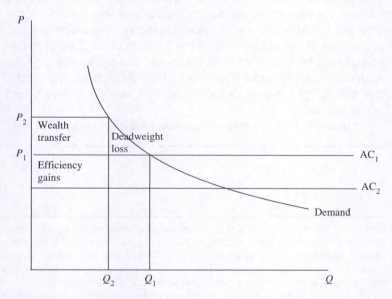

Effects of monopoly power

The court estimated Superior Propane's efficiency gains over a ten-year period at $29.2 million per year, the deadweight loss at less than $3.0 million per year, and the wealth transfer from consumers to producers at approximately $40.5 million per year.[15] The results of applying the total surplus standard are shown in the table.

The total surplus standard

Change in welfare	$m per year
Deadweight loss (−CS)	−$3.0
Wealth transfer(−CS, +PS)	$40.5
Efficiency gain (+PS)	$29.2
Total	$26.2

This merger was upheld on the basis of the BCA. It turns out that the above calculations are incorrect because they incorrectly assume that there was no pre-existing monopoly power. Correct calculations give net benefits from the merger as essentially zero, but these were not available to the Court at the time of the decision.

In any event it is clear that concerns about the welfare of those harmed creates an issue of standing. When the moral sentiments of other Canadian citizens towards those harmed here are included the project would clearly be undesirable based on the corrected benefit–cost calculations. Based on the faulty calculations shown in the above table, if the harm to other Canadian citizens arising from their care about those directly harmed by the merger amounts to about 60 percent of the direct consumer harm, then the merger fails a benefit–cost test even if the incorrect figures are used.

(For a discussion of these issues see Zerbe and Knott, 2004.)

---

[15] Zerbe and Knott (2004). The loss of consumer surplus could be less than the stated amount because of improvements to delivery services by the merged propane company, or increases in quality and improved innovation. In stockholder literature, Superior claimed that services would improve following the merger, but did not use this argument in court and did not give specific examples of improvement (see http://www.superiorpropane.com/html/income.html). We thank Aaron Finkle and Leigh Anderson for this observation.

4.9 SUMMARY

The true measure of whether or not a project is beneficial is based on changes in the utility of affected individuals. The Pareto criterion, the most restrictive criteria for approval of a project, says that if a project increases at least one person's utility without decreasing any other person's utility that project is beneficial, but this criterion is of little use in evaluating actual projects.

Consideration of the net impact of a project on social welfare when there are simultaneously positive and negative impacts on different people requires knowledge of their utility functions and the assumption of some objective social welfare function. Unfortunately, calculation of cardinal utility functions and the changes in utility and comparison of these changes across individuals makes direct use of utility functions and social welfare functions impossible in any realistic way.

By looking instead at net benefits accruing to people and weighting individuals equally, we get a more pragmatic measure of the desirability of a project. In particular, the KH criterion suggests treating all people equally and granting them rights to the status quo for the purpose of analysis. This yields the concept of net benefits as a measure of the economic merit of a project, the most common measure used in BCA. In particular, net benefits should be calculated on the basis of compensating variations, using WTP to value benefits and WTA to value costs.

An alternative pragmatic approach to valuing welfare changes is to look at net gains from trade in markets directly affected by projects. To this end, changes in consumer surplus (net gains to consumers) and producer surplus (net gains to producers) might be estimated for use in calculation of net welfare effects.

The standard KH criterion can be augmented to include moral sentiments. Within the context of KH, if moral sentiments and the willingness to pay for increases in others' utility levels are recognized, the potential effect is to increase the weight attached to net benefits accruing to particular individuals or groups within society.

REFERENCES

Feldstein, Martin (1974), 'Distributional preferences in public expenditure analysis', in Harold H. Hochman and George E. Peterson (eds), *Redistribution Through Public Choices*, New York: Columbia University, pp. 136–61.

Hicks, John R. (1939), 'The foundations of welfare economics', *Economic Journal*, **49**: 696–712.

Kaldor, Nicholas (1939), 'Welfare propositions in economics and interpersonal comparisons of utility', *Economic Journal*, **49**: 549–52.

Olsen, E.O. and D.M. Barton (1983), 'The benefits and costs of public housing in New York City', *Journal of Public Economics*, **20** (3): 299–332.

Willig, Robert D. (1976), 'Consumer's surplus without apology', *American Economic Review*, **66**: 589–97.

Willig, Robert D. and Elizabeth E. Bailey (1981), 'Income distributional concerns in regulatory policy-making', in Gary Fromm (ed.), *Studies in Public Regulation*, Cambridge, MA: MIT Press.

Zerbe, Richard O. (2001), *Economic Efficiency in Law and Economics*, Cheltenham, UK and Northampton, MA, USA: Edward Elgar.

Zerbe, Richard O. and Dwight Dively (1994), *Benefit–Cost Analysis in Theory and Practice*, New York: Harper Collins.

Zerbe, Richard O. and Sunny Knott (2004), 'An economic justification for a price standard in merger policy: the merger of Superior Propane and ICG Propane', *Research in Law and Economics*, **21**: 409–44.

EXERCISES

Questions

1. Imagine a move from state of the world A to state of the world B affecting two people, Dave and Chris. Their WTP and WTA figures are given in the table below.

   The value of a move from A to B

	WTP	WTA
Dave	CV = $100	EV = $130
Chris	EV = −$105	CV = −$120

   Calculate the net benefits of a move from A to B and the net benefits of a move from B to A. Comment on the results.
2. Can you assemble an example similar to that given in the preceding question in which both a move from A to B and a move from B to A are desirable? If not, why not?

Answers

1. For a move from A to B, Dave will enjoy a benefit and Chris will suffer a loss. Dave's benefit should be valued according to his willingness to pay of $100 while Chris's loss should be valued according to his willingness to accept, −$120, for a net benefit of −$20.

   For a move from B to A, Dave will suffer a loss and Chris will enjoy a benefit. Dave's loss should be valued according to his willingness to accept of −$130 while Chris's gain should be valued according to his willingness to pay, $105, for a net benefit of −$25.

   The result is that neither move is beneficial. This may seem to be a contradiction, but the difference between the moves lies in the assignment of property rights in each of the two states of the world and the effect that different property rights have on valuations.
2. As long as the goods involved are normal goods, it will be impossible to construct an example in which both moves are desirable. This is because the magnitude of the willingness to accept will always be greater than the magnitude of the willingness to pay, so the costs of a move from one state of the world to another will be larger than the benefits of a reverse move.

5.   Valuing inputs using market prices

5.1   INTRODUCTION

Inputs are the goods and services used in a project. Examples include the cement and labor used in building a dam, the building materials used in constructing a public housing project or the land used to create a municipal golf course. Most of these will be purchased, hired or rented in some sort of market where the price paid is usually a good measure of their value. However, using market prices to value project inputs offers several challenges. Taxes, externalities and other market distortions must be accounted for correctly. If any inputs are obtained through any means other than direct, voluntary trade, they may need to be valued differently.

There are three implications of using inputs in a project. First, the market price of the input may rise as a result of the increase in demand for that input. Second, other consumers of the input may wind up using less of it because the project has taken some of the input out of the market. Third, producers of the input may make more of it to cover the additional demand of the project. The relative sizes of decreased private consumption and increased production will depend on the relative elasticities of supply and demand.

Both the decrease in private consumption and the increase in production of the input are costs of the project. The decrease in private consumption is a cost because individuals will be consuming less of a good or service they desire. The increase in production is a cost because productive inputs will be shifted from other activities toward increased production of this input.

Proper treatment of input costs can be summarized in two rules:

- The reduction in private use of an input should be measured according to the willingness to pay by other consumers of that input.[1]
- The increase in production of an input should be measured according to the marginal cost of the additional production.

---

[1]   If a project requires that some units of a good be taken from private users, it may be more correct to value this loss using a willingness to accept, or the necessary compensation for the lost consumption. An example of this is land takings through eminent domain, discussed below.

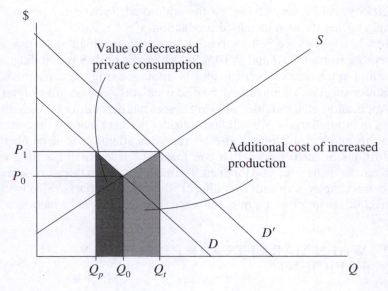

Figure 5.1   Input cost rules

These rules are illustrated in Figure 5.1. The original supply and demand curves are S and D. The project increases demand for the input from D to D'. The increased production, $Q_t - Q_0$, is valued along the supply or marginal cost curve. Decreased private consumption, $Q_0 - Q_p$, is valued along the demand or marginal value curve. The sum of the increased production and decreased private consumption is the total quantity of the input used in the project.

The relative sizes of decreased private consumption and increased production will depend on the relative elasticities of supply and demand.

If demand is relatively elastic and supply relatively inelastic, the increased demand resulting from a project using an input is likely to come mostly from decreased private consumption. One extreme example is land in a city. A project that uses some of the land in a city will necessarily displace some other use of the land. If no additional land can be created, supply is perfectly inelastic and the entire amount necessary for the project will come from decreased private use.

If, on the other hand, demand is relatively inelastic and supply relatively elastic then the increased demand is likely to come mostly from increased production. Imagine that a town is going to install lights at a number of playfields. These lights will use a significant amount of electricity, but if the local power company has excess generating capacity, the supply of electricity will be very elastic, so the additional demand for power will simply be met through increased production.

In what follows we will concentrate on direct willingness to pay and accept measures (WTP and WTA). But all of the problems and diagrams here and in the next chapter can also be approached in the consumer and producer surplus fashion, as will be discussed at the end of this chapter.

Application of these rules will vary somewhat depending on the conditions in input markets. We will first consider markets that are functioning with no major distortions and then turn our attention to a number of distortions or inefficiencies that can make the true cost of inputs very different from the price paid for them. The most important thing to take away from this chapter is an understanding of when market prices are likely to be correct values for project inputs and when they are likely to be incorrect.

5.2   WHEN MARKETS ARE RELATIVELY EFFICIENT

If markets are free of inefficiencies, consumers' WTP should be approximately equal to the marginal cost of production, and both of these will simply be the market price of the input. This suggests a market in which there are no (or negligible) taxes, no externalities and no firms with significant market power and in which both suppliers and consumers have good information. These conditions are consistent with the typical model of perfect competition, but a market does not have to be perfectly competitive in the strictest sense for the principles of this section to be applied. The important consideration here is that there will not be a large difference between the marginal cost of production and the price paid by consumers.

In this simple situation it is not important to determine the relative sizes of increased production and decreased private consumption. The one important consideration will be the quantity of the input demanded by the project relative to the size of the relevant market and whether or not the market price is likely to change as a result of the project. That is, will the project use a small quantity of the input or a large quantity of the input?

The Basic Case: Relatively Large Quantities

The most basic diagram of increased demand for a project input is shown in Figure 5.1. The purchase of the input for the project increases demand from D to D' resulting in an increase in the price from P_0 to P_1 and an increase in the total market quantity from Q_0 to Q_t. The price increase also means that purchases by private consumers, whose demand is given by the original demand curve, fall from Q_0 to Q_p. As described above, the total value of the input is the sum of consumers' WTP for the units they no longer consume (the left side of the shaded area in Figure 5.1) and the additional production costs of private producers who increase their output (the right side of the shaded area in Figure 5.1).

Such a price increase may result because there is no effective national or global market for the input (as may occur with labor in a remote area) or because the project is very large relative to the total supply of some input. Such large projects are probably rare, but in dealing with such a large project, it is critical to use the correct price for major inputs.

When a project will use a quantity of an input sufficient to change the market price, the correct price to use in valuing that input is the average of the pre-project and during-project prices. In terms of Figure 5.1, the project will use a quantity of $Q_t - Q_p$ and the average value of this input is $(P_0 + P_1)/2$, so the total cost of this input would be the product of the two, $(Q_t - Q_p) \times (P_0 + P_1)/2$.[2] For example, if a project will use a large quantity of labor in a remote area of a developing country and wages will be driven from \$8.00/day to \$10.00/day as a result, the correct value to attach to labor used on this project would be the average of these two values, or \$9.00/day.

In estimating the price effects of large projects, one approach is to use an estimate of the price elasticity of demand and the price elasticity of supply of the input in question. Example 5A shows this. The percentage price increase likely to result from a project can be calculated using the following equation:

$$\%\Delta P = \frac{Q_{\text{project}}/Q}{-\text{PED} + \text{PES}},$$

where:

Q = the total quantity of the good being exchanged in the market prior to the project;
Q_{project} = the quantity of the good that will be used in the project;
PED = the price elasticity of demand for the input; and
PES = the price elasticity of supply for the input.

Some practical advice is in order here. While there are numerous estimates of demand elasticity, estimates of supply elasticities are more rare. Lacking reliable estimates of supply and demand elasticities for a market, here are some guidelines for predicting price effects.

---

[2] This formula is only exactly correct when the demand and supply curves are linear, but in most cases this should be a good approximation.

EXAMPLE 5A   THE GUACAMOLE PROJECT

In an effort to promote tourism, a community wants to create the world's largest bowl of guacamole. Town leaders estimate that it will use 20 percent of next year's North American supply of avocados. Economists estimate that the price elasticities of supply and demand for avocados are 0.3 and −1.2, respectively. To calculate the percentage increase in the price of avocados that is likely to result from the project, the formula would be:

$$\%\Delta P = \frac{Q_{project}/Q}{-\text{PED} + \text{PES}} = \frac{0.20}{1.2 + 0.3} = \frac{0.20}{1.5} = 0.133,$$

or about a 13.3 percent increase.

To use this information to determine the cost of the avocados in the project, you need to know the quantity of avocados to be used and their initial price. Imagine that the project will use 50,000 tons of avocados and that the initial price is $4000 per ton. The price with the project in place would be:

$$\$4000 \times 1.133 = \$4532.$$

The correct price to use in valuing the avocados would be the average of the before project price ($4000) and the during-project price ($4532) or $4266.

The total value of 50,000 tons would be $213,300,000. If the initial price were used, this figure would be $4000 multiplied by 50,000 tons or $200,000,000.

In the very short run it may be impossible for suppliers to change the quantity they offer for sale. This would be the case, for example, with the housing stock in a city. Over a matter of months it may be largely impossible for the supply of housing to increase. This implies a short-run supply elasticity of approximately 0. To apply this to the guacamole project described above, imagine that the community doing the project approves and implements the project over a very short period of time. If suppliers are unable to respond by increasing the quantity of avocados supplied over such a short period of time, the price elasticity of supply would be 0. The resulting price increase would then be:

$$\%\Delta P = \frac{Q_{\text{project}}/Q}{-\text{PED} + \text{PES}} = \frac{0.20}{1.2 + 0.0} = \frac{0.20}{1.2} = 0.167,$$

or about a 16.7 percent price increase.

In the long run if new firms can enter a market with no real competitive disadvantages or if production processes can be replicated fairly easily (conditions commonly referring to a constant cost industry) then, given enough time, the price will likely return to its long-run equilibrium level. This implies infinitely elastic long-run supply, meaning that there will be no price increase in the long run.

How long the transition from the very short run to the long run might take depends on the industry and is probably open to some difference of opinion. If there is sufficient excess productive capacity or if new capacity can be built quickly, this transition time might be very short. If there is insufficient excess capacity and construction of new capacity cannot be done quickly (as might be the case with steel production or oil refining) it might be years before the long run is attained. The effect of time is shown in Example 5B.

EXAMPLE 5B THE PEACH PROJECT

A multi-year research project will use a quantity of peaches equivalent to about 10 percent of the domestic market for peaches over at least the next twenty years. It takes about five years for a new peach tree to start bearing fruit. If the price of peaches is generally about $150/unit and the price elasticity of demand for peaches is estimated to be -1.4, what price should be used to value the peaches used in the project?

The first consideration should be whether or not there is an international market for peaches. If there is, then foreign suppliers might be able to accommodate the additional demand of the project with no significant price increase, so the prevailing world price (which should be close to $150 in the absence of trade barriers) would be an appropriate price to use.

If there is no international market for peaches and no surplus in the domestic market, we might assume that the short-run price elasticity of supply is 0. The above formula gives us:

$$\%\Delta P = \frac{Q_{\text{project}}/Q}{-\text{PED} + \text{PES}} = \frac{0.10}{1.4 + 0} = \frac{0.10}{1.4} = 0.07,$$

or about a 7 percent increase from $150 to $160.50. The appropriate value to attach to the peaches would be the average of these two figures, or $155.25. This price would only be relevant in the short run, or about the first five years of the project. After that, when new trees come into production, the price is likely to drop back to $150.

So, the costs of the project would include a price for peaches that is 3.5 percent higher ($155.25) for the first five years and then would revert to the long-run equilibrium price of $150 for the duration of the project.

Relatively Small Quantities

If the project will use a relatively small quantity of the input, its price will not change significantly as a result and the market price prior to the project starting can be used as the cost of the input. What is meant by a 'relatively small quantity' may be a point of some disagreement. If the quantity the project will use is a small percentage of the total quantity of the input consumed in the local area, it is probably a small quantity. If there are good national or global markets for the input and the project is unlikely to have an impact on prices in those markets, the quantity used may also be considered small.

For example, a meals-on-wheels program in an urban area might use some labor for food preparation and delivery, some vehicles and some gasoline. The quantities of each of these will be unlikely to affect market prices, so the pre-project wages and prices would be good values to use for the project inputs. In a well-functioning economy, very few projects are so large that they could reasonably be expected to have a significant effect on market prices, so in most cases it is probably correct to use pre-project prices as the cost of inputs.

5.3   VALUATION OF INPUTS WHEN DISTORTIONS AND INEFFICIENCIES EXIST

Myriad distortions may exist in markets and these can change the valuation of a project's inputs. The rest of this chapter will discuss valuation of inputs in the presence of distortions including taxes, externalities and the existence of firms with significant market power. While the two rules presented above will remain as guiding principles, their application will be slightly more complex in the face of market distortions.

5.4 VALUATION OF INPUTS WHEN THERE ARE TAXES

Most project inputs are likely to be subject to some sort of tax. Labor is subject to payroll and income taxes, construction materials may be subject to sales tax and there may be taxes associated with transfers of land or building used in a project. While it is possible to use market prices as a measure of the cost of taxed inputs, the calculations are slightly more complicated. One consideration is the extent to which the tax should be included in the cost of the input. A second consideration is the relative impact of the project on total production and private consumption of the input. That is, when the project purchases units of the input, how much of that purchase will come from increased production of the input and how much will come from reductions in private purchases?

For purposes of this chapter, it will be assumed that the government collecting the tax has standing in the analysis. The implication is that tax payments are simply transfers from taxpayers to the government and do not count as costs or benefits. An alternative view might be that the government collecting the tax does not have standing. One example of this would be a BCA done from the point of view of residents of a state. Any payments to the federal government might be regarded as costs, even though they might be more properly considered transfers from state taxpayers to the federal government. Another example would be a BCA of a relief program sending supplies to people in a country with an unpopular or oppressive government that will collect taxes on the supplies sent. If the government is seen as corrupt, hostile or illegitimate, any taxes it collects might be considered costs. If the government does not have standing, the analysis should change so that the tax payment is a cost.

The two rules stated earlier in this chapter imply that taxes associated with the input should be included in the value of decreased private consumption but not in the value of increased production. Private consumers will purchase additional units of the output until their marginal value declines to the price *including tax*, because this is the price that consumers must pay. Thus, consumers' marginal value of the input includes the tax they pay, and any decrease in private consumption should be valued at the price including tax, as shown in Figure 5.2. Private suppliers of the input will produce additional units until their marginal cost rises to the price they receive, but this price will not include taxes. Any increase in production should be valued at the marginal cost of production, which will be equal to the price less taxes. The tax that will be paid on the sale of these additional units is merely a transfer to the taxing authority and counts as neither a cost nor benefit.[3]

The Standard Diagram: Relatively Large Quantities

Consider a project that will consume a large quantity of an input, resulting in an increase in its price. This will mean that some private consumers of the input will reduce their consumption and that suppliers will increase the quantity they produce. The situation is depicted in Figure 5.2.

Following the two rules stated above, taxes should be included in the value of decreased private consumption but not in the value of increased production. The marginal value (MV) of the input to private consumers includes the tax they pay and any decrease in private consumption should be valued at the price including the tax. Suppliers of the input will produce additional units until the marginal cost rises to the price they receive from selling an additional unit, but this will be the price excluding the tax. Thus, any extra units produced to provide inputs for a project should be valued at the marginal cost of production, which will be equal to the sales price less taxes. The tax paid on the sale of these additional units is merely a transfer to the taxing authority.[4]

Figure 5.2 illustrates a large project's impact on the market for a taxed input. The original supply curve is given by $S = MC$, the marginal cost of production not including taxes. The effect of the tax is to shift the supply curve to S_t, equal to the marginal cost of production plus the tax. The project's impact is shown as an increase in demand for the input. The effect of the project is to raise the price from P_0 to P_1 and to decrease the quantity sold. The right side of the shaded area shows the cost of increased production of the input, valued according to the marginal cost of production excluding the tax. The left side of the shaded area shows the value of the reduction in private consumption and is valued according to marginal value, the price including the tax.

To calculate the value of this input, the increase in production should be multiplied by the average of the pre- and post-project prices excluding the tax and the decrease in private consumption should be multiplied by the average of the pre- and post-project prices including the tax.

---

[3] Assuming, of course, that the taxing authority has standing.
[4] Assuming, of course, that the taxing authority has standing. If the taxing authority does not have standing, then the tax paid on the additional output would be a cost. This amount is equal to the area of the parallelogram above the additional cost of increased production in Figure 5.2.

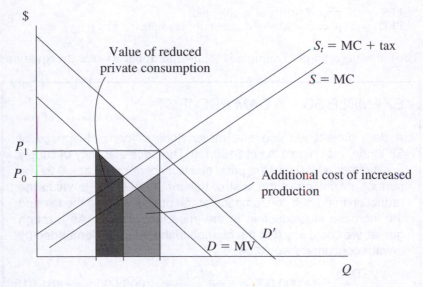

*Figure 5.2   The costs of a government buying program when an excise
tax exists*

The most difficult part of this valuation process will likely be determining
how much of the project's use will be made up through increased production and how much will be made up through decreased private consumption.

The key to determining this is some knowledge of the elasticities of
supply and of demand for the good in question. These are probably most
easily obtained from previous estimates that economists have done. The list
of resources in Chapter 12 may have supply or demand elasticity estimates
for goods you are interested in.

If reliable estimates of the supply and demand elasticities are available,
the changes in the quantities supplied and the quantity privately demanded
may be estimated by the following equations:

$$\frac{dQ_s}{dX} = \frac{\text{PES}}{-\text{PED} + \text{PES}}$$

$$\frac{dQ_D}{dX} = \frac{-\text{PED}}{-\text{PED} + \text{PES}},$$

where:

dQ_s = the change in the quantity supplied;
dQ_D = the change in the quantity demanded by private users;
dX = the quantity of an input used in the project;

PES = the price elasticity of supply; and
PED = the price elasticity of demand (for example, −0.5).

The following example, Example 5C, shows the application of the equation.

EXAMPLE 5C   A DAM PROJECT

A dam project will use one million tons of concrete priced at
$800/ton, including a tax of $100/ton. The price elasticity of supply
is estimated at 0.9 and the price elasticity of demand at −0.2. The
correct estimation of the cost of this input would be to value the
reduction in private consumption at the price including the tax and
the increase in production at the price less the tax. As a rough
guess, we could say that the change in the quantity demanded by
private consumers would be:

$$\frac{PED}{-PED + PES}*1{,}000{,}000 = \frac{-0.2}{0.2 + 0.9} \times 1{,}000{,}000 = -181{,}818,$$

and that the change in the quantity supplied to the market would be:

$$\frac{PES}{-PED + PES}*1{,}000{,}000 = \frac{0.9}{0.2 + 0.9} \times 1{,}000{,}000 = 818{,}181.$$

To simplify the calculations, assume first that the price of concrete does not change as a result of the dam project. The reduction in quantity demanded would be valued at $800/ton and the
increase in production would be valued at $700/ton (the price
excluding the tax) for a total input cost of:

$$181{,}818 \times \$800 + 818{,}181 \times \$700 = \$718{,}181{,}100.$$

It is more realistic to assume that the price of concrete will
increase by some amount. In fact, this is what will drive both the
decrease in private consumption and the increase in production. If
the price increases by $50 (to $750 excluding the tax or $850
including the tax) then the appropriate value for the reduction in
private consumption would be $825 and the appropriate value for
the increase in production would be $725 and the total cost of the
concrete used in the dam would be:

$$181{,}818 \times \$825 + 818{,}181 \times \$725 = \$743{,}181{,}075.$$

Reliable elasticity estimates may be unavailable much of the time. Lacking reliable estimates, here are a few guidelines.

First, if there is excess capacity among suppliers in the market and this capacity can be easily exploited, supply elasticity, even in the short run, may be infinite. That is, all of the input required for the project may simply come from increased production by firms that will be all too happy to make and sell the extra output. If this excess capacity has the same marginal cost as previously used capacity, the market price excluding taxes will be an appropriate cost to apply to the additional units. If this excess capacity has slightly higher marginal cost than usual production processes, this higher marginal cost should be used as the cost of the input.

Second, if there are restrictions on the potential for increased production but consumers have good substitutes available to them so that demand is very elastic, then the quantity of the input required may come from decreased private consumption. In this case, the input should be valued according to consumers' WTP, which will include the tax on the good.

Third, if there seem to be very limited excess capacity and opportunities for substitution among private consumers, it may be reasonable to simply assume that half of the quantity will come from increased production and half will come from decreased private consumption, at least until new productive capacity can come online. Under this assumption, the tax should be included in half of the quantity and excluded from half of the quantity. In any case, the analyst should be clear about the assumptions used.

Extreme Assumption 1: Perfectly Elastic Supply

One extreme, though not necessarily unrealistic, assumption is that supply of the input is perfectly elastic. This assumption is consistent with all of the project's input coming from increased production. Put another way, this assumption says that there will be no decrease in private consumption as a result of the project, only increased production, and the increase in production will be exactly equal to the quantity of input used by the project.

Under this assumption, valuation of the input is easily calculated. Because supply is perfectly elastic, there is no change in the market price. The only effect is an increase in private production, so the project's output should be valued at the marginal cost of production, or the price minus taxes.

This assumption may be most relevant in the short run if suppliers of the input have sufficient excess capacity to meet project demands or in the long run if it is easy for firms to enter the input market. While there may be some price response in the short run, if the project will have a long lifetime the assumption of no long-run price change may be reasonable.

Extreme Assumption 2: Perfectly Elastic Demand

Another extreme, though again not necessarily unrealistic assumption is
that demand for the input is perfectly elastic. This assumption is consistent
with all of an input for a project coming from reduced private consumption. Put another way, this assumption says that there will be no increase in
production as a result of the project, only a reduction in private consumption, and that the reduction in private consumption will be exactly equal to
the quantity used by the project.

Under this assumption, there will be no change in the market price
because demand is perfectly elastic. The only effect is a decrease in private
consumption, so the input should be valued at the price including the tax.
This idea is expressed in Examples 5D and 5E.

EXAMPLE 5D   A PERFECTLY ELASTIC INPUT DEMAND FOR INPUT

A project will employ ten people at an average wage of $20.00/hour.
Because of the small number of people involved it is not expected
that the project will have any impact on equilibrium wages in the
area. Further, there is sufficient frictional unemployment in the area
that it is unlikely that other jobs will go unfilled because of the
project's hiring. The wages paid are subject to state and federal
income taxes, with a combined marginal rate of 40 percent.

If standing for the analysis of this project is universal, the taxes
paid here should be regarded as transfers, and the proper cost of
the labor used is:

$$\$20.00/\text{hour} \times (1 - 0.40) = \$12.00/\text{hour}.$$

If, however, the analysis is done from the point of view of the
agency carrying out the project, payroll taxes may be seen as costs
and the full $20.00/hour would be the cost applied to the labor used.

5.5   WHEN THERE ARE EXTERNALITIES

As mentioned previously, an increase in the production of an input should
be valued according to the marginal cost of the additional production. If
the production or use of an input generates a negative externality, the value

EXAMPLE 5E   A PROJECT USING GASOLINE

A project will involve operating several vehicles that will use gasoline. The best estimate is that the project will use 10,000 gallons of gasoline. The current price of gasoline is $1.50 per gallon, including tax of $0.40/gallon.

If gasoline is supplied in a large, competitive market and there is sufficient excess capacity to allow the increased demand to be met at little additional cost, then the project's demand will be met through increased production. In this case, the correct value to attach to the gasoline used would be the marginal cost of production. If the gasoline industry is reasonably competitive, then the pre-tax price of $1.10 should be a good approximation of the marginal cost and the cost of the gasoline used in the project would be $1.10 × 10,000 = $11,000.

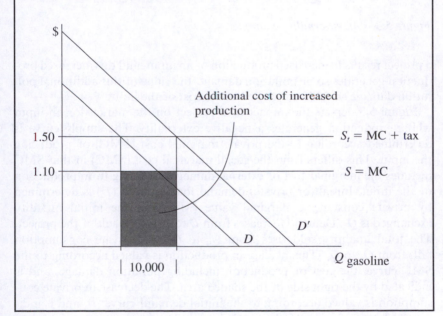

of the external damage should be included in the cost of the additional production of the input. In this case, the private marginal cost of producing the input fails to take into account the full social cost of the input, and the external damages need to be included. To put this more clearly, if

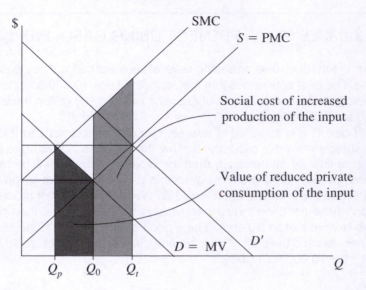

Figure 5.3   An externality example

a project results in increased production of an input, and this increased production generates some pollution damage, the value of this additional pollution damage should be included in the cost of the input.

Figure 5.3 depicts the impact of a project on the market for an input whose production generates a negative externality. The supply curve is determined according to the private marginal cost (PMC) of producing the input. This differs from the social marginal cost (SMC) in that SMC includes the marginal cost of external damages resulting from production of the input. Initial (or private) demand for the input (D) is determined by private consumers' marginal value (MV) and the initial quantity exchanged is Q_0. Demand increases from D to D' as a result of the project. The total quantity sold rises from Q_0 to Q_t and private consumption falls from Q_0 to Q_p. The increase in production is valued according to the SMC curve, the cost of production including pollution damage, and is indicated by the right side of the shaded area. The decrease in private consumption is valued according to the initial demand curve, D, and is indicated by the left side of the shaded area. The market price is used to value the reduction in private consumption because these units will still be produced (so the total amount of pollution damage will remain unchanged), but they will be made unavailable for private use. The optimum result is usually said to be at Q_0. This is, however, not necessarily or even usually the case. We would need to know the most cost effective method to reduce the external damages. A pollution control device might be available, for example, at little cost. The point is that reductions in production are unlikely to be the best or the only method of reducing damage.

External damages are very difficult to estimate accurately. The value of external damages resulting from production or use of an input may depend critically on the exact location, timing and conditions. Very often, if there are significant environmental or other external effects associated with an input, the best an analysis may be able to do is to discuss these qualitatively without applying an explicit monetary value.

An additional consideration is that a tax may be imposed for the purpose of correcting an externality (a so-called Pigouvian tax). In such a case, the tax should be included both in valuing the reduction in private consumption and in valuing additional production because the tax represents the external costs associated with production and/or consumption of the good. To put it another way, the tax represents the cost of unpurchased resources used in production of the input. This point is illustrated in Example 5F.

EXAMPLE 5F   THE OIL REFINERY

A large oil refinery is going to be shut down temporarily to install new pollution control equipment. The effect of this shutdown will be a 20 percent decrease in the supply of oil to a particular region of the country for several months. Over such a short period of time, both supply and demand are relatively inelastic. Best estimates put demand elasticity at -0.2 and supply elasticity at 0.4. Gasoline prices have averaged \$1.25/gallon recently, but this includes taxes of \$0.50/gallon. How should the lost production be valued? Note that in this case the lost production is a cost of the project, even though it is not an input in the usual sense.

There are a number of issues to be addressed in this analysis. The first is to determine the likely increase in the market price. To use the equation presented earlier:

$$\%\Delta P = \frac{Q_{project}/Q}{-\text{PED} + \text{PES}} = \frac{0.2}{0.2 + 0.4} = \frac{0.2}{0.6} = 0.33.$$

A 33 percent increase would mean a price during the project of about \$1.66 including or \$1.16 excluding tax. The average of the pre-project and during-project prices would be \$1.455 and \$0.9455 with and without taxes, respectively.

The second issue is what the marginal cost of production is for gasoline. If the wholesale gasoline market is competitive, then the pre-tax price may be approximately equal to the marginal cost, so we might assume the marginal cost to be $0.75 prior to the project and $1.16 during the project. If, instead, there is significant market power among gasoline refiners, the marginal cost could be well below $0.75 and may be estimated either through knowledge of the industry (engineers may be able to offer approximations) or through economic analysis.[5]

The third issue is whether or not the tax on gasoline is seen as an attempt to address the external costs of production and consumption. If so, the tax is part of the cost of the good and should be included in both the value of decreased private consumption and in the cost of increased production, so the value of each would be $1.455/gallon. If it is not intended to address an externality, the tax should be included only in the value of decreased private consumption ($1.455/gallon) and not in the cost of additional production ($0.9455/gallon). However, doing so would ignore any external costs associated with the production and consumption of gasoline.

Incidentally, because of the relative elasticities of supply and demand we can estimate that one-third of the lost gasoline would be made up through reduction in private consumption and two-thirds would be made up through increased production.[6]

5.6   WHEN THERE ARE OTHER INEFFICIENCIES

Myriad inefficiencies may plague input markets. In determining appropriate values for various situations with some degree of inefficiency the two underlying rules presented at the beginning of this chapter still apply:

- The decrease in consumption of the input should be measured according to consumers' willingness to pay for the additional units.

---

5   Of some use here are markup rules that specify profit-maximizing prices as a function of elasticity and marginal cost. A firm with marginal cost C facing price elasticity of demand ε has a profit-maximizing price of $P = C[\varepsilon/(1 + \varepsilon)]$.

6   This is based on the formulae presented above:

$$\frac{dQ_s}{dX} = \frac{\text{PES}}{-\text{PED} + \text{PES}} = \frac{0.4}{0.6} = 0.67, \quad \frac{dQ_D}{dX} = \frac{-\text{PED}}{-\text{PED} + \text{PES}} = \frac{0.2}{0.6} = 0.33.$$

- The increase in private production of an input should be measured according to producers' marginal cost of the additional units.

While it is true that all markets suffer from some degree of inefficiency, the techniques described here should be used only when the degree of inefficiency seems sufficiently large to warrant the extra trouble.

Monopolists or Firms with Significant Market Power

If a firm supplying an input has significant market power it is likely that the price is greater than its marginal cost. In such a case, the reduction in private consumption should be valued according to the market price. This will be equal to consumers' WTP as measured by the original, pre-project demand curve. Any increased production should be valued at the marginal cost of production.

The difference between the price paid and the marginal cost of additional output is the additional profit earned by the monopolist. As long as the monopolist (or, more accurately, the monopolist's owners or stockholders) has standing, this is simply a transfer from the agency doing to the project to the monopolist. If, however, the monopolist does not have standing, then the entire price paid for the extra output is the appropriate cost.

Figure 5.4 shows a monopolist with marginal cost curve MC supplying an input. The effect of the project is to increase demand (and corresponding

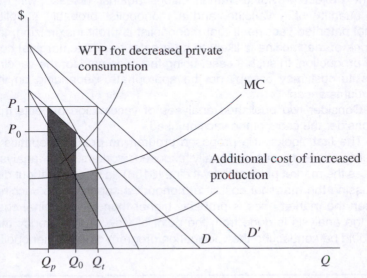

Figure 5.4   Increased demand for the product of a monopolist

marginal revenue) from D to D'. As a result of this increase in demand, the monopolist's profit-maximizing price rises from P_0 to P_1. The total quantity produced rises from Q_0 to Q_t while the quantity demanded by private individuals falls from Q_0 to Q_p. The increased production should be valued according to the marginal cost, as shown by the right side of the shaded area in Figure 5.4. The decreased private consumption should be valued according to the marginal value of private consumers, as shown by the left side of the shaded area.

As with taxes and externalities, calculation of the cost of an input supplied by a monopolist requires an assumption about the relative sizes of the increase in production and the decrease in private consumption. If the project purchases its inputs through regular markets then there is likely to be some division between increased production and decreased private consumption. However, it may be the case that a project purchasing a large quantity of an input from a monopolist will negotiate a price independent of the market price. This is a form of price discrimination by the monopolist and in such a case the project's quantity of the input is likely to come only from increased production with no decrease in private consumption. Consider the following example of a vaccination program (Example 5G).

EXAMPLE 5G   VACCINATION PROGRAM

Any project providing immunizations against disease will use a quantity of a vaccine, and a monopolist probably supplies that patented vaccine. If that monopolist is profit maximizing, the price of the vaccine is likely to be greater than the marginal cost of production. In such a case, using the price paid for the vaccine as its cost may or may not be appropriate, depending on the circumstances.

Consider two published analyses of vaccination projects that consider the costs of the vaccine used.

The first[7] looks at a proposed program to provide hepatitis B vaccinations to occupationally exposed workers. This analysis uses the market price of the vaccine ($108) as its cost without discussing the marginal cost. If a monopolist supplies this vaccine, then the market price is probably higher than the marginal cost. If the analysis is done from the point of view of the agency that would be conducting the vaccination program or if the monopolist

---

[7]   Mauskopf et al. (1991).

that produces the vaccine does not have standing, then using the price as a measure of the cost is appropriate. However, if the monopolist has standing, then the marginal cost of production should be used as the cost of the vaccine. At the very least, there should be some mention of the fact that the marginal cost is likely to be less than the price.

Further, if the agency conducting the program purchases a large quantity of the vaccine through normal markets, the result will probably be an increase in price and a decrease in private consumption. The market price should be used to value decreased private consumption and the marginal cost should be used to value increased production. Assuming that the vaccine is produced at a constant marginal cost of $40 and that the price will rise from $108 to $120 as a result of the program, the additional production of the vaccine should be valued at $40 while the reduction in private consumption should be valued at the average of the pre- and post-project prices, $114.

The second[8] looks at a proposed program to vaccinate children in Spain against a particular strain of influenza. This analysis assumes that the agency doing the program will negotiate a special price with the supplier of the vaccine. This suggests that the supplier (who is likely a monopolist) will price discriminate and that the units used in the program will be entirely the result of increased production. If the analysis does not grant the monopolist standing, then the negotiated price of the vaccine would be used as its cost. However, if the monopolist is granted standing in the analysis, the vaccine should be valued at the marginal cost of production.

Inputs Are Subject to Price Controls

When inputs are traded in markets subject to price controls, there is no guarantee that market prices will reflect either the opportunity costs of production or the marginal WTP of consumers.

If there is an effective price ceiling imposed there is likely to be a shortage of the input. If the project has some prior claim to a quantity of the input,[9] the quantity available to consumers is likely to be directly reduced as a result. In this case, the official price at which the ceiling is set is too low

---

[8] Jimenez et al. (1999).
[9] This means that the project can purchase the input at the controlled price before private consumers get the chance to purchase units of the input.

to use for a proper valuation. The marginal WTP on the part of consumers is likely to be much higher. It may be estimated by black market prices, if these can be reliably determined. Alternatively, if waiting in line is a common form of rationing the controlled good, attaching some value to the average wait might give an estimate of the marginal WTP on the part of private consumers. At the very least there should be some recognition that the ceiling price is too low a value for the input.

If there is an effective price floor maintained by some system of price supports, there will generally be a surplus of the input. Producers will supply additional units until their marginal cost rises to the supported price, but this quantity is likely to be larger than the quantity demanded at the supported price and the marginal cost of production will be greater than consumers' marginal value for the final unit produced. The appropriate price to apply to an input subject to a price floor may have little to do with the supported price. The important question is likely to be what would have happened to units of the input had they not been used in the project. It is also important to remember that an existing system of price supports should be taken as exogenous when considering an independent program.

Proper treatment of the value of a price-supported input depends on the nature of the support program. Some price-support programs purchase surplus units of a product at the supported price and then simply dispose of them in some non-productive manner. If the project uses surplus units of the input that would otherwise have been thrown away, the marginal cost of using them in a project should be zero, or even negative if disposal costs are saved. Other price-support systems pay producers the difference between the supported price and the market price for each unit they produce. Under this sort of program, units of the good used in a project result in reductions in private consumption and should be valued according to the market price, not the supported price, as this is the best measure of private WTP.

If a project uses a large quantity of the good as an input, this may have the effect of raising the market price and reducing support payments. Proper treatment of these reductions in transfer payments depends on who has standing in the analysis. If standing is universal, the support payments to producers are simply transfers and their reduction as a result of a project is neither a cost nor a benefit. If, on the other hand, taxpayers have standing but the producers who would receive support payments do not, then reductions in support payments may be seen as a benefit of the project. The following example of farm subsidies and ethanol, Example 5H, demonstrates this idea.

EXAMPLE 5H   FARM SUBSIDIES AND ETHANOL

Ethanol is a fuel produced from agricultural products, some of which are produced under government subsidy programs. The existence of these programs makes it difficult to do benefit–cost analyses of ethanol programs. Imagine that one grain used in ethanol production sells on world markets at a price of $0.40/bushel but is priced at $1.00/bushel in the United States due to price supports. The proper value to attach to a bushel used in ethanol production depends on how the price support system operates. If the government buys surplus production at the market price of $1.00 and then destroys it, the cost of using this input in ethanol production may be zero or negative. If, on the other hand, the government pays producers the difference between the equilibrium price of $0.40 and the supported price of $1.00 for each unit they produce, then the ethanol program will reduce private consumption of the good and the input should be valued at the prevailing market price of $0.40.

Unemployment

A common variation on the theme of market imperfections occurs when there is unemployment in an area. This may be caused by price controls (a minimum wage) or by some other labor market inefficiency.

A common and incorrect practice is to attach zero value to the labor of unemployed individuals who are employed by a project. In fact, unemployed people may be engaged in other beneficial activities such as child care, home maintenance, training or job searching while not working in the labor market, so the value of their labor should not be counted as zero. It is similarly incorrect to use the wages paid to previously unemployed people as the cost of their labor. The cost of the labor used in a project is its opportunity cost. If people who were previously unemployed choose to work on a project, it must be because the wages paid by the project are greater than the value of their next best alternative. The excess, or the difference between the wage and the value of the next best alternative, is a transfer from the people financing the project to the people it will employ.

An appropriate value to attach to the labor of unemployed people the project hires could be a fraction of the market wage for people with similar skills and backgrounds. If these people were actively seeking work at the going wage then the value of their next best alternative must have been less than the wage. How much less is difficult to say, but a range of percentages (for example, 30, 50, 80 percent) might be tried and included in a sensitivity analysis.[10]

Under most circumstances, wages paid to people employed on a project should not be counted as benefits, although this practice is disturbingly widespread.[11] As mentioned above, the opportunity cost of labor used on a project is the output that that labor would have generated elsewhere, either in paid work or in household production. Including wages paid to labor on a project as a benefit implies that that labor would have produced nothing otherwise and that the agency making the wage payments does not have standing. While employing previously unemployed people may have myriad social benefits including reductions in alcoholism and domestic violence, these benefits should be specifically discussed in an analysis. An illustration is shown in Example 5I.

The Taking of Land through Eminent Domain

The use of land in a project may be analyzed in a somewhat different way. The quantity of land in any area is typically fixed, so the land supply curve may be thought of as a vertical line. However, the land available for private use is equal to the total amount of land available minus the amount of land used in the project. Thus, the project could be seen as reducing the supply of land for private uses, shifting the vertical supply curve to the left with the result that the price will be higher and the quantity available for private use smaller.

If this land is bought in a straightforward manner from people who are willing to sell, the market price (or in the case of a large project, the average of the before and after market prices) is an accurate reflection of the value of the land involved because the price was adequate to get the owners to sell voluntarily.

If, however, governments assert eminent domain over a piece of land in order to force the owner to sell at a 'fair market price' then this price is a lower bound on the value of the land. Indeed, if the owner only valued the land or the improvements upon it at or below the prevailing market value, he/she would have sold it prior to consideration of the project. Instead, the owner who is forced to sell would seem to value the land at more than the fair market value in terms of their willingness to accept for loss of their real

---

[10]   Boardman et al. (2000, pp. 94–5) suggest 100 percent of the going wage as an upper bound and 50 percent as a lower bound.

[11]   See, for example, Sengupta (1987).

EXAMPLE 5I TIMBER TO TRAILS

A program is proposed that would employ out-of-work loggers to build hiking trails in state forests that have been taken out of timber production. The program would build an agreed-upon set of trails using 50,000 person days of labor, almost all of which would be currently unemployed loggers. In the areas where these people live, the market rate for an eight-hour work day is about $40, but unemployment is high. If the other costs and benefits of the project (the value of the trails minus the costs of other inputs excluding labor) are calculated, the project has net benefits of about $1.2 million. Should the project be done? The answer depends on how this labor is valued. It would be incorrect to value the labor at zero as these people are probably providing some beneficial services to their families, but if they are unemployed but actively seeking work, the wage of $40 must be higher than the value of their next best activity. Assigning the labor that would be used in this project a value of $24/day ($1.2m/50,000) would result in zero net benefit, so use of any amount below this would suggest that the project is worthwhile and any amount above this would suggest that the project is not worthwhile.

Incidentally, the wages paid to the people working on the project are merely a transfer from taxpayers to the people working on the project and should be counted as neither a cost nor a benefit.

To add a degree of difficulty to this analysis, if the BCA is done from the point of view of the state, but money would come from the federal government, then any federal money would be counted as a benefit of the project.

Finally, an analysis might note that reducing unemployment in the area could reduce social problems that typically accompany high joblessness. While valuing these benefits may prove difficult, at the very least they should be mentioned so that the reader of the analysis can actively decide whether these benefits could make an otherwise undesirable project worthwhile.

estate. Normally, the value attached to an item should not be more than the price of a close substitute, but in the case of real estate, each location is unique and may have uniquely valuable characteristics or hold great sentimental value for the owner, making the owners' WTA very high indeed.

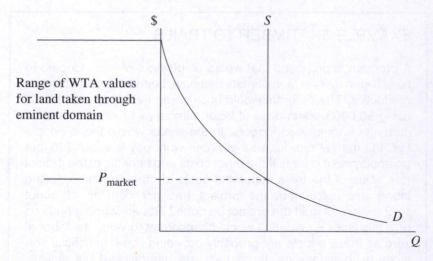

Figure 5.5   Range of WTA values

The value of units of land taken through eminent domain may range from the market price to the final landowner's reservation price, as shown in Figure 5.5.

It is difficult to determine guidelines for assigning proper values to land taken through eminent domain. Market measures cannot estimate the value of the exact parcels of land taken from their owners. At the very least, it may be said that the fair market value paid for the land is a lower bound on its proper value. (See Example 5J.)

EXAMPLE 5J   STANDING AND EMINENT DOMAIN

A city is going to build a swimming pool that will be open to city residents and their guests. The land required for the pool is currently occupied, but will be taken through eminent domain. The owners will be given fair market value for the land at a total cost to the city of $800,000. A number of the residents protested the action, but the city prevailed in court and received approval to take the land.

In a BCA of building the swimming pool, one issue might be the cost of the land involved. If the analysis is done from the point of view of city government, the cost of the land is simply the fair market value that must be paid to its owners, or $800,000. If, however, the residents of the land are also granted standing, then the $800,000 fair market value is a minimum bound on the cost of the land. The fact that some residents protested the taking would suggest that they valued their parcels at more than the declared fair market price, although determining an appropriate value for this may be impossible.

5.7 USE OF PRODUCER AND CONSUMER SURPLUS TO MEASURE GAINS AND LOSSES

The discussion of Figure 5.1 measures gains and losses through the WTP and resource cost changes. This is an intuitive way to think about gains and losses and translates well into quantitative analysis. There is another approach that will give the same answers, but which is sometimes superior for diagramming gains or losses and can be particularly useful in considering secondary effects. This is to calculate the change in consumer and producer surpluses. This approach involves the calculation of horizontal areas on the supply and demand curves.

For convenience we will distinguish government revenue and external effects as a separate category though the student should realize that these categories are also consumer and producer surpluses. With this in mind we can then give a general formula for welfare changes as follows:

$$\Delta W = \Delta CS + \Delta PS + \Delta GR + \Delta EE,$$

where:

W = welfare gained in the specified market;
CS = consumer surplus (the area above price but below the demand curve);
PS = producer surplus (area above supply curve but below price);
GR = government revenue; and
EE = external effects.

In Figure 5.6 we measure horizontally. Before the program, consumer surplus (CS) was areas A + B + C. Producer surplus was areas E + F. There is no government revenue. After the government program, CS is just area A. PS is areas B + C + D + E + F. For the government doing the program, government revenue is the negative of government spending or C + D + F + G + H. The change in CS is then −(B + C). The change in producer surplus is +(B + C + D) and the change in government spending is −(C + D + F + G + H). Combining these gives us just the same area as was found above: area −(C + F + G + H), the cost of using this input in the project.

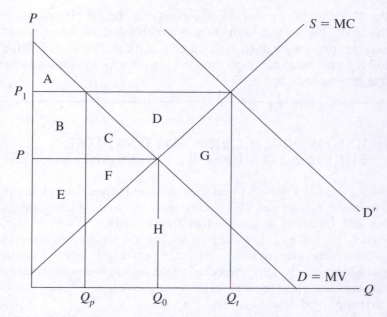

Figure 5.6   Calculating consumer and producer surplus

5.8   SUMMARY

Attaching values to the inputs used in a project should usually be a fairly straightforward process. If markets are operating with reasonable efficiency, the price paid for inputs should be a reasonable measure of the opportunity cost of using them in the project. For most inputs into most projects, the pre-project price of the input is the correct value to use in BCA. If a project will use a very large quantity of an input and its price is expected to rise as a result, the average of the pre- and during-project prices is probably appropriate.

If taxes are paid on the purchase of an input, the extent to which they should be included as a cost depends on whether the collecting agency has standing as well as the division between reduction in private consumption and increase in production.

External damages related to production or use of an input should be included in the cost of an input, but these damages can be difficult to estimate accurately.

The general rule in assigning values to inputs is that any additional production that is generated due to the project should be valued at the marginal cost and any reduction in private consumption should be valued according to the consumers' willingness to pay or, in limited cases, willing-ness to accept.

If they are available, elasticities can be used to determine relative sizes of private consumption decreases and production increases. If elasticities are unavailable, it might be safe to assume some division between the two in the short run and that the long-run supply elasticity is likely to be infinite for most goods. For better or for worse, BCA is an inexact practice.

There may be myriad other inefficiencies present in markets and, when these persist, an analyst should exercise caution in calculating values for inputs and should treat market prices with a healthy dose of skepticism. At the very least, the analysis presented in this chapter should allow an analyst or reviewer of an analysis determine when market prices are likely to be inappropriately high or inappropriately low values for inputs.

REFERENCES

Boardman, Anthony E., David H. Greenberg, Aidan R. Vining and David L. Weimer (2000), *Cost–Benefit Analysis: Concepts and Practice*, Englewood Cliffs, NJ: Prentice-Hall.

Jimenez, F. Javier, Pilar Guallar-Castillon, Carlos Rubio Terres and Eliseo Guallar (1999), 'Cost benefit analysis of haemophilus influenzae type B vaccination in children in Spain', *Pharmaco Economics*, **15** (1), January: 75–83.

Mauskopf, J.A., C.J. Bradley and M.J. French (1991), 'Benefit–cost analysis of hepatitis B vaccine program for occupationally exposed workers', *Journal of Occupational Medicine*, **33** (6): 691–8.

Sengupta, Mritunjoy (1987), 'The choice between coal and nuclear power in India: a cost–benefit approach', *Journal of Energy and Development*, **12** (1): 85–102.

EXERCISES

Questions

1. Imagine that there is an input whose supply and demand curves are given by the following equations:

    $$\text{Demand: } Q_d = 1000 - 2P$$

    $$\text{Supply: } Q_s = 3P - 200.$$

    Imagine that a project will use 100 units of this good as an input. Find the correct value for the cost of this input in the following conditions:

    A. There are no market distortions.
    B. There is a tax of $50/unit paid to a government with standing.
    C. There is a tax of $50/unit paid to a government without standing.
    D. Production of this input results in external marginal damage of $20/ unit.
    E. This input is supplied by a monopolist with marginal cost of $100 (so the supply curve given above is no longer relevant).

2. A project will use 10,000 gallons of gasoline. Because this is a relatively small amount, it is not expected that the market price of gasoline will change as a result of the project. Because of excess capacity in local refineries, supply is assumed to be perfectly elastic. There are two distortions in the gasoline market.

    A. First, the market is not perfectly competitive, so while the marginal cost of supplying a gallon of gasoline is $1.00, the price is $1.75. Also, gasoline is subject to federal and state taxes totaling $0.40/gallon. Discuss what value should be used for the cost of the gasoline used in the project.
    B. Now, imagine that instead of supply being perfectly elastic it is perfectly inelastic. This might be the situation in the short run if there were no excess capacity. How does your answer change?

Answers

1.A. The initial price and quantity are given by the simultaneous solution of the demand and supply functions:

    $$Q_d = Q_s$$

$$1000 - 2P = 3P - 200$$
$$1200 = 5P$$
$$P = 240, Q_d = Q_s = 520.$$

In this case, the quantity demanded will increase by 100 to give the new demand relationship $Q_d = 1000 - 2P + 100 = 1100 - 2P$ and the new equilibrium price will be:

$$Q_d = Q_s$$
$$1100 - 2P = 3P - 200$$
$$1300 = 5P$$
$$P = 260, Q_d = Q_s = 580.$$

Because the price rises from 240 to 260 as a result of the project, the average of these two prices, 250, should be used as the per unit value, for a total cost of $250/unit multiplied by 100 units or $25,000.

Incidentally, the total quantity exchanged in the market rises from 520 to 580, an increase of 60 units. However, because the project uses 100 units of the input, private consumption falls by forty units from 520 to 480.

1.B. Adding the tax to the market involves re-writing the supply curve as:

$$Q_s = 3P - 200 \rightarrow P = Q_s/3 + 66.67$$

and adding the tax to get:

$$P = Q_s/3 + 66.67 + 50 \rightarrow Q_s = 3P - 350.$$

The pre-project equilibrium is:

$$Q_d = Q_s$$
$$1000 - 2P = 3P - 350$$
$$1350 = 5P$$
$$P = 270, Q_d = Q_s = 460$$

and the price not including the tax is 220.

The project increases demand by 100 units and the post-project equilibrium is:

$$Q_d = Q_s$$
$$1100 - 2P = 3P - 350$$

$$1450 = 5P$$
$$P = 290, Q_d = Q_s = 520.$$

So the project increases the total quantity by 60 units, but because the project actually uses 100 units the quantity available for private consumption decreased by 40 units. The 60 unit increase in total production should be valued according to marginal cost, the price excluding the tax, while the 40 unit reduction in private consumption should be valued at marginal value, the cost including the tax.

1.C.   The calculations in this case are identical to the calculations in Part B except that the tax paid on addition units produced should be included because the government collecting the taxes does not have standing. So the 60 unit increase in production should be valued according to the pre- and post-project prices including the tax:

$$\left(60 \times \frac{270 + 290}{2}\right) + \left(40 \times \frac{270 + 290}{2}\right) = 16{,}800 + 11{,}200 = 28{,}000$$

1.D.   There is no tax here, but the \$20/unit external damage should be added to the cost of the additional output. Going back to part A, we have initial price and quantity of $P = 240$, $Q_d = Q_s = 520$ and post-project price and quantity of $P = 260$, $Q_d = Q_s = 580$. The 60 unit increase in production should be valued at the price plus \$20/unit to reflect the marginal damage, so the total value of the input is:

$$\left[60 \times \left(\frac{240 + 260}{2} + 20\right)\right] + \left(40 \times \frac{240 + 260}{2}\right)$$
$$= 16{,}200 + 10{,}000 = 26{,}200.$$

1.E.   The answer here depends on whether or not the monopolist has standing.
       For the initial case, again, the demand curve is:

$$Q_d = 1000 - 2P \rightarrow P = 500 - Q_d/2,$$

so the monopolist's total revenue function is:

$$TR(Q) = P * Q = (500 - Q/2) \times Q = 500Q - Q^2/2$$

and the monopolist's marginal revenue function is:

$$MR(Q) = \frac{dTR(Q)}{dQ} = 500 - 3Q/2.$$

Setting this equal to the marginal cost of 100 give us:

$$500 - 3Q/2 = 100$$
$$3Q/2 = 400$$
$$Q = 267, P = 500 - 267/2 = 367.$$

So the initial or pre-project quantity is 267. The project will increase demand by 100 units to $Q_d = 1100 - 2P$, giving the monopolist a new marginal revenue function of $MR(Q) = 550 - 3Q/2$ and a new profit maximizing quantity of:

$$550 - 3Q/2 = 100$$
$$3Q/2 = 450$$
$$Q = 300, P = 550 - 300/2 = 400.$$

So, the quantity produced increases by 33 units from 367 to 400 but because the project uses 100 units, the quantity available for private use falls by 67 units from 367 to 300.

Now, if the monopolist has standing, the 33 units of increased production should be valued at the marginal cost of 100 while the 67 unit decrease in private consumption should be valued according to the average of the pre- and post-project prices. The additional output is valued according to the marginal cost rather than the price because the difference between the cost of producing the units and the price charged for them is a transfer from the agency doing the project to the monopolist:

$$(33 \times 100) + \left(67 \times \frac{267 + 300}{2}\right) = 3{,}300 + 18{,}994.5 = 22{,}294.5.$$

If, however, the monopolist does not have standing, then the 33 units of increased output should be valued according to the price charged instead of the marginal cost. The difference between the price and the marginal cost is a cost, rather than a transfer, because the monopolist does not have standing:

$$\left(33 \times \frac{267 + 300}{2}\right) + \left(67 \times \frac{267 + 300}{2}\right)$$
$$= 9{,}355.5 + 18{,}994.5 = 28{,}350.$$

It should be noted that the cost of the project is higher when the monopolist does not have standing.

2.A. If supply is perfectly elastic, the price will not change as a result of the project and there will be no decrease in the quantity of gasoline available for private consumption; the entire quantity used by the project will come from increased production.

   If there is global standing (that is, if all governments collecting taxes and the gasoline suppliers have standing) then the appropriate value to attach to the gasoline used by the project is simply the marginal cost of $1.00/gallon or a total of $10,000.

   If the governments have standing but the gasoline supplier does not, then appropriate value is the price paid for the gasoline, not including taxes, or $1.75/gallon or a total of $17,500.

   If the gasoline supplier has standing but the governments do not then the appropriate value would be the marginal cost plus tax, of $1.40/gallon or a total of $14,000.

   Finally, if neither the governments nor the gasoline supplier have standing, the appropriate cost of the gasoline would be the entire price paid of $2.15/gallon or a total of $21,500.

2.B. If there is no excess capacity, the gasoline used in the project will come entirely from reduced private consumption. If there is no price increase,[12] then gasoline used in the project should be valued according to private willingness to pay, or the full price of $2.15/gallon or a total of $21,500.

---

[12] It is a bit of a mystery why private consumption would decrease in the absence of a price increase.

6. Valuing outputs using market prices

6.1 INTRODUCTION

Outputs are the goods and services produced by a project. Examples include electricity generated by a dam, apartments contained in a public housing project and recreational benefits associated with a municipal golf course. In the private sector, goods and services are sold in markets where the price paid is usually an accurate measure of their value. If a project's outputs are sold in markets to the highest bidders, market prices can be used to value these outputs. However, using market prices to value project outputs offers several challenges. Taxes, externalities and other standard market distortions must be accounted for correctly.

There are three implications of a project generating outputs and supplying them to the market. First, the market price of the output may fall as a result of the increase in supply. Second, other, private producers of the output may wind up supplying less of it because of the reduced price. Third, consumers of the output may purchase more of it if the project's output results in a lower market price.

Both the decrease in private production and the increase in total consumption of the output are part of the project's benefits. The decrease in private production is considered a benefit from a societal point of view because it frees the resources that would have been used in private production for other activities.[1] The increase in private consumption is a benefit because consumers are getting more of goods or services that they value.

The relative sizes of decreased private production and increased consumption will depend on the relative elasticities of supply and demand.

If demand is relatively elastic and supply relatively inelastic then the extra output generated because of the project will go mostly to increased consumption. For example, a project that generates more office space in an area will, in the short run, result in an increase in the total quantity of office space consumed and a fall in its price, but little or no decrease in the

---

[1] This fact is unlikely to be of any comfort to businesses shut down and workers laid off as a result of a competing government project.

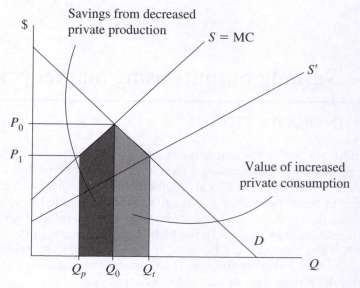

Figure 6.1   Output cost rules

quantity supplied by private suppliers because in the short run supply is
likely to be very inelastic.

If, on the other hand, demand is relatively inelastic and supply relatively
elastic then the project's output will result in reduced private production of
that good. While private producers of the good are likely to be hurt by this,
their reduced production costs are a cost savings resulting from the project.
One example might be a project that produces food in a country. Demand
for food is inelastic, but if food producers are free to export to other countries, then the supply of food in that country is probably elastic. The project
will increase the supply of food and drive prices down. Consumers will
consume about the same amount of food, but private producers will
respond by decreasing the quantity they sell domestically and increasing
their exports to other countries.

Proper valuation of the project's output can be summarized in two rules:

- The increase in consumption of the output should be measured
  according to consumers' willingness to pay for that output.[2]
- The decrease in private production of an output should be measured
  according to producers' marginal cost of the decreased production.

---

[2]   WTP is indicated by the demand curve, which is also an indication of marginal
      value.

These rules are illustrated in Figure 6.1. The original supply and demand curves are S and D. The project increases supply of the input from S to S'. The increased consumption, $Q_t - Q_0$, is valued along the demand or marginal value curve. Decreased private production, $Q_0 - Q_p$, is valued along the supply or marginal cost curve. The sum of the increased consumption and decreased private production is the total quantity of the output generated by the project. This chapter discusses the proper application of these rules to a variety of situations.

Application of these rules will vary somewhat depending on the conditions in input markets. We will first consider markets that are functioning with no major distortions and then turn our attention to a number of distortions or inefficiencies that can make the true value of outputs very different from the price paid for them.

6.2 WHEN MARKETS ARE RELATIVELY EFFICIENT

If markets are free of inefficiencies, consumers' WTP should be approximately equal to suppliers' marginal cost, and both of these will simply be the market price of the output. This suggests a market in which there are no (or negligible) taxes, externalities and market power and in which both suppliers and consumers have good information. These conditions are consistent with the typical model of perfect competition, but a market does not have to be perfectly competitive in the strictest sense for the principles of this section to be applied. The important consideration is that there will not be a large difference between the marginal cost of production and the price paid by consumers.

In this simple situation it is not important to determine the relative sizes of decreased private production and increased consumption. The one important consideration will be the quantity of the output produced by the project relative to the size of the relevant market and whether or not the market price is likely to change as a result of the project. That is, will the project produce a small quantity of the output or a large quantity of the output?

The Basic Case: Relatively Large Quantities

The most basic diagram of increased supply of a project output is shown in Figure 6.1, above. The sale of the project's output on the open market increases supply from $S = \mathrm{MC}$ to S', resulting in a decrease in the price from P_0 to P_1 and an increase in the total quantity purchased from Q_0 to Q_t.

The price decrease also means that output by private producers, whose supply is given by the original supply curve, falls from Q_0 to Q_p. As described above, the total value of the project's output is the sum of consumers' WTP for the additional output (the right side of the shaded area in Figure 6.1) and the reduction in production costs of private producers who reduce their output (the left side of the shaded area in Figure 6.1).

Calculation of this area is not difficult if the relevant quantities and prices are known. The total value of output is equal to the project's total output $(Q_t - Q_p)$ multiplied by the average of the before- and after-project prices, P_0 and P_1, respectively. Put another way, each unit of the project's output should be valued at the average of the price prior to the project and the price after (or during) the project. For example, if a project will generate 1000 units of an output whose price is expected to fall from $5.00 to $4.00 as a result of the increase in supply, the proper value to attach to this output is $4.50/unit, or a total value of $4500.

As in Chapter 5, estimating the price effects of large projects, one approach is to use an estimate of the price elasticity of demand and the price elasticity of supply of the input in question. The percentage price decrease likely to result from a project can be calculated using the following equation, which was also used in Chapter 5, and Example 6A provides an illustration of this equation at work:

$$\%\Delta P = \frac{Q_{\text{project}}/Q}{-\,\text{PED} + \text{PES}}$$

where:

Q = the total quantity of the good being exchanged in the market prior to the project;
Q_{project} = the quantity of the good that will be produced by the project;
PED = the price elasticity of demand for the input; and
PES = the price elasticity of supply for the input.

As in Chapter 5 some practical advice is in order here. If you do not have reliable estimates of supply and demand elasticities for the market you are interested in, here are some guidelines that can help you predict price effects.

In the very short run it may be impossible for suppliers to change the quantity they offer for sale. As in Chapter 5, this would be the case, for example, with the housing stock in a city. Over a matter of months it may be largely impossible for the supply of housing to increase. This implies a short-run supply elasticity of approximately 0. If this were the case with the bicycle example presented above, the resulting price decrease would be:

$$\%\Delta P = \frac{Q_{project}/Q}{-\,PED + PES} = \frac{0.15}{1.3 + 0.0} = \frac{0.15}{1.3} = 0.115,$$

or about an 11.5 percent price decrease.

EXAMPLE 6A   JOB-TRAINING PROGRAM

A job-training program will involve setting up a factory to produce bicycles that will be sold locally. In the local bicycle market, there are usually 10,000 bicycles sold per year. The quantity of bicycles the project is expected to produce each year is 1500, or about 15 percent of the local market. Economists estimate that the price elasticities of supply and demand in the local bicycle market are 0.8 and −1.3. The issue for analysis of the project is what value should be attached to the bicycles produced.

To calculate the percentage decrease in the price, the formula would be

$$\%\Delta P = \frac{Q_{project}/Q}{-\,PED + PES} = \frac{0.15}{1.3 + 0.8} = \frac{0.15}{2.1} = 0.071.$$

So, the price of bicycles could be expected to fall by about 7.1 percent as a result of the project.

To use this information in valuing the bicycles produced, you need to know the price of bicycles prior to the project.[3] Imagine that the median price of a bicycle is $400. Based on this, you can estimate that the price of bicycles after the project starts operating will be:

$$\$400 \times (1 - 0.071) = \$371.60,$$

and the correct value to attach to the bicycles produced by the project would be the average of the before price ($400) and the after price ($371.60) or $385.80.[4]

---

[3]   This may be tricky due to the fact that bicycles are heterogeneous goods that vary greatly in their characteristics.

[4]   It is probably worth noting that if an analysis of the project is being prepared for the agency that will actually do the project, they may only be concerned with the revenue that will be generated. In this case, the value attached to the bicycles would be the lower price ($371.60) even though, from a social perspective, this value would be too low.

In the long run if firms can exit a market costlessly then, given enough time, the price will likely return to its long-run equilibrium level. This implies infinite long-run supply elasticity, meaning that there will be no price decrease in the long run.

How long the transition from the very short run to the long run might take depends on the industry and is probably open to some difference of opinion. A guideline might be to consider the amount of time it would take an entrepreneur to decide to enter the market, make the fixed investments necessary, begin operations and become competitive. Alternately, you might consider how long it would take an existing firm that was losing money to decide to shut down, liquidate its inventory and close up shop. Example 6B demonstrates these ideas:

EXAMPLE 6B　GOVERNMENT PRODUCTION OF ASPIRIN

A government project will set up a large factory to produce aspirin, a drug with no patents in effect that is basically produced and sold competitively. The quantity of aspirin to be produced is anticipated to be about 18 percent of the domestic market. If the price for a 50-tablet container of aspirin is $1 and the price elasticity of demand for aspirin is −0.4, what price should be used to value the aspirin produced by the project?

The first consideration should be whether or not there is an international market for aspirin. If there is, then domestic supply should be very elastic as suppliers could simply ship their aspirin to other countries. In this case, the pre-project price of $1 would be an appropriate value.

If there is no international market for aspirin, we might assume that the short-run price elasticity of supply is 0. That is, domestic producers will maintain their level of production, at least in the short run. The above formula gives us:

$$\%\Delta P = \frac{Q_{\text{project}}/Q}{-\text{PED} + \text{PES}} = \frac{0.18}{0.4 + 0} = \frac{0.18}{0.4} = 0.45,$$

or about a 45 percent decrease in price from $1 to about $0.55. The relevant value to attach to the aspirin produced would be the average of these two figures, or about $0.775.

In the long run, some private aspirin producers will shut down and the price of aspirin will rise back to its previous equilibrium level of $1. From this point in time, the appropriate value to attach to the aspirin produced would be $1. How far in the future the long run lies will depend on how long it might take some aspirin producers to totally abandon the market.

Relatively Small Quantities

If the project will produce a relatively small quantity of the output, its price will not change significantly and the market price prior to the project starting can be used as the value of the output. What is meant by a 'relatively small quantity' may be a point of some disagreement. If the quantity the project will produce is a small percentage of the total quantity of the output consumed in the local area, it is probably a small quantity. If there are good national or global markets for the output and the project is unlikely to have an impact on either global or local prices for the good, it may be treated as a small quantity. If, however, there are significant restrictions that prevent movement of the output outside of a local market, then a project's effects on local prices could be important even if it will have no global impact.

For example, a project that will yield 100,000 gallons of crude oil annually would be unlikely to affect market prices because crude oil is traded in very large international markets. On the other hand, the construction of a municipal golf course in an area with very few golf courses may well drive down the equilibrium price of a round of golf because the relevant market for golf is local rather than national or global.

In a well-functioning economy, very few projects are so large as to have a significant effect on market prices, so in most cases where there are no market distortions it is probably reasonable to use pre-project prices as the value of outputs.

6.3   VALUATION OF OUTPUTS WHEN DISTORTIONS AND INEFFICIENCIES EXIST

Myriad distortions may exist in a market, and these can change the valuation of a project's outputs. The remainder of this chapter will discuss valuation of outputs in the presence of distortions including taxes, externalities and the existence of firms with significant market power. While the two valuation rules presented above will remain as guiding principles, their application will be slightly more complex in the face of market distortions.

6.4 VALUATION OF OUTPUTS WHEN THERE ARE TAXES

The analysis for outputs is similar to that for inputs treated in Chapter 5. A large percentage of goods and services are subject to taxation. In the United States, labor, fuel and most non-food consumer goods are subject to some sort of tax. Valuation of project outputs that are subject to taxes is slightly more complicated than for untaxed goods. For goods that are taxed, it is necessary to estimate the relative sizes of the changes in production and consumption because the reduction in private production and the increase in consumption will be valued differently.

As in Chapter 5, it is still assumed that the government collecting the tax has standing in the analysis. The implication is that tax payments are simply transfers from taxpayers to the government and do not count as costs or benefits. An alternative view might be that the government collecting the tax does not have standing. This might be the view taken if the government (and this term might be used loosely) collecting the tax is seen as either illegitimate or hostile. If the government does not have standing, the analysis will change slightly in that the tax payment on additional output should be regarded as a cost.

In the more usual case where a government has standing, the two rules stated earlier in this chapter imply that taxes should be included in the value of increased consumption but not in the value of decreased private production. Private consumers will purchase additional units of the output until their marginal value declines to the price *including tax*, because this is the price that consumers must pay. Thus, consumers' marginal value of a project output includes the tax they pay, and any increase in private consumption should be valued at the price including tax, as shown in Figure 6.2. Private suppliers of the output will produce additional units until the marginal cost rises to the price they receive, but this price will not include taxes. Any reduction in private production should be valued at the marginal cost of production, which will be equal to the market price less taxes. The tax that would have been paid on the sale of these additional units is merely a reduced transfer to the taxing authority and is neither a cost nor a benefit as long as the taxing authority has standing.

The Standard Diagram: Relatively Large Quantities

Consider a project that will produce a large quantity of some output, resulting in a decrease in its price. This will mean that some private producers of the output will reduce their production and that some consumers of the output will increase their consumption. The situation is depicted in Figure 6.2.

Taxes should be included in the value of the increase in consumption because the private WTP includes the tax on the good. As an example, imagine a project that will produce some gasoline. If the price of gasoline is $1.50/gallon including $0.40 of taxes, then people are consuming a quantity of gasoline such that their marginal value is $1.50. An increase in consumption of gasoline means that consumers will be enjoying more of something they value at $1.50/gallon.

Taxes should not be included in the value attached to decreases in private production because they are not part of the cost of the resources that would have been used to produce the output. If, as above, the price of gasoline is $1.50/gallon, but this includes $0.40 of taxes, the marginal cost of production of gasoline in an otherwise competitive and well-functioning market will be about $1.10. If private suppliers wind up producing less gasoline because of the project, the resources saved will have a value of about $1.10/gallon.

This goes back to the two rules about valuing inputs. The change in private consumption is valued at the price including taxes because individual WTP is equal to the price including the tax. The change in private production is valued at the price excluding taxes because the marginal cost of this additional production is the cost of the resources that go into it and

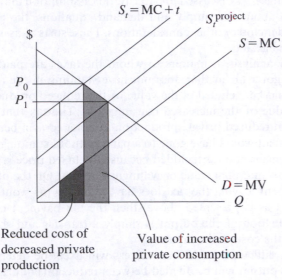

Figure 6.2   Gains and losses when taxes are present

not the tax paid on its sale. If the firms producing the output are profit max-imizing and competitive, then their marginal cost should be approximately equal to the price less the tax.

Figure 6.2 illustrates the impact of a project on the market for a taxed output. The original supply curve is given by $S = MC$, the marginal cost of production not including taxes. The effect of the tax is to shift the supply curve to S_t, the marginal cost of production plus the tax. The project's impact is shown as an increase in supply. The effect of the project on the supply curve may be either larger or smaller than the effect of the tax; in this diagram it is shown as being smaller than the impact of the tax so that the price resulting from the project is higher than the price would have been in absence of the tax. The effect of the project is to lower the price from P_0 to P_1 and to decrease the quantity sold by private suppliers. The right side of the shaded area shows the value of increased consumption of the output and is valued according to consumers' WTP. The left side of the shaded area shows the value of the reduction in private production and is valued according to producers' marginal cost.

To calculate the value of this output, the increase in consumption should be multiplied by the average of the pre- and post-project prices including the tax, and the decrease in production should be multiplied by the average of the pre- and post-project prices excluding the tax.

Because additional consumption is valued differently from reduced pro-duction, it is important to make some assumption about the relative sizes of these changes. As discussed previously, this assumption may be based on information about the supply and demand equations, the elasticities of supply and demand or other considerations. These sorts of assumptions are bound to be inexact.

As in any analysis, it matters to whom the taxes are paid. If a tax is levied by a government that does not have standing in the analysis then the tax should be included in the value of the reduced production as well as in the value of the increased consumption. The tax that would have been paid on reduced private production is included as a benefit because the tax payment would have gone to a party without standing. The tax on increased consumption is included because the taxed price is the measure of consumers' marginal value or willingness to pay. On the other hand, if the government levying the tax does have standing (as would usually be the case and as is presented above) then the tax payment on decreased private production of the output is simply a transfer and should not be included in the cost of the input.

The most difficult part of this process will likely be determining how the project's output will be divided between reductions in private produc-tion and increases in consumption. The key to determining this is some knowledge of the elasticities of supply and demand for the good in question. These are probably most easily obtained from previous demand or supply elasticity estimates that economists have done and some knowledge of the characteristics of suppliers in the market. The resources described in Chapter 12 may have supply or demand elasticity estimates for goods you are interested in.

If reliable estimates of the supply and demand elasticities are available, the changes in the quantities supplied and demanded may be estimated by the following equations:

$$\frac{dQ_s}{dX} = \frac{PES}{-PED + PES}$$

$$\frac{dQ_D}{dX} = \frac{-PED}{-PED + PES},$$

where:

dQ_s = the change in the quantity supplied by private producers;
dQ_D = the change in the quantity demanded by consumers;
dX = the quantity of an output produced by the project;
PES = the price elasticity of supply; and
PED = the price elasticity of demand (for example, -0.5).

The next section will discuss two extreme cases.

Extreme Assumption 1: Perfectly Elastic Supply

An extreme, though not necessarily unrealistic, assumption is that supply is perfectly elastic. This assumption is consistent with all of the project's output displacing private supply. Stated another way, this assumption says that there will be no increase in consumption as a result of the project, only decreased private production, and the decrease in private production will be exactly equal to the quantity of output produced by the project.

Under this assumption, valuation of the project's output is easily calculated. Because there is no change in the total quantity of the output supplied to the market, there is no change in the market price. The only effect is a decrease in private production, so the project's output should be valued at the price minus taxes.

This assumption may be most relevant over longer periods of time if private firms face low costs of exit. Finding their profits reduced by lower prices in the short run, they may choose to exit the market with the long-run effect of reducing supply and bringing the price back up to its long-run equilibrium level. While there is some price response in the short run, if the project has a long lifetime, the assumption of no price change and only a decrease in private production may be reasonable.

In the Nevada wine example, Example 6C, if the 120,000 cases produced by the project were offset by decreases in private production of 120,000 cases, the wine produced by the project would be valued at the pre-project price excluding taxes, or $112.00/case, for a total value of $13,440,000.

Extreme Assumption 2: Perfectly Elastic Demand

Another extreme, though again not necessarily unrealistic, assumption is that demand is perfectly elastic. This assumption is consistent with all of the project's output being consumed in addition to the existing private production. Put another way, this assumption says that there will be no decrease in private production as a result of the project, only an increase in consumption, and the increase in consumption will be exactly equal to the quantity produced by the project.

Under this assumption, there will be no change in the market price because consumers will simply buy the additional output at the pre-project price. The only effect will be an increase in consumption, so the project's output should be valued at the price including the tax.

In the Nevada wine example, if the 120,000 cases produced by the project were consumed in addition to the previously existing private production, the wine produced by the project would be valued at the pre-project price including taxes, or $132.00/case, for a total value of $15,840,000. Two additional examples follow (Examples 6D and 6E).

EXAMPLE 6C   WINE PRODUCTION IN NEVADA

An experimental project investigating large-scale wine production in Nevada will produce 120,000 cases of a rare variety of wine. Wine is subject to a tax of $20/case.

Case A: You have estimates of the supply curve (including the tax) and demand curve for this market. They are:

$$Q_D = 600,000 - 2,000P$$

$$Q_s = 3,000P - 60,000.$$

The pre-project equilibrium price and quantity are $132.00/case and 336,000 cases. When the project supply is added to the market, the quantity supplied will increase by 120,000 cases to:

$$Q_s' = 3,000P - 60,000 + 120,000$$

$$Q_s' = 3,000P + 60,000,$$

giving a new market equilibrium price and quantity of $108.00 and 384,000, with private production falling to 264,000 cases: 384,000 cases minus the 120,000 supplied by the project.

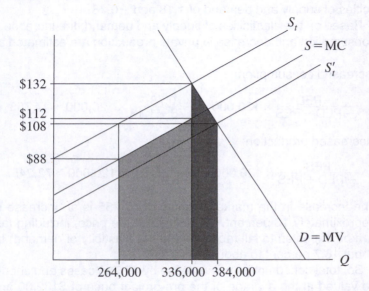

So, total consumption will go from 336,000 cases to 384,000 cases, an increase of 48,000 cases valued at the average of the pre-project price of $132.00 and the post-project price of $108.00 for a total value of:

$$48,000 \text{ cases} \times \$120.00/\text{case} = \$5,760,000.$$

Private production will fall from 336,000 cases to 264,000 cases, a decrease of 72,000 cases[5] valued at the average of the pre-project

---

[5] Note that the decrease in private production plus the increase in consumption equals the quantity provided by the project.

and post-project prices minus the $20 tax, $112.00 and $88.00, respectively, for a total value of:

$$72,000 \text{ cases} \times \$100.00/\text{case} = \$7,200,000.$$

So, the total value attached to the wine produced by this project should be the sum of the value of the increased consumption and decreased private production, or $12,960,000.

Case B: You know that the initial equilibrium price and quantity are $132.00 and 336,000 cases. You have estimates of the elasticities of supply and demand of 1.18 and −0.78.

Based on the elasticities of supply and demand, the increase in consumption and decrease in private production are estimated at:

Increased consumption:

$$\frac{-\text{PED}}{-\text{PED} + \text{PES}} \times 120,000 = \frac{0.78}{0.78 + 1.18} \times 120,000 = 47,755$$

Decreased production:

$$\frac{\text{PES}}{-\text{PED} + \text{PES}} \times 120,000 = \frac{1.18}{0.78 + 1.18} \times 120,000 = 72,245.$$

The increase in the market quantity of 47,755 is an increase of approximately 13 percent,[6] meaning that the price, including tax, can be expected to fall (according to the elasticity of demand) by about 16.7 percent to about $111.70.[7]

So, total consumption will increase by 47,755 cases and should be valued at the average of the pre-project price of $132.00 and the post-project price of $111.70 for a total value of:

$$47,755 \text{ cases} \times \$121.85/\text{case} = \$5,818,947.$$

Private production will fall by 72,245 cases and should be valued at the average of the pre- and post-project prices minus the $20 tax, $112.00 and $91.70, respectively, for a total value of:

$$72,245 \text{ cases} \times \$101.85/\text{case} = \$7,358,153.$$

---

[6] Calculated by dividing the increased quantity, 47,755, by the average of the pre- and post-project quantities of 336,000 and 383,755.

[7] Calculated by the same process.

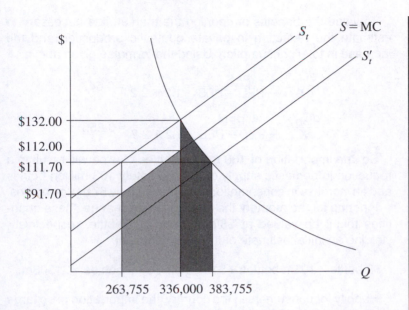

So, the total value attached to the wine produced by this project should be the sum of the value of the increased consumption and decreased private production, or $13,177,100.

EXAMPLE 6D   A PROGRAM TO REMOVE WINE IMPORT BARRIERS

A country with protective barriers against wine imports is considering removing these barriers. They currently consume 1600 million bottles of wine annually. It is expected that 160 million bottles or 10 percent of the current market would be imported if the tariff barriers were lowered. The current price for a bottle of wine is $12, including $4 of taxes. The best estimate of the price elasticity of demand is −1.2. Domestic wine producers have the option of exporting and as a result supply elasticity is estimated at 2.2.[8]

---

[8] The fact that domestic winemakers might continue to produce, but for export rather than domestic consumption, simply means that their resources are not involved in production for the domestic market and are freed for another use, wine production for foreign markets.

To value the benefits of opening the market, it is necessary to estimate the reduction in private domestic production and the increase in total consumption. Using the formulae given above:

$$\frac{dQ_s}{dX} = \frac{PES}{-PED + PES} = \frac{2.2}{1.2 + 2.2} = 0.647$$

$$\frac{dQ_D}{dX} = \frac{-PED}{-PED + PES} = \frac{1.2}{1.2 + 2.2} = 0.353.$$

So, the importation of 160 million bottles of wine will result in a reduction in domestic supply of approximately 103 million bottles and an increase in consumption of approximately 57 million bottles.

Ignoring for the moment the resulting price change, these quantities might be valued at $8/bottle and $12/bottle, respectively, yielding an initial estimate of the total benefit of:

$8/bottle $\times$ 103m bottles + $12/bottle $\times$ 57m bottles = $1508m.

Happily for consumers in the country, the importation of so large a quantity of foreign wine will result in lower prices. From the analyst's perspective, this will reduce the value of wine in the analysis and reduce the benefits of lowering protective tariffs.

The 10 percent increase in quantity will be divided as above into a 6.47 percent decrease in quantity supplied and a 3.53 percent increase in quantity demanded.

The impact of a 6.47 percent decrease in quantity supplied on the marginal cost of production will be:

$$PES = \frac{\%\Delta Q}{\%\Delta P}$$

$$2.2 = \frac{-6.47\%}{\%\Delta P}$$

$$\%\Delta P = -2.94\%.$$

A reduction of 2.94 percent would bring the marginal cost of production down from $8.00 to $7.76. The appropriate value to use in the analysis is the average of these, or $7.88/bottle rather than the $8/bottle used above.

The impact of a 3.53 percent increase in quantity consumed on consumers' marginal value would be:

$$PED = \frac{\%\Delta Q}{\%\Delta P}$$

$$-1.2 = \frac{3.53\%}{\% \Delta P}$$

$$\% \Delta P = -2.94\%.$$

A reduction of 2.94 percent would bring the marginal value of wine consumption down from $12.00 to $11.65. The appropriate value to use in the analysis is the average of these, or $11.825/bottle rather than the $12/bottle used above.

Including the price change, the estimated benefits are:

$7.88/bottle × 103m bottles + $11.825/bottle × 57m bottles
= $1485.66m.

This second estimate of the benefits takes into account the fact that prices will fall as a result of the imports. However, the small price change means that the difference between the two estimates (the first giving benefits of $1508 million and the second giving benefits of $1485.66 million) will be similarly small.

EXAMPLE 6E   A PROGRAM TO PRODUCE GASOLINE

An alternative approach to addressing uncertainties about foreign oil supplies might be to create a program to produce more gasoline domestically from internally available resources. Imagine that gasoline sells in a competitive market at a price of $1.50 including $0.50 in taxes, implying that the marginal cost of production is $1.00.

In this case, the effect of the program is to increase the supply of gasoline, decreasing the price and increasing the total quantity consumed. The quantity of gasoline produced by private suppliers would be reduced as a result of the program. If the project produces 10 million gallons of gasoline each day, the sum of increased consumption and reduced private production will be 10 million gallons.

The increase in consumption should be valued according to consumers' marginal value, the price including the tax. The reduction in private production should be valued at the marginal cost, approximately equal to the price not including the tax.

The trick in evaluating this project is determining the relative amounts by which total consumption will rise and private production will fall. If taxes are a large percentage of the sales price, this determination may be very important to the results of the analysis.

An analyst might reason that demand for gasoline is generally thought to be inelastic, especially in the short run. The supply of gasoline, on the other hand, may be very elastic because the inputs used in making gasoline, crude oil and refinery capacity, may be diverted to the production of other petroleum products. If demand is inelastic and supply is elastic, then the additional gasoline produced by the project will simply be offset by decreases in private production and should be valued at $1.00/gallon, the marginal cost of private production.

Another analyst might claim (perhaps with little empirical support) that the demand for gasoline is elastic and that suppliers of gasoline, reluctant to sacrifice market share, might not reduce production when prices fall. Under these assumptions, the entire output of the project would go toward increased consumption and should be valued at $1.50/gallon, the marginal value of gasoline.

6.5   WHEN THERE ARE EXTERNALITIES

As mentioned previously, a decrease in the private production of a project output should be valued according to the marginal cost of the reduced production. If the private production of a project's output generates a negative externality, the value of the avoided external damage should be included in the value of reduced private production. To put this more clearly, when a project begins producing some output, private production of the output falls and the associated pollution damage falls as well. One benefit of the project is the reduction in the social cost of the reduced production, the reduced private costs plus the reduced pollution damage.

Figure 6.3a depicts a standard negative externality. We assume that a reduction in production is the most cost-effective way to reduce the externality. That is the only available control technology is a reduction in output, or alternatively we assume the social marginal cost is what remains after all of the efficient actions to reduce the externality have been made. There is some demand or marginal value ($D = MV$) for the output. There is an increasing private marginal cost (PMC) curve and the intersection of PMC and the demand curve yields a market quantity, q_0. At this quantity, the market price will be equal to the private marginal cost, but the social mar-

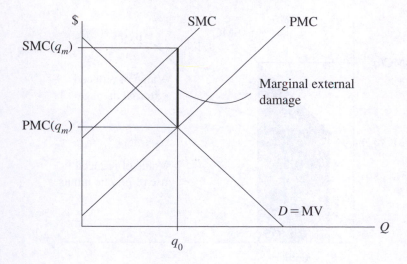

Figure 6.3a   Social and private marginal costs

ginal cost (SMC) will be equal to the private marginal cost plus some marginal external damage. SMC is the total cost of resources used in private production of one additional unit of output.[9]

Suppose the public project will increase total production without externalities. In this case the cost of the increase in production is found in the PMC curve. If a project produces a large quantity of this good, the price will fall and, as a result, private production will also fall. The cost savings from this reduction in private production should be valued along the social marginal cost curve. So, any reduction in private production is a benefit and should be valued at the market price plus the value of the marginal external damage, as shown in Figure 6.3b. The reduction in private production from q_0 to q_p reduces use of private inputs and social inputs by an amount equal to the shaded areas.

The entire effect of a project's output is considered in Figure 6.3c. The project produces additional output beyond q_0. The original quantity in the market was q_0 prior to the project. As a result of the project, the quantity produced by private suppliers falls from q_0 to q_p while the total quantity supplied to the market rises to q_t. The value of the output is shown as the

[9] Although it is not important to the analysis here, it should be mentioned that because price is not equal to the social marginal cost of production, the market quantity q_0 will be inefficient and there will be a deadweight loss.

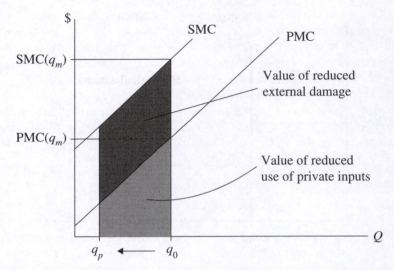

Figure 6.3b   Effect of a change in production

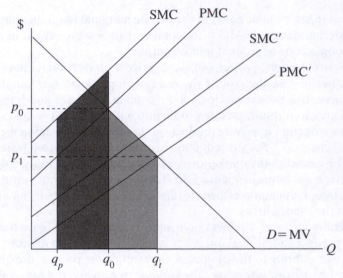

Figure 6.3c   Substituting non-polluting production for polluting production

shaded area in the figure and may be divided into two parts. The left side of the shaded area is the cost savings resulting from decreased private production. As shown in Figure 6.3b, this cost savings contains both private and external costs. The right side of the shaded area is the value to consumers of the additional output, valued along the demand curve.

As a result of the project, market price will fall from p_0 to p_1, but simply using these prices to value the project's output ignores the reduction in external damages (the reduced pollution damage) resulting from diminished private output. Refer to Example 6F for a demonstration of this idea.

EXAMPLE 6F A PROGRAM TO IMPORT ELECTRICITY

Imagine a country whose primary method of generating electricity is burning high sulfur coal, an activity that results in acid rain and significant environmental damage. The country is considering opening its borders to electricity from neighboring countries that are able to generate power by other means. The current price of electricity in the country is $50 per megawatt-hour, but it is anticipated that with the free import of electricity the price will fall to about $40, the prevailing price in neighboring countries. At this lower price, consumers will demand an extra 100,000 megawatt-hours annually. Further, it is expected that the lower price will put a number of inefficient coal-burning plants out of business, resulting in a decrease in domestic generation of 70,000 megawatt-hours.

The total quantity of power that would be imported if domestic markets were opened to foreign generators is estimated to be approximately 170,000 megawatt-hours, the sum of increased consumption and decreased private domestic production. Using the average of the pre- and post-project prices ($50 and $40, respectively) would yield benefits of:

$$170,000 \text{Mwh} \times \left(\frac{\$50 + \$40}{2}\right)/\text{Mwh} = \$7,650,000,$$

or $7.65 million. However, this ignores the value of the reduced pollution damage resulting from decreased domestic generation, so this number should be regarded as a lower bound. How much larger the benefits will be when environmental benefits are included will depend on the resulting reduction in acid rain and the value attached to that reduction.

If an additional megawatt-hour of generation results in $8 of external damage, the reduction in private domestic generation will yield an additional $560,000 in benefits:

$$70{,}000\,\text{Mwh} \times \$8\,/\,\text{Mwh} = \$560{,}000.$$

If there is uncertainty or dispute about the value of the environmental damage done by burning high sulfur coal to generate a megawatt of electricity, an analysis might take the approach of reporting the additional benefit for different values of the external damage from a megawatt-hour of generation and let the reader choose the value he/she prefers.

The market price can be used to value increased private consumption of the output because consumers' marginal value is equal to the market price with no consideration of the external damages.

An additional consideration here is that if a tax is imposed for the purpose of correcting an externality (a so-called Pigouvian tax) then the amount of the tax should be included both in valuing the increase in private consumption and in valuing the decrease in private production. This is because the tax should be representative of the external costs associated with production and/or consumption of the good. To put it another way, the tax represents the cost of unpurchased resources used in production of the output.

The more likely case is one in which there exists a technology that can reduce the externality through some means other than a reduction in output of the good. For example, coal-burning power plants can reduce emissions of particulates and sulfur dioxide through the use of various types of control devices, commonly known as scrubbers. In these cases, the SMC curve when such devices are used becomes the costs of the most effective externality control device plus any residual value of externality damage. The best externality tax is now that levied on the externality directly, for example, on pollution discharge rather than on the good for which the pollution is a by-product. This is a general rule: tax the externality directly, not the good associated with it. In the case in which a reduction in production of the good is the only control mechanism, a tax on pollution discharge will produce the same result as taxing the good, as shown above by a tax equal to the difference between the private and the social marginal cost. When the externality is taxed, as with a tax on pollution, the tax should equal the marginal damage per unit of pollution. This tax will then determine the level of pollution discharge (zero in some cases) and the costs of control as well as the residual damage from any remaining pollution are built into the long-run social marginal cost curve. The pollution tax will equate the private marginal cost and the social marginal cost and the economically optimal equilibrium will result. As before, the intersection of the SMC and demand curves will determine the socially efficient outcome.

6.6   WHEN THERE ARE OTHER INEFFICIENCIES

Myriad inefficiencies can plague output markets. In determining appropriate values for various situations with some degree of inefficiency, the two underlying rules presented at the beginning of this chapter still apply:

- The increase in consumption of the output should be measured according to the willingness to pay by consumers of that output.
- The decrease in private production of an output should be measured according to the marginal cost of the decreased production.

All markets will have some degree of inefficiency. The techniques described in this section should be used only when inefficiencies seem sufficiently severe to warrant the extra consideration.

Monopolists or firms with Market Power

If a project's output is sold in a market in which there are significant barriers to entry and the incumbent firms exercise some market power, it is likely that the market price is above the marginal cost. This may be a monopoly with only one seller or an oligopoly in which a small number of firms divide the market. For purposes of illustration, we will use the standard monopoly model to analyze this situation.

Figure 6.4 shows a monopolist with marginal cost curve MC supplying a market with demand given by $D = MV$. The profit-maximizing quantity, Q_0 will be determined by the intersection of the marginal revenue curve[10] with the marginal cost curve. The price, as given by the demand curve at this quantity, is P_0. The effect on the monopolist of the sale of a project's output will be a reduction in the demand faced by the monopolist. This reduction in the monopolist's demand is shown as a shift of the demand curve from $D = MV$ to D'.[11] At the new, lower demand curve, the monopolist will

---

[10]   This is the steeper line descending from the point where the demand curve intercepts the vertical axis. It is unlabeled in this diagram because of space constraints.

[11]   The horizontal shift in the demand curve is equal to the quantity of output produced by the project. In the diagram, this is equal to $Q_t - Q_p$.

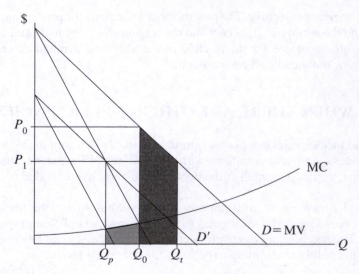

Figure 6.4   Increased production in a monopoly market

choose to supply the smaller quantity Q_p at price P_1. The reduction in the monopolist's costs are given by the left-hand section of the shaded area and are valued along the marginal cost curve, MC. Total output increases from Q_0 to Q_t and the value of the additional consumption is the right-hand side of the shaded area. Of course, if the MC curve also reflects the cost of the project, the darker area under it from Q_0 to Q_t would be a cost of the project.

Outputs Subject to Price Controls

When outputs are sold in markets subject to price controls, there is no guarantee that market prices will reflect either suppliers' opportunity costs of production or consumers' marginal WTP.

If there is an effective price ceiling on an output there is likely to be a shortage, with the implication that the marginal value of an additional unit of output is higher than the controlled price. In this case, the official price at which the ceiling is set is too low to use for a proper valuation. The marginal WTP on the part of consumers is likely to be much higher. It may be estimated by black market prices, if these can be reliably determined. Alternatively, if waiting in line is a common form of rationing the controlled good, estimating a value for the average wait in line and adding this to the controlled price might give an estimate of the marginal WTP on the part of private consumers. At the very least an analysis should recognize that the ceiling price is too low a value for the input.

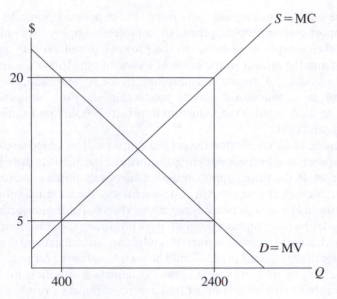

Figure 6.5   A government support program

For example, Figure 6.5 depicts a situation in which a good is subject to a price ceiling of $5, with the result that 400 units are supplied to the market, but at this quantity consumers' marginal value or marginal WTP is $20. The output from a small project that produced and sold one unit of this good should be valued at more than the $5 ceiling price. If the unit produced is somehow distributed to a person whose marginal value is $20, then the value of the project's output should be $20. This would be the case if the project's output were somehow excluded from the price ceiling and sold at a market-clearing price. If, on the other hand, the project's output were distributed by a lottery and the winners were not allowed to resell the goods, then the value would be something less than $20.

If a project output is subject to an effective price floor maintained by some system of price supports, the appropriate value to attach to this output can be difficult to determine and may depend on the exact structure of the support system.[12] In most cases, the existence of the price support system should be taken as given in analysis of a project unless, of course, the analysis is of the support program itself.

Given the existence of a system of price supports, producers will

---

[12] It is curious that there might be a project to produce more of a good whose price is already supported by an existing system of price supports, but such a situation is not unimaginable.

produce until their marginal costs rise to the supported price. As long as the support system persists, private (non-project) suppliers are unlikely to reduce their output in response to the project's output, so any potential benefit from the project would come in increasing the total quantity of an output available for private consumption. If, for some reason, the project did result in a reduction in private production, then the supported price should be used to value the reduction in private production as this will be the marginal cost.

The more likely case is that the project output will be added to either the surplus purchased by the supporting authority or the quantity distributed in the market. If the price support program effectively purchases excess production and then disposes of it in a non-useful way, the marginal value of the output should be zero, or possibly negative if disposal of the project's output is costly. If the price support program pays producers some amount in addition to what they receive at market, this payment is a transfer and the market price (not the supported price) should be used to value the output.

For example, imagine that Figure 6.5 depicts a situation in which a good is subject to a price support that assures suppliers a price of $20. As a result, private suppliers provide 2400 units to the market. A small project produces an additional one unit of the good. Proper valuation of the project output depends on how the support program is run. If the government purchases the entire surplus at $20 (in this case the surplus would be $2400 - 400 = 2000$ units) and disposes of it, then the output of the project will only be thrown away and should be valued at zero. If, on the other hand, the government pays suppliers the difference between the prevailing market price and the $20 price floor, suppliers will produce additional units until the marginal cost rises to $20, and the quantity privately supplied will be 2400 units. Under this type of support system, if a project produces one unit of this good, it will be sold in the market at $5 and a $15 payment will be made by the government to the agency doing the project (assuming the agency is eligible for the payment), but the appropriate value to attach to the output is the consumers' marginal value of $5. The $15 payment from the government to the agency doing the project is simply a transfer.

6.7 DISTRIBUTION THROUGH NON-MARKET METHODS

This chapter focuses on the valuation of project outputs when those outputs are distributed through markets to those people willing and able to pay the most for them. There are projects that distribute their output in other ways, perhaps by giving them away to a certain group of people, selling them at below-market prices or, perhaps, issuing them through a lottery.

If, for some reason, the output is offered in such a way that the price paid is not a reflection of the true market value of the output, then the dollar value may not be a good measure of the project's benefits. In addition, if a project's output is not sold to the people willing and able to pay the most for it, then the benefits of the project, strictly speaking, will not be as large as possible. The benefits of the project will be larger if the output is distributed to a person willing to pay more for it. Consider the case of public housing in Example 6G.

EXAMPLE 6G NON-MARKET DISTRIBUTION OF PUBLIC HOUSING

Imagine a public housing project that constructs some apartments similar to those offered for rent by private landlords but that are offered to low-income families on a waiting list for public housing at below-market rates. Using these below-market rental rates as the value of the units may be incorrect because these units are equivalent to those offered by the private sector and should be valued at a price equal to that of private units. The difference between the higher private rate and the lower rate charged for a project apartment is merely a transfer to families that rent the project's apartments. On the other hand, if the families that get the project's apartments were not living in similar private apartments, they obviously do not value the apartments at the full private rate, so using the private rate to value the project's apartments may be incorrect. In any case, it may be wrong to simply take the rent charged on the project's apartments as a measure of their value.

To extend this idea, imagine that a public housing project will generate one apartment that is similar to apartments that rent for $700 in the private market, but which will be rented out at the rate of $300 to a family meeting some criteria. If the family that rents the apartment previously had no home, then their willingness to pay (a concept conditioned upon their ability to pay) must have been less than $700. Because they chose to rent the apartment, their marginal WTP must be greater than $300. It would be difficult to infer anything beyond the range of their willingness to pay for the public housing unit, although the average of the low and high values, $500, might be a reasonable guess as to their actual WTP.

While this method of distribution will not maximize the net benefits of the project in terms of the potential compensation or Kaldor–Hicks criteria, it may be that the units wind up being distributed to low-income families whose social marginal utility of income (SMUY) is greater than the SMUY of the people who would rent the units at market rates. This greater SMUY could more than make up for the lesser amount that low-income families would be willing and able to pay.

6.8   SUMMARY

Attaching values to project outputs sold in markets should usually be straightforward. If markets are operating with reasonable efficiency, the market price is an appropriate value. For most outputs from most projects, the pre-project price is the correct value to use in BCA. If a project will produce a very large quantity of an output and its price is expected to fall as a result, the average of the pre- and post-project prices is an appropriate value.

If sales of the project output are taxed, the extent to which these taxes should be included in the value of the output depends on whether the collecting agency has standing as well as the division between increase in consumption and decrease in private production.

In addition to taxes, there are numerous factors that may distort markets and complicate analysis of projects. External damages related to private production of an output should be included in the value of reduced private production. A monopolist's markup over marginal cost should be included in the value of net increases in the quantity of a project's output exchanged in the market, but not in the value of the reduction in the monopolist's output. Price controls may have a variety of impacts depending on the exact nature of the control.

The general rule in assigning values to outputs is that any additional output that is generated due to the project should be valued at the consumers' WTP as given by the demand curve. Any reduction in private production should be valued according to the marginal cost.

If they are available, elasticities can be used to determine relative sizes of private production decreases and consumption increases. If elasticities are unavailable, it might be safe to assume some division between the two in the short run and that the long-run supply elasticity is likely to be infinite for most goods. For better or for worse, BCA is an inexact practice.

EXERCISES

Questions

1. Draw a diagram analogous to Figure 6.2 in which the good supplied is taxed but in which the effect of the project on supply is greater than the effect of the tax on supply. Indicate which area is the value of the project's output.

2. Redo the example of wine tariffs using identical values except that price elasticity of demand is −0.7 and price elasticity of supply is 1.1. How do your answers change and how does this demonstrate the importance of estimating and including price changes resulting from a project in the analysis of that project?

3. Imagine that a project will produce 120 units of a good and sell it in a market with demand and supply curves given by:

$$Q_D = 960 - P/2$$

$$Q_s = P - 120.$$

   A. Calculate the appropriate value to attach to the project's output.
   B. Now, imagine that a $30/unit tax is imposed on the market. Calculate the appropriate value for the project's output.
   C. Imagine an analysis simply used the price of the good, including the tax, as the value of the output. By how much would this analysis overstate or understate the value of the project's output?

4. Imagine that a project will produce 240 units of a good whose private production results in a negative externality. The marginal value of the external damage resulting from a unit of private production is $30 and the supply and demand curves for the good are given by:

$$Q_D = 840 - 2P$$

$$Q_s = P - 120.$$

   Calculate the appropriate value of the project's output.

5. Imagine that a project will produce 100 units of a good that will be sold in a market currently served by a monopolist with a marginal cost of $20. Demand in the market is given by:

$$Q_D = 960 - 2P.$$

A. Solve for the initial profit-maximizing price and quantity of the monopolist.

B. Calculate the value of the project's output. How does it compare to the value that would have been attached to it had the monopolist's profit-maximizing price from part A simply been used?

Answers

1.

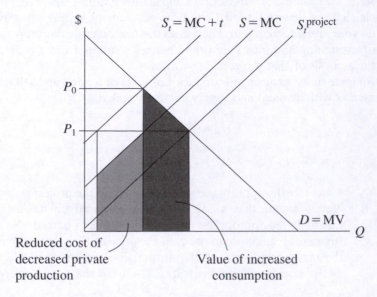

Reduced cost of decreased private production

Value of increased consumption

2. A country with protective barriers against wine imports is considering removing these barriers. They currently consume 1600 million bottles of wine annually. It is expected that 160 million bottles or 10 percent of the current market would be imported if the tariff barriers were lowered. The current price for a bottle of wine is $12, including $4 of taxes. The best estimate of the price elasticity of demand is −0.7. Domestic wine producers have the option of exporting and as a result supply elasticity is estimated at 1.1.

To value the benefits of opening the market, it is necessary to estimate the reduction in private domestic production and the increase in total consumption. Using the formulae given above:

$$\frac{dQ_s}{dX} = \frac{PES}{-PED + PES} = \frac{1.1}{0.7 + 1.1} = 0.611$$

$$\frac{dQ_D}{dX} = \frac{-\text{PED}}{-\text{PED} + \text{PES}} = \frac{0.7}{0.7 + 1.1} = 0.389.$$

So, the importation of 160 million bottles of wine will result in a reduction in domestic supply of approximately 98 million bottles and an increase in consumption of approximately 62 million bottles.

Ignoring for the moment the resulting price change, these quantities might be valued at $8/bottle and $12/bottle, respectively, yielding an initial estimate of the total benefit of:

$8/bottle × 98m bottles + $12/bottle × 62m bottles = $1528m.

Happily for consumers in the country, the importation of so large a quantity of foreign wine will result in lower prices. From the analyst's perspective, this will reduce the value of wine in the analysis and reduce the benefits of lowering protective tariffs.

The 10 percent increase in quantity will be divided as above into a 6.11 percent decrease in quantity supplied and a 3.89 percent increase in quantity demanded.

The impact of a 6.11 percent decrease in quantity supplied on the marginal cost of production will be:

$$\text{PES} = \frac{\%\Delta Q}{\%\Delta P}$$

$$1.1 = \frac{-6.11\%}{\%\Delta P}$$

$$\%\Delta P = -5.55\%.$$

A reduction of 5.55 percent would bring the marginal cost of production down from $8.00 to $7.56. The appropriate value to use in the analysis is the average of these, or $7.78/bottle rather than the $8/bottle used above.

The impact of a 3.89 percent increase in quantity consumed on consumers' marginal value would be:

$$\text{PED} = \frac{\%\Delta Q}{\%\Delta P}$$

$$-0.7 = \frac{3.89\%}{\%\Delta P}$$

$$\%\Delta P = -5.56\%.$$

A reduction of 5.56 percent would bring the marginal value of wine consumption down from \$12.00 to \$11.33. The appropriate value to use in the analysis is the average of these, or \$11.67/bottle rather than the \$12/bottle used above.

Including the price change, the estimated benefits are:

$$\$7.78/bottle \times 98m\ bottles + \$11.67/bottle \times 62m\ bottles = \$1486m.$$

This second estimate of the benefits takes into account the fact that prices will fall as a result of the imports. However, the small price change means that the difference between the two estimates (the first giving benefits of \$1508 million and the second giving benefits of \$1486 million) will be similarly small.

In this case, the difference between the value of the project's benefits without consideration of the price change and with consideration of the price change is fairly small, about 1.5 percent.

3.A.   The initial price and quantity are found by setting the quantity demanded equal to the quantity supplied and solving for price and the substituting the price back into the original equations to solve for the quantity:

$$960 - P/2 = P - 120$$
$$1080 = 3P/2$$
$$P = 720,\ Q = 600.$$

The project will increase the quantity supplied at all prices by 120, giving a new supply curve with the equation:

$$Q_s' = P - 120 + 120 = P,$$

and a new equilibrium of

$$960 - P/2 = P$$
$$960 = 3P/2$$
$$P = 640,\ Q = 640.$$

The 120 units of output should be valued at the average of the two prices or \$680/unit, for a total value of \$81,600.

3.B.   To add the tax to the supply curve, rewrite the supply relationship to get price as a function of quantity, add the tax and then rewrite the equation to get quantity as a function of price.

$$Q_s = P - 120$$
$$P = Q + 120 + 30$$
$$Q_s^t = P - 150$$

$$960 - P/2 = P - 150$$
$$1110 = 3P/2$$
$$P = 740, Q = 590$$

$$Q_s'' = P - 150 + 120 = P - 30$$
$$960 - P/2 = P - 30$$
$$990 = 3P/2$$
$$P = 660, Q = 630.$$

So, as a result of the project, the total quantity traded has risen from 590 to 630, an increase of 40 units. Because the project produced 120 units, this means that private production decreased by 80 units. The increase in consumption of 40 units should be valued at the average of the two prices including tax, which would be $700. The decrease in production of 80 units should be valued at the average of the two prices less the $30 tax, or $670. The total value of the output, then, would be:

$$40 \text{ units} \times \$700/\text{unit} + 80 \text{ units} \times \$670/\text{unit} = \$81,600.$$

3.C. If only the initial price ($720 without the tax or $740 with the tax) were used, the resulting values for the output would be $86,400 and $88,800, respectively. Recognizing that the price will fall as the project's output enters the market results in the calculated value of the output falling by $4800 or $7200. However, in this case, the value of the project's output did not change as a result of a tax being added to the market.

4.   The initial price and quantity are:

$$840 - 2P = P - 120$$
$$960 = 3P$$
$$P = 320, Q = 200.$$

With the project, the supply curve becomes:

$$Q_s' = P - 120 + 60 = P - 60$$

and the new equilibrium is:

$$840 - 2P = P - 60$$
$$900 = 3P$$
$$P = 300, Q = 240.$$

Total quantity exchanged or consumed increases by 40 units, but because the project produces 60 units, this means that private production falls by 20 units.

The increase in consumption should be valued according to the average of the two prices, but the decrease in private production should be valued at the average of the two prices plus the marginal external damage. The total calculated value of the project output is:

$$40 \text{ units} \times \$310/\text{unit} + 20 \text{ units} \times \$340/\text{unit} = \$19{,}200.$$

5.A. To solve for the monopolist's profit-maximizing price and quantity, rewrite the demand equation to get price as a function of quantity:

$$P = 480 - Q/2,$$

then multiply by Q to get the revenue function:

$$\text{TR}(Q) = 480Q - Q^2/2$$

and take the derivative to get the marginal revenue function:

$$\text{MR}(Q) = d\text{TR}(Q)/dQ = 480 - Q.$$

Setting this equal to marginal cost gives a profit-maximizing result of:

$$480 - Q = 20$$
$$Q = 460, \; P = 250.$$

5.B. The effect of the project will be to reduce the quantity demanded from the monopolist by 100 units, changing the monopolist's demand curve to:

$$Q_D = 960 - 2P - 100 = 860 - 2P.$$

Rewrite the demand equation to get price as a function of quantity:

$$P = 430 - Q/2,$$

then multiply by Q to get the revenue function:

$$\text{TR}(Q) = 430Q - Q^2/2,$$

and take the derivative to get the marginal revenue function:

$$MR(Q) = dTR(Q)/dQ = 430 - Q.$$

Setting this equal to marginal cost gives a profit-maximizing result of:

$$430 - Q = 20$$
$$Q = 410,\ P = 225.$$

So, as a result of the project producing 100 units of the good, the monopolist has reduced production by 50 units. This means that consumption increased by $100 - 50 = 50$ units.

The reduction in production should be valued according to the monopolist's marginal cost of $20 while the increase in consumption should be valued along the demand curve at the average of the before- and after-project prices, $237.50:

$$50\text{ units} \times \$20/\text{unit} + 50\text{ units} \times \$237.50 = \$12,875.$$

Had the initial profit-maximizing price been used as the value of the project's output, the total value would have been:

$$100\text{ units} \times \$250 = \$25,000.$$

This is nearly double the more properly calculated value and it illustrates the importance of accounting for the fact that the price will fall as a result of the project and, more importantly, to recognizing the gap between marginal cost and price for a firm with market power.

7. Assigning monetary values using shadow values

7.1 INTRODUCTION

Whenever possible, primary market prices should be used to value inputs and outputs in benefit–cost analysis. When markets are relatively free of distortions, prices are the best indication of the willingness to pay for an output or the marginal cost of an input and the analysis should be restricted to these primary markets. For example, the benefits of a project providing electricity to an area that previously had none will be captured in the electricity market. The availability of electricity will increase residents' demand for electrical devices such as lights and televisions, but these secondary markets should usually be excluded from any analysis.

Sometimes, however, primary market prices are not available and some alternative method must be used to value a good. A value calculated through some alternative method is referred to as a shadow value. There are a variety of situations in which shadow values might be used. One example is a project that will create a new national park. While people may pay an admission fee to enter the park, this fee is not usually an accurate measure of the park's value. A second example is a project that will reduce the risk of death faced by a large group of people. There are no markets that trade directly and explicitly in human life, so attaching a value to the lives saved must be done through another method. A third example is a project that will either improve or degrade the air quality in an area. Clean air is not sold in any market, but is clearly important to people. The problem is accurately estimating its value. A fourth example is a project that will preserve the natural habitat of a popular endangered species. If people care about the species, they will attach some value to increasing the probability of its continued survival, but because this probability is not traded there is no market value for it.

The correct technique for determining shadow values varies by situation. This chapter will describe several techniques for estimating values by indirect means. While not exhaustive, the list of approaches described here is suggestive of techniques that may be employed.

7.2   TRAVEL COST

The travel cost method (TCM) is a process for estimating the value of amenities (generally recreational or health related) that people must physically visit in order to enjoy. Originating from an idea proposed in a letter from Harold Hotelling to the National Parks Service in 1946 in response to a solicitation for ways in which to estimate the value of national parks,[1] it has been used to value a variety of attractions as well as their constituent characteristics.

The underlying idea is that different people face different costs for traveling to an attraction. The cost of a visit includes not only the admission or use price, but also the cost of round trip travel, including the value of travel time. People living further away generally face higher travel costs. Because different consumers face different costs, the quantity demanded (in terms of visits per person per year, for example) at these different costs can be measured and a demand curve can be estimated. This demand curve can then be used to value the attraction.

We will first consider the zonal TCM, how it is done and the various assumptions and problems associated with it. We will then briefly describe an extension, the hedonic travel cost method, which can be used to estimate the value of particular characteristics of a group of similar attractions.

The Zonal Travel Cost Method

The goal of TCM is to estimate a demand curve for visits to some sort of attraction such as a park, a ski resort or a medical facility. Demand is the number of visits a person would choose to make over some time period (such as a year) depending on the cost of each visit. If the cost of a visit is dependent on the round trip distance traveled to make that visit, then the quantity demanded may also be thought of as a function of the distance.

As a simple example,[2] imagine that a park is visited only by residents of two cities, one is 50 miles away and the other is 200 miles away. Round trip travel costs from the two cities are $20 and $80, respectively, and it is known that people from the nearer city average five trips per year while people from the further city average two trips per year. If the park charges no admission fee, the only cost of visiting is the travel cost, and the data provide two points on the demand curve for the park. Assuming that the demand curve is linear, we have the diagram as shown in Figure 7.1.

---

[1]   According to McConnell (1985).
[2]   A more detailed example may be found in Johansson (1987, p. 117).

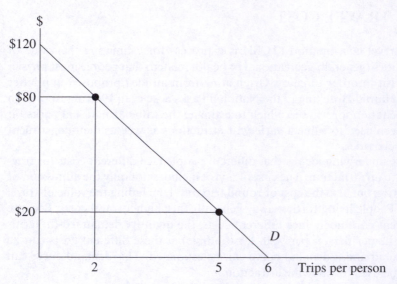

Figure 7.1   The travel cost method

The annual value of the park to a person living at its entrance (who would face zero travel cost for a visit) would be his/her consumer surplus at a price of zero. This is equal to the entire area under the demand curve which is $360. The annual value of the park to a person living in the nearer of the two cities would be the consumer surplus associated with a price of $20 and a quantity of five visits, or $250. The annual value of the park to a person living in the further of the two cities would be the consumer surplus associated with a price of $80 and a quantity of two visits, or $40.[3]

Of course, there are generally a number of towns or cities from which visitors may originate. As a result, the areas surrounding an attraction may be broken into zones based on distance from the attraction, essentially creating concentric circles about the attraction. Mean travel costs and visitation rates could be calculated for people coming from each of the zones and the analysis described above could be duplicated.

The area surrounding an attraction might be divided into five zones, the nearest being Zone 1 and the furthest being Zone 5. A very simple version of this is shown in Figure 7.2. Visitors to the attraction can be surveyed to determine from which zone they came. If the population of each zone is

---

3   The consumer surpluses in this case are the areas of the triangles under the demand curve above the $20 line and above the $80 line.

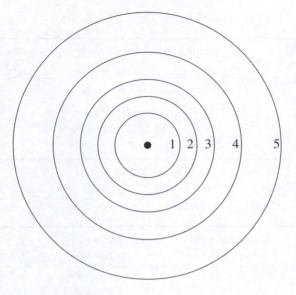

Figure 7.2　Travel cost zones

known, a visit rate (annual visits per capita) can be calculated. Assuming a travel cost from each zone, the demand relationship can then be estimated.

The value of the park to the people who might visit it depends on their cost of traveling to the park and the admission fee, if any. To consider extreme cases, a park that was prohibitively expensive to visit or to enter would have very little value.[4]

A simple example

As an example, imagine that 1 percent of the visitors to a state park are surveyed to determine their zone of origin (Table 7.1a). If the population of each zone is known, an annual visitation rate can be calculated for each zone, as shown in Table 7.1b.

The next step is to assign a travel cost per trip from each zone. This cost will probably depend on the average driving distance from that zone to the site. To this end, zones may be defined on the basis of driving rather than linear distances. The mean travel cost and annual visitation rate can then be combined to yield the demand relationship, as shown in Table 7.1c, which can then be graphed, as in Figure 7.3.

---

[4]　For example, the value of a park on the moon would be zero despite the fact that it might have spectacular mountains and canyons.

Table 7.1a   Visitors zone of origin

Zone	Number sampled	Estimated total number of visits
1	100	10,000
2	1,800	180,000
3	2,300	230,000
4	900	90,000
5	20	2,000

Table 7.1b   Annual visitation rate

Zone	Estimated total number of visits	Zone population	Annual visitation rate
	10,000	25,000	0.40
2	180,000	600,000	0.30
3	230,000	1,150,000	0.20
4	90,000	900,000	0.10
5	0	200,000	0.00

Table 7.1c   Demand curve relationship

Zone	Mean round trip distance in miles	Cost per mile	Mean travel cost	Annual visitation rate
1	20	$0.30	$6.00	0.40
2	50	$0.30	$15.00	0.30
3	80	$0.30	$24.00	0.20
4	110	$0.30	$33.00	0.10
5	140	$0.30	$42.00	0.00

The value of the park to the people in any zone may be calculated as the consumer surplus at the cost and quantity applicable for that zone. For example, the people living in Zone 5 with travel costs of $42.00 and zero visits have consumer surplus of zero. People living in Zone 4 with travel costs of $33.00 and a visit rate of 0.1 have consumer surplus that is approximately equal to $0.45 per person or, because there are 900,000 residents in Zone 4,

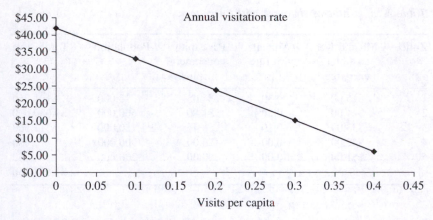

Figure 7.3   Demand curve for visitors

Table 7.1d   Value of the park

Zone	Mean travel cost	Annual visit rate	Per capita consumer surplus	Population	Total value
1	$6.00	0.40	$7.20	25,000	$180,000
2	$15.00	0.30	$4.05	600,000	$2,430,000
3	$24.00	0.20	$1.80	1,150,000	$2,070,000
4	$33.00	0.10	$0.45	900,000	$405,000
5	$42.00	0.00	$0.00	200,000	$0
					$5,085,000

a total consumer surplus of $405,000. Values for the remaining zones are shown in Table 7.1d. The total value of the park is calculated as $5,085,000.

The above analysis assumes that once a person has traveled to the park, entry is free. If an entry fee were charged, this would have the effect of increasing the cost of a visit, just as would happen if travel cost rose by the same amount. Imagine that, in addition to the travel cost, an entry fee of $9.00 were imposed, raising the cost of attendance and reducing the visit rate for each zone, in this case, to what it had been for the next zone out. The effect would be, as shown in Table 7.1e, to reduce the value of the park to $1,698,750.

A more complicated travel cost example can be found in the appendix at the end of this chapter.

Table 7.1e   Value of the park with entry fees

Zone	Mean travel cost plus entry fee	Annual visit rate	Per capita consumer surplus	Population	Total value
1	$15.00	0.30	$4.05	25,000	$101,250
2	$24.00	0.20	$1.80	600,000	$1,080,000
3	$33.00	0.10	$0.45	1,150,000	$517,500
4	$42.00	0.00	$0.00	900,000	$0
5	$51.00	0.00	$0.00	200,000	$0
					$1,698,750

Problems with the zonal travel cost method
Estimating the value of an attraction based on travel costs is complicated
by a number of potential problems. While each of these issues should be
addressed or at least mentioned in a good study, there may be no real solu-
tions to these problems.

The first issue is determining the cost of travel to the site from the various
zones.[5] While an average dollar amount per mile of round trip travel may
be used, this ignores the fact that people traveling different distances may
tend to use more or less costly methods of transportation. Visitors from
nearby may cram into small cars for the trip while those traveling longer
distances may demand more comfortable and more expensive transportation. People visiting from very far away may arrive by a combination of
private automobile and commercial air travel, greatly complicating a cost
per mile assumption. Further, travel to the site may be part of the attraction, especially if the drive takes a visitor along scenic roads. For example,
a motorcyclist may get as much value from the ride to a national park as
he/she does from any experiences in the park. People who fly first class will
incur significantly higher travel costs, but the premium paid is for amenities
enjoyed during the flight. To say that traveling is merely a cost of visiting
an attraction may ignore an important aspect of traveling.

A second issue is multi-purpose trips that take a visitor to a number of
other attractions in addition to that whose value is being measured. For
example, residents of Michigan may take a trip for the specific purpose of visiting Mackinac Island in northern Lake Huron. The total cost of their trip
would reflect the value they attach to the island. Visitors from Germany who
are traveling across the United States and visiting many sites along the way

---

[5]   For an extended discussion, see Randall (1994).

would report a huge cost for visiting Mackinac Island, but this would probably include a trans-Atlantic flight and many miles of driving en route to many destinations including the island. How these total travel costs should be divided between the many destinations or many purposes of the trip is a difficult question.

A third issue is how to treat visits of different lengths. People visiting an attraction may choose to stay for different lengths of time. Visits of different lengths imply different values for the attraction. The proper measure of use in a study may be the number of visit days instead of simply the number of visits.

A fourth issue is the possibility of heterogeneity across zones. That is, demand for the attraction could, and probably does, vary between zones. People who live close to an attraction may do so because they attach a high value to visiting it. Those who live further away may value the attraction less and would visit it less frequently even if they lived nearby. The estimation of one demand curve for the attraction relies on the assumption that the demand relationship between cost of visits and number of visits is the same across zones, or that the populations are homogeneous. If this assumption is violated, estimation of the demand curve, or even the theoretical existence of only one demand curve, may be unreasonable.

Finally, if a demand curve is to be reliably estimated, a good range of travel costs should be available. This means that observations should include people who have traveled from a variety of distances and have incurred a wide range of travel costs. The wider the range of legitimate travel costs, the more reliably the demand curve can be estimated. If only a narrow range of travel costs can be reliably observed, demand estimates will be unreliable.

The Hedonic Travel Cost Method

An extension of TCM is the hedonic travel cost method.[6] The hedonic TCM goes beyond valuing one particular attraction and seeks to value particular characteristics of sites by looking at travel to a large number of similar attractions with varying sets of characteristics. In the words of Brown and Mendelsohn (1984, p. 427), 'the travel cost method can measure the value of the Colorado River, the hedonic travel cost method can value scenic quality, fish density, crowdedness, etc.'.

For example, imagine two national parks that are identical except that one offers opportunities for fly fishing while the other does not. The

---

[6] See Brown and Mendelsohn (1984).

increased amount that people pay to travel to the park with fly fishing would be a measure of the value of that activity.

As another example, imagine that there are several trailheads in an area offering access to hiking and backpacking areas. If people tended to travel further to get to less crowded trailheads, the cost of the additional travel would be a measure of either the value of greater solitude or the cost of greater crowding.

Although it offers great potential for determining values of attributes, the hedonic TCM has data and technical requirements that are likely to be prohibitive in most cases. For a discussion of some of the challenges in using the hedonic TCM, see Smith and Kaoru (1987).

7.3   VALUE OF LIFE RISKS

Many projects have the effect of reducing the risk of death faced by the affected population. Examples include programs to offer vaccinations, improvements in highway safety, bicycle helmet laws and the equipping of passenger airliners with defibrillators. Although the effect of these programs is to reduce the risk of death faced by a number of people, the benefits are usually assessed in terms of the number of lives saved. In these situations, conducting a benefit–cost analysis requires that a dollar value be attached to the lives saved.

Several qualifications are important in considering the value of lives saved or lost as a result of a project. First, the analysis presented here is for a statistical life saved. This means that a person is saved as a result of a reduced risk of death faced by a group of people. Before the project is carried out, it is not known exactly who would die if the project were not carried out, only that on average a certain number would die without the project and a smaller number will die with it. Situations in which the life to be saved is not statistical but is, instead, a specific individual or a certain life, are generally assessed very differently. The benefits of saving a certain life are usually much greater than the benefits of saving a statistical life. Second, if execution of a project involves some risky activities, it is generally assumed that the people hired to do these things receive a compensating wage differential for the risk faced. That is, the value of the risk they face is included in the cost of the project as part of the labor cost, so additional calculations for the lives lost among those hired to carry out the project are not necessary.[7]

---

[7]   If, for some reason, there is no compensating differential, perhaps because workers were unaware of the risks involved in the project, then any deaths occurring over the course of the project should be included in the analysis.

Third, if a project results in reduced risk faced by people at work, one result of the project may be that employees receive lower wage rates after the project than they did before. As a result, the benefits of such a project are actually enjoyed by employers who are now able to hire people at lower wage rates than was previously possible. The implication is that worker safety regulations may offer greater benefits to employers than they do to workers because worker safety regulations impose a mandated substitution of safety for income.[8] Example 7A provides an illustration of this:

EXAMPLE 7A   SEARCH AND RESCUE

To illustrate the difference between a certain and a statistical life, imagine that a person has become lost on a hiking trip in very rugged terrain. It is expected that if that person is not found within several days, he/she will die of exposure.

A search and rescue effort is launched with 200 people covering the area. Due to the rough terrain, there is some risk to the search and rescue personnel. If the area in which they were searching were so dangerous that each searcher faced a probability of 0.01 of suffering a fatal accident during the search, the expected number of fatalities among the rescuers would be:

$$200 \text{ people} \times 0.01 \text{ fatalities/person} = 2 \text{ fatalities.}$$

Under these conditions, if the search and rescue effort were carried out, the implication may be that the two statistical lives were of less value than one certain life.

While risks and statistical lives are not explicitly traded in markets, a variety of market goods and services are associated with varying degrees of risk. The most common examples come from labor markets. Different jobs are associated with different probabilities of death. Other things being equal, jobs associated with higher probabilities of death will pay higher wage rates to compensate employees for the additional risks involved. This additional payment is a measure of the value attached to that additional

---

[8] If it is the case that employers actually resist a set of worker safety rules, it may simply be that the costs exceed the benefits for those rules.

risk.[9] A second approach to estimating the value of changes in risk is to look at the price of products for which safety is an important considera- tion. Safer automobiles, for example, should have higher sale prices, other things being the same, and the price difference between two otherwise similar cars should be a measure of the value of the difference in risk assoc- iated with driving one or the other. By analyzing such things as wage pre- miums for riskier jobs and price premiums for safer products, it is possible to infer the value that people attach to marginal changes in their risk of death. As marginal reductions in risk are the mechanism through which public projects (at least those subject to BCA) typically save lives, inferences about individual decisions regarding life risks are a good way of valuing the benefits of such projects.

One criticism of wage-based estimates of risk reductions is that they are based on the behavior of people who actually take risky jobs and, as such, may be too low a value to attach to the general population, most of whom choose not to take risky jobs and, as revealed through their behavior, value their lives more highly than those who actually do take risky jobs.

The Hedonic Wage Model

The most common method used to estimate the value of a marginal change in the risk of accidental death is the hedonic wage model. The hedonic wage model is based on the idea that the wage or salary paid to an employee is a function of the characteristics of that employee and the characteris- tics of his or her job. One of the characteristics of a job is the risk of a work- related death over the course of a year. Other things being the same, riskier jobs should offer higher pay rates. If done properly, analysis of data should provide estimates of the average willingness to accept in exchange for a marginal increase in the probability of accidental death.

Given appropriate data, the basics of the analysis are fairly straightfor- ward. The rate of pay is regressed on a set of personal characteristics such as age, educational attainment and work experience and on a set of job characteristics such as relative unpleasantness of working conditions, level of responsibility involved, level of exertion required, flexibility of hours worked and the probability of a fatal (or perhaps non-fatal but serious) accident over the course of a year. The estimated coefficient on the probability of an accident is an estimate of the willingness to accept for a marginal increase in risk.

---

9   A compensating wage differential is a measure of willingness to accept for a marginal increase in risk and, as such, will likely be larger than willingness to pay.

For example, if a regression of hourly wage on various explanatory factors and the mortality rate (measured in fatalities per 1000 full-time workers) yielded a coefficient of 0.55 on the fatality rate, this would suggest that as the probability of death increases by one in one thousand, the wage should increase by about $0.55/hour or, over a 2080 hour work year, about $1144. If this marginal change in risk were applied to 1000 workers over the course of a year, the expected impact would be one additional fatality and the value of this one statistical life would be the product of $1144 and 1000, or $1,144,000.

There are a number of technical issues that complicate estimation of the wage premium.[10] First, it may be that workers' or employers' perceptions of the risk involved in a job are inconsistent or inaccurate. If workers do not know the level of risk to which a job exposes them, the observed wage differential will underestimate the value of that risk. Indeed, such risk data can be difficult to find and will likely be aggregated to some extent. For example, data on accident rates in the commercial fishing industry may include not only deck hands (whose working conditions are extremely hazardous) but also office personnel. As a result, average accident rates for the industry will understate risk for deck hands and overstate it for office workers.

Second, getting a consistent measure of the level of compensation received by employees may be a challenge. While it may be possible to directly obtain or construct an hourly wage in some cases, industries in which hours are irregular may present a challenge. Further, if benefits are an important part of compensation, their value should be included.

Third, there will be unobserved variables for individuals and occupations. For example, it is impossible to observe or measure a person's work ethic, a potentially important factor in explaining earnings. A particular problem is that characteristics that make a person more or less valuable under dangerous conditions (grace or clumsiness) may have impacts for the wage in risky jobs but not in relatively safe jobs.[11] Similarly, data on some occupations will likely exclude some aspects of the job that are critical to determining the associated wage.

Fourth, there will likely be collinearity in the data resulting from the fact that more dangerous jobs will also tend to have other undesirable characteristics, such as being physically demanding, subjecting the worker to long hours or extremes of heat, cold or noise, or requiring work in remote

---

[10] Many of the potential difficulties listed here are technical econometric issues and the reader is referred to Studenmund (1997), Kennedy (2003) or any of many other fine texts for guidance.

[11] See Garen (1988).

areas.[12] It is almost certainly the case that the rate of fatal accidents is cor-related with the rate of non-fatal injuries across jobs. Separating the wage effects of bad working conditions from those of increased risk, and sepa-rating the effects of increased risk of death versus increased risk of injury may be impossible.

Numerous attempts have been made at estimating the value of marginal changes in risk and, based on the results, imputing a value for a statistical life.[13] Despite myriad potential problems in these estimations, studies usually seem to arrive at overall estimates that are at least in the same neighborhood.

Labor Market Calculations of the Value of a Statistical Life

Despite the difficulties involved in estimating the wage premium associated with increased risk of job-related death, many studies have used this approach to calculate the value of a statistical life (VSL). The most reli-able studies looking at recent labor market data in the United States gen-erally find a VSL in the range of $5 million to $12 million, with a median value of about $7 million.[14] There are a number of qualifications for this number.

First, VSL has a positive income elasticity that has been estimated in the range of 0.2 to 1.0, but is most likely in the neighborhood of 0.5.[15] Because this is positive, as a person's income rises, so does the value that they attach to risk. Other things being the same, people with lower incomes are willing to take additional risk in exchange for a lower payment than are people with higher incomes. Put another way, safety appears to be a normal good. As income rises by 1 percent, the amount of money necessary to compen-sate a person for a marginal increase in risk rises by about 0.5 percent. Studies done in lower-income regions or countries are likely to yield lower VSL estimates.

Second, VSL may be age dependent in a way that makes it more produc-tive to speak of the value of a statistical year of life. For example, if a project will reduce risks of early childhood mortality (perhaps through improved neo-natal care for at-risk populations) then the number of statistical life years saved per life saved will be very large. On the other hand, a project that will address one cause of mortality among people with numerous other

---

[12]   These characteristics are consistent with the working conditions of pilots, miners, construction workers, timber cutters and commercial fishermen, people who face among the highest rates of job-related injuries and fatalities.

[13]   A listing and analysis of these papers is given in Viscusi and Aldy (2002).

[14]   Ibid., pp. 24–5.

[15]   Ibid., pp. 43–4.

severe conditions will yield a small number of statistical life years saved per life saved. A program that saves a smaller number of lives could be preferable to a program that saves a larger number of lives if the first program saves more expected years of life. The value of a life year may be calculated by viewing VSL as the present value of a stream of life years and using annuity formulae to calculate the value of one year in that stream. If, for example, wages paid to 35-year-old males were used to calculate a VSL of $7 million, this could be combined with the fact that the life expectancy for a 35-year-old male is approximately 41 years[16] and a discount rate of 1 percent to yield an annual value of $208,957. Aldy and Viscusi (2004) conduct an analysis along these lines and arrive at the conclusion that the VSL follows an inverted U-shape relative to age, peaking in the prime working years at a value of approximately $7 million for a 30-year-old and declining to just over $2.5 million for a 60-year-old. It should be noted that this approach to valuing lives is almost certainly inexact as a number of factors, including health status, are correlated with age. Further, even if technically flawless, such estimates are likely to be very controversial.

Finally, calculations of VSL based on WTA for the added risk of more dangerous jobs are based on observations of the people who actually take those jobs. Many people work in safer occupations because, in part, they perceive risk premiums as insufficient for the additional risk. VSL figures are based on observations of people who, as revealed through their behavior, attach less value to risk than do other people in the economy. As a result, estimates of VSL may be too low for the general population.

Other Approaches to VSL

In addition to estimates based on labor market data, estimates of VSL have been made using other market data. The general approach is to use a hedonic price equation in which the price of a good is modeled as a function of its various characteristics including the risk of death or injury associated with its use.

For example, the price of an automobile may be estimated as a function of its characteristics including measures of safety. Other things being the same, safer automobiles should command a higher price and this higher price may be used as an estimate of the marginal risk reduction. Using this approach, Atkinson and Halvorsen (1990) calculate a VSL of $5.13 million while Dreyfus and Viscusi (1995) find values ranging from $3.8 million to $5.4 million.

---

[16]   Arias (2002, Table 2).

Estimates of VSL based on observed behavior outside of labor markets tend to be a bit smaller than those based on labor market data, but are of comparable magnitude.[17]

The VSL values presented here are, of course, subject to some dispute. Ashenfelter and Greenstone (2004) analyze the decision by individual states to raise speed limits from 55 miles per hour and infer from this the VSL based on the value of travel time saved per additional fatality. They arrive at an estimated VSL of approximately $1.5 million (in 1997 dollars) and point out several important biases that could seriously diminish the reliability of other estimates. The first of these is the problem of omitted variable bias, the idea that there are factors that should be included in VSL analyses that are excluded, usually because the necessary information is unavailable. For example, in valuing lives based on travel time saved at higher speeds, the fact that people drive more slowly when conditions are dangerous needs to be taken into account. That is, travel speed is endogenous and dependent upon risk and failure to recognize that behavior changes in the face of perceived risk can bias estimates of VSL. Second, they suggest that there might be a bias in VSL from published academic papers if the publishing journals prefer papers with statistically significant results. They show that situations with statistically significant estimated coefficients related to VSL also tend to attach higher values to VSL. It may be that there are unpublished papers that find lower VSL values. While these two factors do not necessarily bias VSL estimates in one direction or the other (in fact they work in opposite directions) they do point out two potential weaknesses in VSL calculations.

7.4   HEDONIC ANALYSIS OF PROPERTY VALUES

Some projects will have local impacts that cannot be directly valued through markets. This may be because the benefits of the project are not distributed through markets or because the project generates some sort of externality or public good. For example, the establishment of a city park creates an amenity that residents of a city may use at no charge. Construction of a highway creates a nuisance that affects nearby residents whether or not they choose not to use the highway. Improvements in a city's police or fire department will be beneficial but difficult to value because these services are not directly traded in markets. Valuing the effects of projects such as these cannot be done directly through markets because things

---

[17]   Viscusi and Aldy (2002, p. 29).

such as public parks, highway noise and police protection are not directly exchanged in markets. However, all of these projects have local impacts that may be reflected in property values. If a park is a valuable amenity, property values in the neighborhood surrounding the park should rise relative to property values elsewhere when people learn that that park will be established. Similarly, property values may fall when residents learn that a highway will be constructed nearby. Improvements in municipal services may be reflected in property values as residents become aware of improvements, something that may happen immediately or over time. The critical element in these cases is that property is inextricably linked to the area of the project's impact. Property may not be moved out of the area of impact of a negative externality, nor may property be moved into the area of a positive amenity.

The impact of a project on local property values may be estimated using hedonic analysis, a type of multiple regression in which property values are expressed as a function of the characteristics of the property itself and of the neighborhood or surrounding area. Characteristics explaining the value of a house may include such things as its square footage, the size of the lot on which it sits, whether or not it has a view, the number of bedrooms and bathrooms, its age and whether or not it has a garage. Neighborhood characteristics may include proximity to a school, park or shopping, crime rates and noise or pollution levels. Under certain conditions, multiple regression analysis allows the impact of each characteristic on the value of a house to be estimated.

Hedonic analysis may be used in two ways to estimate the value of a project. Data from other locations may be used to predict the effect of a project *ex ante*. For example, the benefit of establishing a new city park might be calculated by using existing data to estimate the effect that proximity to a park has on property values. The necessary assumption is that the effect of the new park will be similar to that of existing parks.

Alternatively, hedonic analysis may be used to estimate the effect of a project *ex post*. For example, imagine that a municipal trash incinerator has been located in a particular neighborhood. To determine the impact on local housing values, data might be collected on characteristics and sales prices of houses around the city, both in the affected neighborhood and elsewhere, from before and after announcement of the incinerator's location. The difference in the rate of change for prices in the affected neighborhood and the rate of change for prices in the rest of the city may be attributed to the incinerator. If this differential in rate of change is multiplied by the initial value of property in the affected neighborhood, the value of the incinerator's impact can be estimated. There may, of course, be other changes in the neighborhood affecting house prices and confounding the analysis.

The equation to be estimated in a hedonic regression of property values has price (or some transformation of price) as the dependent variable and characteristics of the property and the surrounding area as explanatory variables. More specifically, it is common to estimate a double log model in which logged values of both the dependent variable (price) and quantitative explanatory variables are used. When a double log model is used, the estimated coefficients are elasticities of the purchase price with respect to each explanatory factor.[18] Alternatively, the estimated coefficient on a qualitative explanatory factor represented by a dummy variable is the percentage impact of that characteristic on purchase price. This percentage may be applied to the total value of property in the affected area.

As an example, imagine that the logged purchase price of houses in a city is regressed on a variety of explanatory variables including the log of the square footage of the house and the log of the typical air pollution level in the neighborhood. Excluding other variables, the regression results might be:

$$\text{lnPrice}_i = 0.65*\text{lnSqFootage} - 0.15*\text{lnAirPoll}.$$

One implication is that the elasticity of price with respect to square footage of a house is 0.65, so that a 1 percent increase in the square footage of a house is associated with a 0.65 percent increase in its price. The other implication is that the elasticity of price with respect to air pollution levels is −0.15, so that a 1 percent reduction in pollution levels is associated with a 0.15 percent increase in purchase prices of houses. If a project would have the impact of reducing air pollution levels by 20 percent, it could be expected that the impact on property values in the affected area would be to increase them by 3 percent. Thus, the benefits of the program could be calculated as being equal to 3 percent of the value of the property in the affected area.

As a second example, imagine that the logged purchase price of houses is regressed on the same set of explanatory variables plus a dummy variable for whether or not the neighborhood includes a public park, the existence of which is indicated by a dummy variable. As above, the estimated coefficients might be:

$$\text{lnPrice}_i = 0.65*\text{lnSqFootage} + 0.02*\text{Park},$$

where 'Park' is a dummy variable that takes the value 1 if there is a park in the neighborhood of the property and 0 if not. In this case, the implication is that a park increases the value of houses in the neighborhood by

---

18   See Studenmund (1997, p. 217).

2 percent. The benefits of establishing a park could be calculated as being 2 percent of the value of the property in the neighboring area. Caution should be exercised in the interpretation of these variables. It may be that parks are located in neighborhoods that have other nice characteristics as well, or that houses closer to parks are, adjusting for size, nicer than houses further away from parks. In this case, the 'Park' variable would capture the effects on a house's value of a park plus all of the other effects. Without specifically including these other factors in the analysis it may be impossible to attach a value to the specific effect of a park.

Determining the effect of a project *ex post* would involve a variable describing whether or not the property was affected by the project whose effects are being examined. If sales price data were available on a number of houses from before information about the project became known and after the project was completed (or perhaps after it becomes common knowledge that the project will occur) the rate of change of prices, adjusted for other factors, could be compared between the area affected by the project and areas unaffected. The difference in the rates of change of properties affected by the project and those not affected may be attributed to the project.

As an example, imagine that data are collected on sales prices of houses in a city one year before and one year after announcement and construction of a monorail transit system. Houses located within half a mile of the monorail route are compared with those located more than a mile away to see what differences there are in the rate of increase of prices. The usual explanatory variables for the houses and the neighborhood should be included, along with dummy variables indicating whether the house was sold before or after the monorail was announced and built, whether the house is within half a mile of the monorail and a third dummy variable that is the product of the first two. The estimated coefficient on this variable will be the difference in the rate of appreciation between houses near the monorail and those further away. In addition to the other explanatory variables, the estimated coefficient on these explanatory variables might be:

$$\ln Price_i = 0.25 * After - 0.11 * Monorail + 0.05 * MonoAfter,$$

where:

> After is a dummy variable taking the value 1 if the sale occurred after the monorail was announced and/or built and 0 otherwise;
> Monorail is a dummy variable taking the value 1 if the house is near the monorail and 0 otherwise; and
> MonoAfter is the product of After and Monorail, so it takes the value 1 only if a sale involved a house near the monorail and that sale occurred after the monorail.

There are several implications. First, houses increased in value by 25 percent from the pre- to the post-monorail period, correcting for all of the explanatory variables not explicitly included above. Second, houses near the monorail were initially valued at 11 percent less than houses else-where. Third, houses near the monorail increased at a rate that was 5 percent greater than the rate of increase of houses elsewhere. The result that prices for houses near the monorail increased at a greater rate than did prices for houses elsewhere suggests that there are benefits of the monorail beyond those captured in the prices people pay to ride it, and this extra value (or consumer surplus) might be estimated at 5 percent of the value of the real estate near the route.

If sufficient data are available, the results of hedonic analysis are stronger when the analysis is restricted to houses that were sold both prior to and after the project. If there are houses adjacent to the project and further away from the project that were sold within a few years of announcement of the project and then were sold again after announcement or after com-pletion of the project, comparison of rates of change in the values of these houses may better reveal the impact of the project.

7.5   CONTINGENT VALUATION

The preceding techniques all relate to program effects that a person will experience directly. There are, however, projects whose impacts are not directly felt or experienced by people with standing. For example, a project that will improve the chances for survival of an endangered plant or animal species may have value to people that care about that species, even if those people never expect to see a specimen of the species. A project that will pre-serve a wild and scenic river will have value to people who visit it, but may also have value to people who simply enjoy knowing that it exists. These are values attached to things that are not only untraded, but whose values are not even indirectly reflected in an expenditure or asset. These values exist only internally within people's minds and, as such, there may be no way to measure them other than by asking people.

The technique of asking people about the values they attach to things that they will not, or indeed cannot, purchase, is referred to as *contingent valuation* (CV). Use of this technique is controversial.[19] While it provides the only way of estimating some very important values, its estimates are

---

[19]   A presentation of the arguments surrounding contingent valuation is given in the *Journal of Economic Perspectives*, **8** (4), 1994 (see Diamond and Hausman, 1994; Haneman, 1994, Portney, 1994).

based on people's statements rather than their expenditures. At best, people will make an honest attempt to value things they will never have the opportunity to purchase. At worst, they may lie strategically, either overstating or understating the value they attach to a good or service in hopes of influencing public policy. Despite these problems, CV has been used to estimate values in a variety of analyses.

Types of Values Captured by Contingent Valuation

Contingent valuation studies attempt to elicit values for such things as preservation of natural areas and species, reductions in pollution levels, improvements in groundwater purity and general reductions in risk to a population of people. While the values people attach to such things may not be reflected in any market, there are a variety of psychological bases for them and some goods may have values that are the result of several motivations.

The first type of value that may be captured by CV is *use value*, a stated WTP based on some type of use of the natural area, species or environmental amenity in question. Use value may be divided into *active use value* and *passive use value*. Active use value is derived from a person making direct use of something him-/herself. People may have a positive WTP to preserve air quality in an area because they live there and breathe the air every day. They may value a recreation area where they hike or snowmobile. They may be willing to pay some amount to preserve a species if they like to hunt or photograph that species. Passive use, on the other hand, comes from a person using something indirectly. For example, people who enjoy seeing documentaries and reading articles about geothermal phenomena might be willing to pay to preserve the Kamchatka peninsula because it has a large number of geysers and active volcanoes. These people will not visit and make active use of the scenery and geology of Kamchatka, but will use it in this indirect sense. As another example, people living near a large scenic mountain may be willing to preserve it in a relatively pristine condition because they enjoy seeing it from a distance on a daily basis, even if they never actually visit it.

The second type of value that may be captured by CV is *non-use value*, values that people attach to things that they are not currently using. Non-use value may be divided into *option value* and *existence value*. Option value is the value that people place on the preservation of an area or a species because they believe that they might want to use it in the future. By preventing the irreversible destruction of a natural location or extinction of a species, the option for future use is preserved. As with financial options, this option has some value that may be reflected in a CV study. One example would be the preservation of a wild and scenic river with rapids suitable for kayaking or rafting. A person who enjoys these activities but who has never been on the particular river in question might attach a value to the option to use that river at some point in the future.

Existence value is the value placed on something that the respondent will never use in any way. It is merely the value of knowing, for example, that a species will continue to exist or that a natural wonder will be preserved in pristine condition. A CV study assessing WTP to preserve or improve the quality of deep ocean waters would be focused entirely on existence value. Virtually no people will ever visit these deep waters or derive any use from the species that are found there.

The concepts of use and non-use values may be extended. Respondents may have a WTP for a location, a species or some environmental amenity not because they personally attach a use or non-use value to it, but because other people about whom they care attach a value to it. *Altruistic option value* is a value based on the idea that while the respondent will never use the thing in question, other people might. The option is preserved for someone else, but the respondent attaches value to the option on behalf of someone he/she cares about.[20] If the people for whom the option or the amenity is preserved are future generations, this may be referred to as *bequeath value*. Indeed, use or non-use values may be related to altruism or bequeath motives. A respondent may attach value to something solely because he/she suspects that other people, either those currently alive or members of future generations, will use, would like the option to use, or might attach existence value to that species, feature or environmental amenity.

Criticisms of Contingent Valuation

Contingent valuation is a relatively new area of economics that differs from the standard paradigm in some important ways. As such, it is subject to a number of criticisms and is either partially or completely rejected by some economists.

The first and most fundamental criticism of CV is that instead of inferring values from actual behavior involving scarce resources and budget constraints, CV simply (or sometimes not so simply) asks people about their WTP for things such as preservation of a species or a natural area, improvements in water or air quality or perhaps elimination or mitigation of some risk. It asks people only to imagine that there are scarce resources involved and does not actually force them to allocate these resources among different

---

[20]   Inclusion of altruistic values in BCA may be done more generally, but can become problematic. See, for example, Zerbe et al. (2006).

uses. This is radically different from the usual practice in economics and the values that people state in CV studies may completely ignore the fundamental concept of scarcity.

Second, the people responding to CV surveys, even if they are thoughtful and honest, have no experience valuing the things they are asked to value. They have probably never bought or sold anything like the goods in question and, so, have no experience as consumers or suppliers of these goods in the usual sense. It is as if a person who has tasted wine but never priced or purchased it were asked to attach a value to a bottle of a particular variety. Even if people have good knowledge of the wine, it is unlikely that they would arrive at the same value that they would if they were experienced buyers or sellers.

Third, the values that people give in CV studies are particularly sensitive to the form of the question asked. For example, when people are asked about a particular type of environmental damage, their stated WTP to prevent future incidents is typically much smaller than their stated WTA measure of compensation for previous damage. The order in which questions are asked or the exact wording of the question may impact the stated valuation. Values calculated from CV studies may be at least as dependent on how questions were asked as they are on the nature of the thing that was supposed to have been valued.

A fourth criticism of CV is that a question asked about one thing may elicit a response that includes values for many other things. For example, if you ask people to state a WTP to prevent extinction of a particular fish species in a river, the stated value may reflect the value they attach not only to that fish species in that river, but perhaps to many other species in that river, various uses of that river, and perhaps a WTP to prevent species loss in general. This phenomenon, known as *embedding*, can dramatically inflate values, even if respondents believe that they are honestly stating values for the thing about which they are being asked.

One approach to investigating the problem of embedding is a scope test. This asks different sets of respondents to value slightly different goods. For example, one group of respondents might be asked about WTP to prevent damage to several bird species, another about WTP to prevent damage to several fish species, and a third about WTP to prevent damage to both fish and bird species.[21] Ideally, the WTP to prevent damage to fish and birds separately should be less than the WTP to prevent damage to both fish and birds, but if the CV study is not done carefully the estimated WTP figures could be the same for all three respondent groups.

---

[21] Carson et al. (1996).

A fifth criticism of CV is that respondents who suspect the results of the study will be used in making policy decisions will give *strategic responses* in hopes of forcing policy one way or another. Imagine that policy makers are considering setting aside a parcel of land as a wilderness area to improve the likelihood of survival of an endangered species. A respondent who knows this and is in favor of the wilderness area may state that his/her willingness to pay to preserve the species is $10,000 per year[22] in hopes of generating a huge estimate of the benefit of the wilderness area. Alternatively, a respondent opposed to establishment of the wilderness area may state a zero or even a negative WTP to preserve the species, even if his/her WTP is positive, in hopes of reducing the likelihood of the wilderness area being established. If respondents in CV studies are allowed to freely state a dollar value for a good, strategic responses may be a serious threat to the credibility of the results.

A sixth criticism of CV is that the values stated by respondents may be very sensitive to the information provided in the interview and, in the case of telephone or in-person interviews, the presence of the interviewer him/herself. Just as people may be hesitant to state unpopular opinions, they may be reluctant to state values for environmental goods or species preservation that they think will seem too low to the interviewer, even if they do not personally care about those things. This problem may be exacerbated if the interviewer gives the respondent the impression that he/she is in favor of preservation.

While not comprehensive, this list is suggestive of the criticisms most commonly made of CV. While CV certainly has its problems, some contend that because it is the only way of estimating many kinds of values, it has a place in BCA.[23] If, indeed, these values are important in an analysis, the best hope may be to do a CV study, but to be sure it is done well so that its results will be credible.

The Basics of a Good CV Study

There are several fundamental elements to a CV study, and each of these elements may have numerous variations. This subsection discusses each of these elements and offers recommendations on how to best execute them.[24] The recommendations offered here address many of the criticisms listed above.

---

[22] For this reason, responses in excess of some percentage of median annual income are often excluded from analysis.

[23] This is the position taken by Haneman (1994) in the *Journal of Economic Perspectives* debate.

[24] These recommendations are largely based on those given in the 'Report of the NOAA Panel on Contingent Valuation' (Arrow et al., 1993).

First, a CV study must be based on a sample of people taken from the population with standing. Ideally, this will be a random sample, meaning that each person with standing will have the same probability of being sampled.[25] The sample should be large enough to generate enough completed, usable interviews for the analysis to be done, mindful of the fact that there will be some percentage of people who either will not respond or will respond in some unusable manner.

Second, obtaining a statement from a person about the value they attach to something requires some sort of interview with them. A number of options exist for interviews, including personal interviews, telephone interviews, mail surveys and on-line surveys. Of these, personal interviews are preferred, in part because they generate the highest response rates, because they allow respondents to easily ask for clarification of questions and provide explanations of their responses, and they allow interviewers to assess the respondents' level of understanding and provide clarification where necessary. Further, personal interviews may offer better opportunities to present respondents with information regarding the program or proposal being considered. Of course, personal interviews are also the most expensive option as both interviewers and respondents must be in the same place at the same time. Given a fixed budget for interviews, other methods may be preferable.

Mail surveys are frequently used in CV studies. For a fixed sample size, the cost of administering a mail survey is much lower than the cost of personal interviews and this will allow for a larger sample. Mail surveys suffer from a number of disadvantages including relatively low response rates, even when subjects are repeatedly contacted and are offered incentives for participation. Those people who do respond may not represent a random sample of the population but may, instead, be those people who are particularly interested in the issue being discussed.[26]

Phone and on-line surveys are options that involve a built-in bias in that they will sample from people who have either phones or computers, respectively. These techniques may also have a higher probability of response from individuals with a lower value of time.

Third, eliciting a value for something like a species or a natural amenity should be done by describing a credible preservation program that will prevent a loss in the future and then asking the respondent if he/she would vote to impose a tax or other fee on him-/herself to fund that program, given

---

[25] Recommendations for selecting a good random sample are provided in Salant and Dillman (1994, Chapter 5).

[26] An example of this is given in Rubin et al. (1991) in which respondents to a survey on valuing preservation of the Northern Spotted Owl had more education and lower incomes than the typical state resident.

some annual cost. This is the *referendum approach* to eliciting values and is generally thought to yield the most credible results. Varying the annual cost across respondents (that is, telling some respondents that the annual cost will be $5, some that it will be $20 and others that it will be $50) and calculating approval rates at each price will yield an estimate of overall willingness to pay for the program. Describing a particular program helps respondents to focus on the exact item to be preserved and to separate it from more general issues of environmental quality or species preservation, thus helping to eliminate the embedding problem. Making the program credible reduces the chance of a zero valuation that really reflects doubts about the program rather than a lack of concern for the issue. Finally, describing the funding of the program through a tax or a price increase for a commonly purchased item (an increase in a gasoline tax, for example) may help respondents better consider the expense that they will incur as a result of this program. The values elicited through the referendum approach will likely be conservative, but this approach is designed to address some of the more common criticisms of CV.

An important part of the referendum approach is that respondents be given the chance to explain why they voted yes or no on the referendum. This may allow for exclusion of respondents who voted yes or no for reasons unrelated to the valuation of the environmental amenity addressed in the survey. For example, a respondent may actually value a species highly, but choose to vote no on a proposal that increases its chance of survival because he/she does not believe that the government should have the right to do things included in the proposal or does not believe that the proposed program will actually be effective.

Fourth, a good CV study will use a survey instrument that has been pretested. Pre-testing, administering the survey to a number of people and then discussing it with them afterward, allows researchers to determine the validity and accuracy of the instrument. Validity is the extent to which the survey measures the concept that it claims to measure. A CV study may seek to elicit values for a particular species or area, for example, but it may be revealed in talking with pre-test respondents that the values they stated were for a variety of other things as well. If, for example, respondents were asked about the value of bird deaths avoided through oil spill prevention, their response might include many other benefits of oil spill preventions as well, including avoided deaths of other species and improvements in general environmental quality. It may also be the case that respondents reject the proposal simply because they find the proposed program incredible, because they do not believe the government is capable of solving the problem, or because they believe that someone else should pay for the solution. In these cases, the value elicited is more dependent on the described program than on the species or amenity in question and the survey instrument should be modified.

Accuracy of the instrument refers to how well it measures an individual's value. In a referendum format, each respondent has the opportunity to reject or accept the proposed project at some cost drawn from a range of costs. If this range is too low (so that many people are willing to pay even the largest amount) or too high (so that most reject even the smallest amount) then the resulting values will not be an accurate reflection of people's values. Ideally, the highest cost presented to respondents should result in rejection most of the time while the lowest cost presented to respondents should result in acceptance most of the time. This topic is illustrated in Example 7B:

EXAMPLE 7B ESTIMATING THE VALUE OF AN IMPROVEMENT IN WATER QUALITY

A local environmental group is trying to estimate willingness to pay for an improvement in the quality of the water in an important regional river. For purposes of conducting a CV study to estimate this value, they create a proposal to upgrade a local water treatment plant that will have the effect of improving water quality in a particular river from a level of quality appropriate for boating to a level of quality appropriate for swimming. The upgrade will be funded through increased rates on sewer services. In pre-tests, respondents indicate that they believe that the upgraded treatment facilities will improve water quality and that they are able to focus on the river described without embedding other environmental goods.

In the survey, the annual cost of the project to a typical household varies. There are five values, $5, $10, $20, $50 and $100 that respondents might see listed as the cost of the project and each is equally likely. To be clear about this, 20 percent of respondents are told the project will cost a typical household $5 per year, 20 percent are told it will cost $10 per year and so on. The approval rates for each cost group are:

Cost	% Approval
$5	95%
$10	85%
$20	65%
$50	30%
$100	5%

A primer for benefit–cost analysis

If there are one million people with standing (perhaps because they live within some distance of this river) these percentages can be used to construct an aggregate demand curve for this water quality improvement.

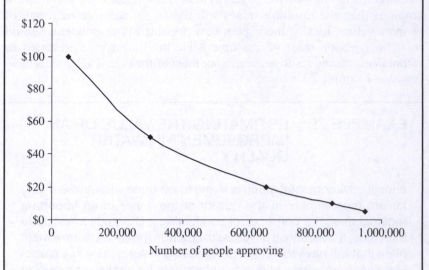

The area under the curve may be interpreted as being the total willingness to pay for this project. It can be approximated as four trapezoids with areas:

$$(300{,}000 - 50{,}000) \times \frac{\$100 + \$50}{2} = \$18{,}750{,}000$$

$$(650{,}000 - 300{,}000) \times \frac{\$50 + \$20}{2} = \$12{,}250{,}000$$

$$(850{,}000 - 650{,}000) \times \frac{\$20 + \$10}{2} = \$3{,}000{,}000$$

$$(950{,}000 - 850{,}000) \times \frac{\$10 + \$5}{2} = \$750{,}000.$$

The total value is the sum of each of these, or about $34,750,000.

This value is an estimate of the value of this improvement in water quality, regardless of how it is achieved. The mechanism described may, of course, be only one option for achieving this improvement.

Fifth, a study should present the respondent with the information needed to reach a valuation of the thing in question without biasing that valuation. Achieving this task is a tremendous challenge and there are bound to be differences of opinion as to what information is appropriate. For example, McConnell (1997) describes a survey asking people if they would be willing to pay a given tax increase in order to eliminate gill netting, a practice which sometimes kills harbor porpoises in New England. Some of the people were told that the harbor porpoise is never actually seen, others were not. This information had a significant impact on the probability that a person would be willing to pay the tax increase. At the very least, information provided should be factually correct. Were it not, a study could, for example, generate a positive WTP to preserve a fictitious species.

It should be acknowledged that, from the point of view of BCA, the value of a species is totally dependent on the value that human beings attach to it. This has at least two implications. First, species that people perceive as threats or nuisances (the smallpox virus, for example) will have negative values attached to their existence. Second, a species whose existence is unknown or unsuspected is likely to have zero value simply because of ignorance. As a result, if the survey makes a person aware of the existence of a species or a natural area of which they previously had no knowledge, the survey itself may change his/her valuation or WTP to preserve it.

The best guideline to presenting necessary but not biased information in a survey is probably to pre-test it to determine the extent to which different elements affected people's values and then to eliminate those elements that are most distorting.

Sixth, a study should remind respondents that there are substitutes to the thing being valued. A particular natural area may be only one of many in a region. A species may have many close relatives that are nearly identical to or indistinguishable from it. An improvement in water or air quality may generate recreational or health benefits that could be achieved through other means. In some way, respondents should be explicitly reminded of possible opportunities for substitution within the survey.

Seventh, respondents should be reminded that any money or resources spent on the program in question would not be available for other goods or services, including other environmental amenities. In the words of Arrow et al. (1993, p. 4609), 'This reminder should be more than perfunctory, but less than overwhelming. The goal is to induce the respondents to keep in mind other likely expenditures, including those on other environmental goods, when evaluating the main scenario'.

Following these guidelines will not assure accuracy or acceptance of the results of a CV study, but it will improve its quality and increase the probability that skeptics will find its values credible. It should be noted, however, that most of these guidelines tend to diminish the estimated value yielded by the study. This is largely a reflection of the fact that most criticisms of CV relate to its estimated values being unreasonably high.

7.6 SUMMARY

Ideally, values used in BCAs will be based on observed market prices for the goods and services in question. Unfortunately, there are a variety of goods and services that, while important, are not traded directly. Valuation of these things necessarily involves an alternative approach.

The travel cost method is generally used to value an attraction to which people must travel and whose admission price does not capture all of or even most of the visitors' value. Estimation of the value of a statistical life allows valuation of changes in uncompensated risks resulting from a project. Estimation of property values through hedonic analysis allows the effects of projects affecting local conditions to be estimated when a large number of properties will be affected. Finally, contingent valuation allows for valuation of amenities that, in addition to not being exchanged in markets, may not even be used in the traditional sense.

This chapter presents four alternative approaches to valuation that may be used in a variety of situations. While not exhaustive, the list presented here is illustrative of strategies that might be used when more straightforward valuation techniques are impossible.

REFERENCES

Aldy, Joseph E. and W. Kip Viscusi (2004), 'Age variations in workers' value of statistical life', John M. Olin Discussion Paper No. 468, Harvard University.

Arias, Elizabeth (2002), *National Vital Statistics Reports*, **51** (3), Center for Disease Control, Hyattsville, MD.

Arrow, K., R. Solow, E. Leamer, P. Portney, R. Radner and H. Schuman (1993), 'Report of the NOAA Panel on Contingent Valuation', *Federal Register*, **58** (10): 4601–14.

Ashenfelter, O. and M. Greenstone (2004), 'Estimating the value of a statistical life: the importance of omitted variables and publication bias', *American Economic Review*, **94** (2): 454–60.

Atkinson, S.E. and R. Halvorsen (1990), 'The valuation of risks to life: evidence from the market for automobiles', *Review of Economics and Statistics*, **72** (1): 133–6.

Brown, Gardner M., Jr and Robert Mendelsohn (1984), 'The hedonic travel cost method', *Review of Economics and Statistics*, **60** (3): 427–33.

Carson, Richard T. et al. (1996), 'Was the NOAA Panel correct about contingent valuation?', Resources for the Future Discussion Paper 96–20, Washington, DC.

Diamond, Peter A. and Jerry A. Hausman (1994), 'Contingent valuation: is some number better than no number?', *Journal of Economic Perspectives*, **8** (4): 45–64.

Dreyfus, M.K. and W.K. Viscusi (1995), 'Rates of time preference and consumer valuations of automobile safety and fuel efficiency', *Journal of Law and Economics*, **38** (1): 79–105.

Garen, J. (1988), 'Compensating wage differentials and the endogeneity of job risk-iness', *Review of Economics and Statistics*, **70** (1): 9–16.

Haneman, W. Michael (1994), 'Valuing the environment through contingent valu-ation', *Journal of Economic Perspectives*, **8** (4): 19–43.

Johansson, Per-Olov (1987), *The Economic Theory and Measurement of Environmental Benefits*, Cambridge: Cambridge University Press.

Kennedy, Peter (2003), *A Guide to Econometrics*, 5th edn, Cambridge, MA: MIT Press.

McConnell, K.E. (1985), 'The economics of outdoor recreation', in A.V. Kneese and J.L. Sweeney (eds), *Handbook of Natural Resources and Energy Economics*, Amsterdam: North-Holland, pp. 677–722.

McConnell, K.E. (1997), 'Does altruism undermine existence value?', *Journal of Environmental Economics and Management*, **32** (1): 22–37.

Portney, Paul R. (1994), 'The contingent valuation debate: why economists should care', *Journal of Economic Perspectives*, **8** (4): 3–17.

Randall, Alan (1994), 'A difficulty with the travel cost method', *Land Economics*, **70** (1): 88–96.

Rubin, J., G. Helfand and J. Loomis (1991), 'A benefit–cost analysis of the north-ern spotted owl: results from a contingent valuation survey', *Journal of Forestry*, **89** (12): 25–30.

Salant, Priscilla and Don A. Dillman (1994), *How to Conduct Your Own Survey*, New York: John Wiley & Sons.

Smith, V. Kerry and Yoshiaki Kaoru (1987), 'The hedonic travel cost method: a view from the trenches', *Land Economics*, **63** (2): 179–92.

Studenmund, A.H. (1997), *Using Econometrics: A Practical Guide*, 3rd edn, Reading, MA: Addison-Wesley.

Viscusi, W. Kip and Joseph E. Aldy (2002), 'The value of a statistical life: a critical review of market estimates throughout the world', John M. Olin Discussion Paper No. 392, Harvard University.

Zerbe, Richard O. Jr, Yoram Bauman and Aaron Finkle (2006), 'An aggregate measure for benefit–cost analysis', *Ecological Economics*, (forthcoming).

APPENDIX: A MORE COMPLICATED TRAVEL COST EXAMPLE

As an example of a travel cost study, imagine that over the course of a year, visitors to an attraction are sampled at a rate of 1 in 100 to determine their zone of origin. The data and the estimated totals are given in Table 7A.1.

If the population of each zone is known an annual visitation rate can be calculated for each zone, as shown in Table 7A.2.

The next step is to assign a travel cost per trip from each zone. This cost will probably depend on the average driving distance from that zone to the site. To this end, zones may be defined on the basis of driving rather than linear distances. The mean travel cost and annual visitation rate can then be combined to yield the demand relationship, as shown in Table 7A.3, which can then be graphed, as in Figure 7A.1.

Further, the calculated value of the park depends on the shape of the demand curve above the highest point shown. If the demand function were horizontal, indicating that no one is willing to pay more than $90 to visit the park, this would represent a minimal or most conservative estimate of the park's value. A less conservative assumption is that the demand curve

Table 7A.1   Visitors zone of origin

Zone	Number sampled	Estimated total number of visits
1	532	53,200
2	1,247	124,700
3	1,898	189,800
4	429	42,900
5	2,943	294,300

Table 7A.2   Annual visitation rate

Zone	Estimated total number of visits	Zone population	Annual visitation rate
1	53,200	354,700	0.15
2	124,700	959,200	0.13
3	189,800	1,898,000	0.10
4	42,900	536,250	0.08
5	294,300	5,886,000	0.05

Table 7A.3   Demand curve relationship

Zone	Mean round trip distance in miles	Cost per mile	Mean travel cost	Annual visitation rate
1	20	$0.30	$6.00	0.15
2	40	$0.30	$12.00	0.13
3	80	$0.30	$24.00	0.10
4	160	$0.30	$48.00	0.08
5	300	$0.30	$90.00	0.05

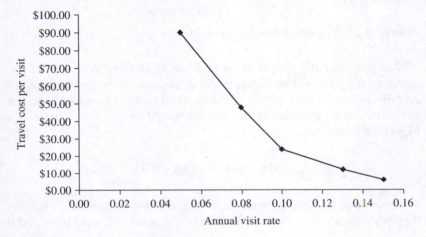

Figure 7A.1   Estimated demand relationship

will continue with the slope it demonstrated between visit rates of 0.08 and 0.05, intersecting the vertical axis at a price of $160.

Consider the people living in Zone 5. If the top part of the demand curve is assumed to be horizontal, then people living in Zone 5 would receive no consumer surplus from their visits, but if the top portion of the demand curve is assumed to be upward sloping, people living in Zone 5 would receive per capita consumer surplus equal to the area of the triangle under the demand curve but above the $90 line shown by area A in Figure 7A.2, or,

$$CS_5 = \frac{1}{2} \times (\$160 - \$90) \times (0.05) = \$1.75.$$

If there are 5,886,000 people living in Zone 5, the total value they would place on the park, if entry were free, would be $10,300,500.

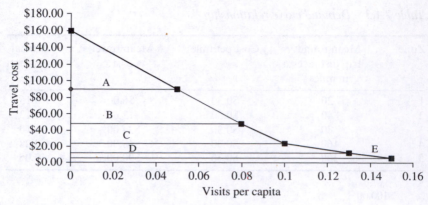

Figure 7A.2   Estimated demand for visits

Now, consider the people living in Zone 4. The per capita value they attach to the park will be higher because they are closer and face a lower cost of visiting. If the top part of the demand curve is assumed to be horizontal, the per capita consumer surplus would be the area labeled B in Figure 7A.2, or,

$$CS_4 = \tfrac{1}{2} \times (\$90 - \$48) \times (0.08 + 0.05) = \$2.73.$$

If the top part of the demand curve is assumed to be downward sloping, their per capita value would be the sum of the areas indicated by A and B,

$$CS_5 = \tfrac{1}{2} \times (\$160 - \$48) \times (0.08) = \$4.48.$$

If there are 536,250 people living in Zone 4, the total value they would place on the park, if entry were free, would be $1,463,962.50 under the conservative assumption that the top portion of the demand curve is flat or $2,402,400 under the assumption that the top portion of the demand curve is downward sloping.

The value of the park to people living in the other zones is given in Table 7A.4. If standing is restricted to people living in the five zones, the value of the park may be calculated as the sum of the total value of the people in each of the zones.

It is, of course, possible that were a sixth, more distant zone added to the analysis, the estimated demand curve could become steeper above $90. If this were the case, the estimated value of the park would be even greater than the larger of the two calculated values.

Table 7A.4   Value of the park

Zone	Mean travel cost	Annual visit rate	Per capita surplus, horizontal demand	Per capita surplus, sloping demand	Population	Total value, horizontal demand	Total value, sloping demand
1	$6.00	0.15	$7.11	$8.86	354,700	$2,521,917	$3,142,642
2	$12.00	0.13	$6.27	$8.02	959,200	$6,014,184	$7,692,784
3	$24.00	0.10	$4.89	$6.64	1,898,000	$9,281,220	$12,602,720
4	$48.00	0.08	$2.73	$4.48	536,250	$1,463,963	$2,402,400
5	$90.00	0.05	$0.00	$1.75	5,886,000	$0	$10,300,500
						$19,281,284	$36,141,046

The above analysis assumes that once a person has traveled to the park, entry is free. If an entry fee were charged, this would have the effect of increasing the cost of a visit, just as would happen if travel cost rose by the same amount.

As an example, consider people living in Zone 3 assuming that the upper portion of the demand curve is downward sloping. With zero cost of admission, the per capita value they attach to the park is $6.64. If park officials were to impose an admission fee of $12.00, the cost of a visit from Zone 3 would rise to $36.00 and the estimated visit rate would be reduced from 0.10 to 0.09. The reduction in the value that people from Zone 3 attach to the park would be $1.14 per person or $2,163,720 overall. This effect is shown in Figure 7A.3.

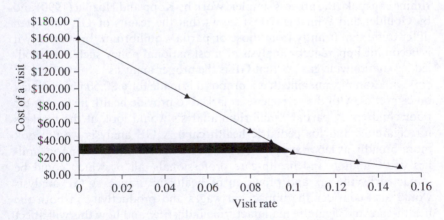

Figure 7A.3   Reduction in per capita value to Zone 3

8.   General equilibrium analysis

8.1   INTRODUCTION

Thus far, we have analyzed the effects of programs by looking at only one market. If a project uses labor or generates electricity, for example, we have looked only at the labor market or at the electricity market and have inherently assumed that the effects of the project did not extend beyond these markets. This approach is known as *partial equilibrium* analysis.

The alternative to partial equilibrium analysis is to consider how a project affects the entire economy starting with its effect in the primary markets (the labor market or electricity market in the paragraph above) and then in other markets in the economy based on the interrelationships between markets. This sort of analysis is called *general equilibrium* (GE) analysis and it attempts to account for the simultaneous determination of prices and income throughout all of the markets in an economy. In theory, a GE analysis might model all of the markets in an economy and the relationships between them to determine the entire effect of a project on an economy. Lest the reader find this a thoroughly daunting proposition, it should be noted that most GE models include only a small number of important markets and assume that the remaining markets are affected so little that they can be ignored. Moreover the availability of simplified algorithms can make the process simpler. Work by Kopp and Hazilla (1990) and by Goulder and Williams (2003) shows that the results of GE will often differ quite significantly from those of partial equilibrium. Increasingly it is becoming apparent for analysis of most national policy such as embodied in a nationwide gas tax that GE is the proper analysis.

As an example, imagine that a proposal is made for a $0.50 per pack tax on cigarettes, with the revenues earmarked to provide health insurance for poor children. A partial equilibrium analysis would look at the markets for cigarettes and for pediatric health care. A GE analysis would look more broadly at labor supply decisions of smokers, heads of poor families with children and health-care professionals, all of which could be impacted by the tax and provision of health insurance. A GE analysis would also consider the impact on wages and productivity in both the health-care and cigarette manufacturing industries and how this will affect wage determination and productivity in other industries as labor and capital shift from one sector to another. Because GE analysis considers potential effects on labor supply and capital allocation across sectors, there is the potential for considering changes in the long-run rate and pattern of economic growth.

A full technical discussion of GE modeling and its role is a matter for econometric treatment. Here we consider its use solely in benefit–cost analysis. We offer a general description of the GE approach, some more examples of its use in BCA, and some opinions about the extent to which it might or might not affect the numbers reported in and eventual decision of a BCA. Those seeking a more thorough treatment of econometric modeling are directed to references given in this chapter.

8.2 THE BASICS OF GENERAL EQUILIBRIUM MODELS

A GE model is a complete mathematical description of the behavior in and the relationships between every market in an economy. While there are a wide variety of GE models, most contain the following elements. The first element is the utility functions and budget constraints of the households in the economy. These can be used to describe households' behavior and, as with the presentation of individual welfare analysis and compensating and equivalent variations earlier in this text, can be used to accurately value the impacts of changes in prices or allocations of goods. For the sake of simplicity and tractability it is often assumed that households' utility functions follow a particular mathematical form and are identical. The second element is the technology and production function of each firm in the economy. These allow modeling of firms' hiring and output decisions based on the cost of various inputs including labor. As with households, these production functions are likely to be assumed to take a particular mathematical form and to be identical. The third element is the government's budget constraint. As public projects will almost necessarily be a net cost or a net gain for the government, the effect on the government's budget, its spending on other programs and resulting changes in taxes could be important in the analysis. Of course, these changes will be reflected in both households' and firms' decisions. The fourth element is the resource constraints of the economy, or the set of productive resources that are available and will be available if the project is enacted. The fifth element is the nature of the markets in the economy and whether they are competitive, monopolistic, oligopolistic and so on. This most often impacts the relationship between price and marginal cost in the model. For example, it is often assumed that markets in an economy are perfectly competitive, one implication of which is that price is equal to marginal cost in all markets. If instead it is assumed that firms in all markets or in a set of markets exercise some degree of market power, then the assumption might be that the price in those markets is some multiple of marginal cost.

The goal of these elements is to determine how a project, which will have some predictable influences in a small number of primary markets, will ultimately affect households once all of the various complex inter-relationships are accounted for. One issue that might be reflected in a GE model is a shift in the households' consumption from one good to another, a substitute perhaps, and how this affects the households welfare. A second issue that might arise is a change in how the households allocate time, either among productive options or between labor and leisure. This will also have welfare implications for households. A third issue that might arise is changes in the technology that firms use for production, shifting perhaps between labor and capital. The GE model would determine the eventual impact that this shifting would have on wages and returns to capital and to the owners of firms. Because households both provide labor to and own firms, these will impact households' budget constraints and spending decisions and ultimately have welfare effects on the households. Such complicated interactions are missed by partial equilibrium analysis and might have important effects on an analyst's assessment of a project.

8.3   EXAMPLES OF GE IN BENEFIT–COST ANALYSIS

We now present two examples of GE analysis applied to BCA. The main idea of these examples is to show how partial equilibrium and GE analysis differ in their approach and to acquaint you with the basic components of a GE model.

A Robinson Crusoe Example

Consider the following model of a simple Robinson Crusoe economy with one person, Crusoe, who engages in the production of two goods, coconuts and fish.

First, Crusoe has some preferences over food and fish, described in Figure 8.1 by an indifference curve. Crusoe has constant returns to scale (CRS) technologies for producing both coconuts and fish and a fixed amount of labor effort (or time) each day to allocate to production of

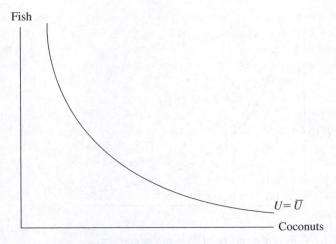

Figure 8.1 Indifference curve for fish and coconuts

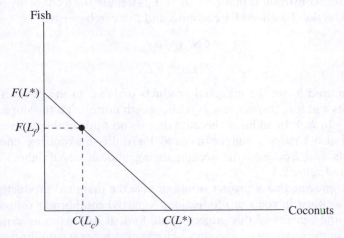

Figure 8.2 Production possibility frontier

either good. Because the production technologies are CRS his production possibilities frontier (PPF) is a straight line. The total amount of time or labor effort he has available is L^*. If he allocates all of his time to coconut production he can have $C(L^*)$ units of coconuts and if he allocates all of his time to catching fish he can have $F(L^*)$ units of fish. At some interior point, as shown in Figure 8.2, he will allocate L_c to coconut production and L_f to fish production and wind up with the bundle $[C(L_c), F(L_f)]$.

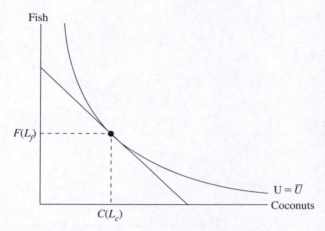

Figure 8.3   Consumer choice of fish and coconuts

His time constraint is that $L^* = L_c + L_f$. Because the technology is CRS, the production functions for coconuts and fish can be written as:

$$C(L_c) = a_c L_c$$

$$F(L_f) = a_f L_f,$$

where a_c and a_f are the marginal products of labor in the production of coconuts and fish, respectively. It is also worth noting that the slope of the PPF is $-(a_f/a_c)$. In addition, because there is no trade in this economy the PPF is also Crusoe's budget line and his utility-maximizing choice of coconuts and fish (and the accompanying allocations of labor) are as shown in Figure 8.3.

Now, imagine that a project would double the marginal productivity of Crusoe's efforts in coconut production. A partial equilibrium approach to valuing the benefits of this project would look at its impact in terms of a change in the quantity of coconuts.[1] However, a general equilibrium approach will consider the impacts on both coconut and fish production, recognizing that with the higher marginal productivity in coconut production, Crusoe is likely to shift some of his effort from one activity to the other. The overall impact will be assessed through either the compensating variation (CV) or the equivalent variation (EV) in Crusoe's utility-maximization diagram.

So, as mentioned above, imagine that a project, perhaps a machine that Crusoe can construct, will increase the marginal productivity of his efforts

---

[1]   If there were trade in this economy, we would also consider the impact on the price of coconuts.

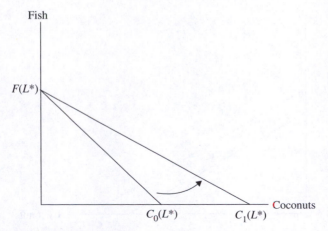

Figure 8.4   The production possibility curve

in coconut production and will cause his PPF to pivot outward to reflect his greater total capacity to produce coconuts, as shown in Figure 8.4.

However, this project will come at a cost. Crusoe will have to expend some effort building the machine, an expenditure that is analogous to increased tax payments that are necessary to fund the construction of a more typical public project. Because Crusoe is free to take time from either coconut production or fish production to build the machine, the effect is a parallel inward shift of his new budget line, as shown in Figure 8.5. This is analogous to funding a public project through a lump-sum tax.

The net impact on Crusoe's budget line is shown in Figure 8.6. The overall impact on Crusoe's utility will depend on the cost of the project in terms of the amount of effort it will require, its impact on coconut production and consumption and its impact on fish production and consumption. Simply looking at coconuts would have ignored the effect on fish, a potentially important omission.

The net benefit of the project will depend on the change in Crusoe's utility level, as shown in Figure 8.7. This may be valued using either the CV or the EV.

An Example of Cost of Funds with Environmental Externalities[2]

One aspect of a BCA of a project is the marginal cost of funds (MCF) used in the project. Most projects will require the agency that conducts them to

---

2   The example is a simplified summary of Brendemoen and Vennemo (1996).

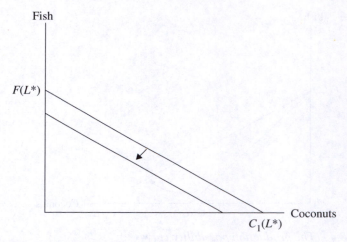

Figure 8.5   A shift in the budget line

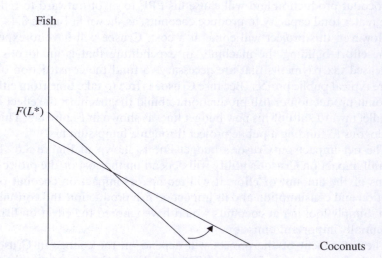

Figure 8.6   Net impact on budget line

borrow money or raise tax revenue to carry out the project. The opportunity cost of doing this depends on what the money that is borrowed
would have been used for if it had not been used in the project, and how
behavior will change as a result of taxes being raised for the project.

Imagine that a project might be funded through either labor taxes
or energy taxes. A labor tax would result in producers substituting energy
for labor while an energy tax would result in producers substituting labor

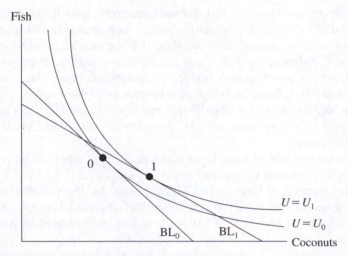

Figure 8.7   Change in level of satisfaction

for energy. If there are negative externalities associated with energy use and no negative externalities associated with labor use, then it could be argued that the marginal cost of funds raised through energy taxes is lower than the cost of funds raised through labor taxes.

Brendemoen and Vennemo (1996) use a GE model to estimate the MCF for a project that will consume some materials, electricity and fossil fuels when the funds are raised from a variety of taxes and when there are environmental externalities, and look specifically at the Norwegian economy. Their model includes several elements. First, household utility is based on consumption of 13 different goods, leisure and environmental quality. Among the goods consumed is energy, which is composed of electricity and fossil fuels. Second, production is modeled as a function of capital, labor, energy and materials inputs. Two important components of production are the total amount of production done in the economy and the energy intensity of that production. Energy use might fall either if total production falls or if the intensity of energy use falls. Third, the resources available for production are generally considered to be widely available on global markets with the exception of labor and capital, which must be hired in national markets and whose supply will depend on the after-tax wage, household wealth and income taxes. Fourth, markets are considered to be competitive, so price equals marginal cost plus tax and inputs are paid the value of their marginal product. Finally, consumption of fossil fuels creates national and global negative externalities and impacts household utility. As the authors point out, the residuals from fossil fuel use are the main link between economic activity and environmental quality. The government's budget constraint is not explicitly included in their model, because they use the model to examine the impacts of different types of taxes rather than a particular project that will impact the government's budget, although one particular project is briefly described. By using standard economic models of utility and production and estimates of elasticities and environmental effects for the Norwegian economy, they are able to calculate values for MCF for a variety of taxes.

The taxes considered include an equal percentage marginal increase in all taxes, a lump-sum tax, an income tax, a value-added tax (VAT), gasoline taxes, mineral oil taxes and a CO_2 emissions tax. The way in which the GE analysis uses each of the components of the model to estimate the impact of a particular type of tax increase can be illustrated by a couple of examples.

A lump-sum tax will take a fixed amount of money from each household and will reduce household wealth. A household with reduced wealth will demand a reduced quantity of leisure and other normal goods and, in theory, supply an increased quantity of labor.[3] This increase in labor supply will lead to greater production and with it greater use of fossil fuels, thus leading to more environmental damage and resulting reductions in household utility. Use of a GE model allows for consideration of the effects of a lump-sum tax on labor supply and the resulting impacts on production, fossil fuel use and environmental damage. Application of empirical estimates from the Norwegian economy (notably the low income elasticity of labor supply) allows for defensible dismissal of these possible impacts and leads to a conclusion that the MCF raised through a lump-sum tax is somewhat moderate.

An income tax, on the other hand, will take income from households based on their income from labor and will reduce their effective wage rate. A household facing an increased income tax rate will supply a smaller amount of labor, assuming that at the margin the substitution effect outweighs the income effect, which studies of the Norwegian economy suggest is the case. The reduction in labor supply will reduce the size of the economy and reduce income tax revenue from labor but, because labor and energy use are substitutes in the model, the smaller economy will make more intensive use of energy and will actually generate increased environmental damage and further reductions in household utility. The environmental

---

[3]   In fact, the income elasticity of leisure demand (or labor supply) is sufficiently small in Norway that the authors estimated that there would be no appreciable change in the quantity of labor supplied.

damage coupled with increased inefficiencies in the labor market makes the MCF raised through an income tax very high.

It is worth noting that the different types of taxes might have different equity effects. Lump-sum taxes, though efficient, place a much heavier burden on poor people than on rich people. Income taxes are relatively inefficient, but are usually much more equitable in that they impose a more even burden on rich and poor. Of course, taxes on fossil fuels will most heavily impact big users of fossil fuels, but the equity effects are ambiguous and depend on whether those big users tend to be rich or poor.

8.4 GE ANALYSIS

Sizing the Difference Between Partial Equilibrium and General Equilibrium Estimated – How Much of a Difference Does GE Really Make?

Although GE models have the potential for greater completeness and accuracy relative to partial equilibrium analyses, they are much more difficult and time consuming to calibrate and estimate. The extra resources necessary for a GE analysis would seem to be justified *ex ante* only if the expected results are likely to differ greatly from those of a partial equilibrium analysis. Put more clearly, is GE analysis is worth the extra trouble?

Apparently in many cases it is. Estimates of the differences between partial equilibrium and GE results generally show quite substantial differences when considering issues of national policy, as we mentioned earlier. Moreover, GE thinking can illuminate and show quite different qualitative results when considering public policy. For example in antitrust analysis, in which the direction of efficiency effects are important, a GE point of view can lead to quite different results from partial equilibrium (see Zerbe, 2005).

Goulder and Williams (2003) demonstrate that failure to include GE results can have a predictable and significant impact on the cost of funds raised for projects. They show under reasonable assumptions that partial equilibrium analyses will underestimate the excess burden of taxes by between 16 and 92 percent, depending on the exact type of tax considered and the value of elasticity parameters. This suggests not only that GE is a significant improvement over partial equilibrium analysis, but also that partial analysis has the potential to fail miserably.

A Practical Approach to GE

The simplest way to think about GE is to note that effects in markets other than the primary market are important for economic efficiency only if there are distortions in these other markets. Distortions are divergences from marginal cost pricing due to taxes, monopoly or external effects. For primary markets the net welfare effects (the excess burden) is found by the following formula:

$$B = -\frac{1}{2} t_k^2 \frac{dx_k}{dt_k},$$

where t_k is the tax in the primary market. This is the partial equilibrium formula. If there are no distortions, nothing need be added to this.

The full GE formula developed by Harberger (1964a, b) for a comprehensive measure of excess burden is:

$$EB = -\frac{1}{2} t_k^2 \frac{dx_k}{dt} - \sum_i t_i \frac{dX_i}{dt_k}$$

where EB is the excess burden of the tax on good k, X_i is the quantity of commodity i and t_k is the new tax, and also the pre-existing taxes or other distortions, on goods k. We can take t_k as not just the tax but the amount of any distortion, such as from subsidies, monopoly or externalities. The formula, as we have written it, assumes that there is no pre-existing tax on good k. If there is, then k is simply added as one of the i goods. The formula also assumes that the size of the distortion remains constant through the quantity changed induced by the new tax. If not, a reasonable approximation would be the average size of the distortion over the quantity change. Clearly the results from using the full GE formula can differ very substantially from those of the partial equilibrium formula.

Let us consider these results diagrammatically. The diagram treatment is not particularly intuitive so the student should carefully consider the following.

Consider a world in which there are only two markets, butter and margarine. The government wishes to raise tax revenues through a butter tax. The new supply curve for butter including the tax will shift to the left and the price of butter including the tax will rise. Consumer surplus will fall in the butter market. There will be the usual excess burden and loss of consumer and producer surplus accompanied by the gain in tax revenues that partially offset the losses of producer and consumer surpluses, as shown in Figure 8.8. If there are no distortions in the related margarine market, this is the end of the story. There are no net efficiency effects in the margarine market.

How can this be? There are certainly effects in the margarine market. The key to understanding why we need not count effects in the margarine market is that they are already taken into account in the butter market. They are taken into account through the fact that the existence of the margarine market has already affected the demand for butter and vice versa.

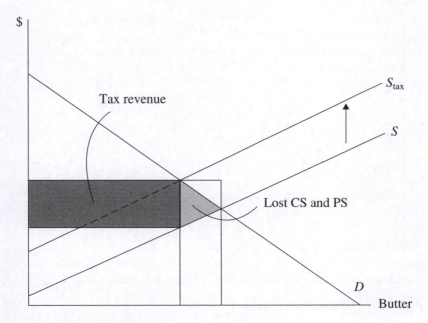

Figure 8.8   Welfare change from a butter tax

The higher price of butter increases the demand for margarine, a substitute for butter. Suppose that there is a flat supply curve for margarine so that the higher price for butter does not increase the price for margarine. There is no welfare change in the margarine market as the price has not changed. The apparent increase in consumer surplus in the margarine market, shown in Figure 8.9, illustrates the value of having margarine as a substitute for butter. That is, area X is not an increase in consumer surplus resulting from the new butter tax. Rather, it is a measure of the value of having the margarine market exist. If the margarine market were not to exist, the demand for butter would be higher and the loss of consumer surplus in the butter market resulting from a decrease in the supply of butter would be greater. This is shown in Figure 8.10.

With the existence of the margarine market, the loss of consumer surplus will be just area A. Without the existence of the margarine market, the loss of consumer surplus in the butter market would instead be A + B. The apparent increase in consumer surplus in the margarine market will equal the greater quantity that would have been lost in the butter market had the margarine market not existed. That is, area B from Figure 8.10 will equal area X from Figure 8.9. The net social cost of the increase in costs of producing butter is wholly shown in the butter market alone. If there were no

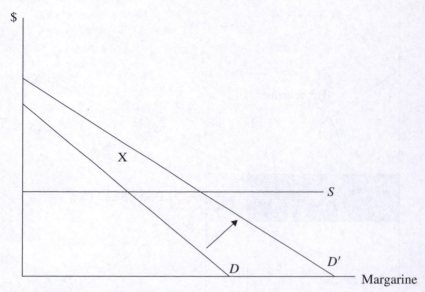

Figure 8.9   The margarine market

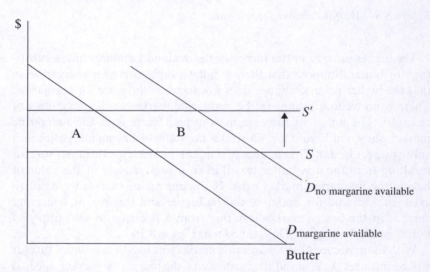

Figure 8.10   The effect of the margarine market on demand for butter

margarine market at the time of the cost increase for butter, there would be
a higher demand for butter and the loss from the cost increase for producing butter would be greater. The gain that arises from the existence of the
margarine market is already shown in the butter market.

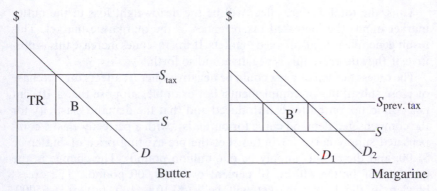

Figure 8.11   General equilibrium welfare effect

Now if the supply of margarine is upward sloping there will be a gain of producer surplus but an equal offsetting loss of consumer surplus in the margarine market. The gain in producer surplus is found in the usual way by riding the higher price up the supply curve. The loss of consumer surplus is found by also riding up the price increase between the old and new demand curves in a way that just offsets the gain in producer surplus. These effects may be important distributional effects but are not net efficiency effects of the butter tax.

Suppose however, that there was a pre-existing distortion in the margarine market, say a tax, as shown in Figure 8.11. The change in welfare will be:

$$\Delta W = \Delta CS + \Delta PS + \Delta TR + \Delta EE,$$

where CS is consumer surplus, PS is producer surplus, TR is tax revenue and EE are external effects.

From the previous discussion we know that the net loss in the butter market will be the excess burden triangle and that this change and the change in consumer and producer surplus in the margarine market will offset each other. We are assuming that there are no external effects. The excess burden for butter, shown in Figure 8.11, will be area B. There will, however, also be an increase in government revenues in the margarine market. This increase in government revenues will then be a positive welfare effect. In Figure 8.11, the increase in government revenues is shown by area B′. This positive increase in tax revenues for margarine could be great enough to more than offset the excess burden in the butter market so that the net excess burden from the tax on butter is negative. This would be the case when B′>B. This effect is a result of the theory of second best: when there are distortions in some markets, it may pay to symmetrically distort related markets, given that the original distortion cannot be changed.

Thus, the total welfare effect will be the deadweight loss in the butter market minus the increased tax revenues in the margarine market. This result generalizes to all affected markets. If tax revenues increase this is positive, if they decrease this is negative, and so forth.

The excess burden of a tax could be negative where it affects the purchase of close substitutes or complements. For example, suppose that a 10 cent per pound tax on butter is introduced and that the demand elasticity for the compensated demand curve for butter is 1 with a perfectly elastic compensated supply curve for butter. Let the pre-existing price of butter be $1.00, and the pre-tax supply be one million pounds. The change in the quantity of butter will be 10 percent or −100,000 pounds. The excess burden in the butter market will be ½($0.10)(−100,000) or −$5000. Suppose, however, that the tax results in an increase in margarine of 40,000 pounds and that the tax on margarine is 20 cents a pound. This will increase tax revenues in the margarine market by $8000 so the net welfare effect (excess burden) is ($8000 − $5000) or $3000. The partial equilibrium welfare loss was $5000 but the GE excess burden is not a loss but a gain of $3000. The gain arises from the fact that with margarine already taxed and a substitute for butter, the new tax on butter reduces the distortion of choice between butter and margarine.

Goulder and Williams (2003) point out that the GE excess burden of a new tax will exceed the partial equilibrium burden when the effect is to reduce the quantity of labor. This is because labor is heavily taxed and a reduction in labor usage will reduce tax revenues. Labor supply is one of the goods affected by a commodity tax and labor is already heavily taxed. A new tax reduces the quantity of labor and thus tax revenues. They provide a formula to estimate the effect of labor on the GE welfare excess burden. This formula assumes that the taxes on labor are the most important GE effects to be considered. The GE excess burden then will be the triangle loss on the originally taxed commodity plus the loss from the labor taxes. They compare the results from their formula which considers only labor taxes with results from a full GE model. This loss can be calculated from the consumption share for the taxed good and labor supply elasticity. They present an example in which the simple welfare triangle estimation for a 14 percent national cigarette tax will understate the true value of the excess burden by 88 percent. The error using their GE formula will overestimate the true excess burden by only 4.4 percent. These findings are similar for a national gas tax of 5 percent. In making these calculations they consider no other commodity taxes other than those on energy and cigarettes. The important results are that their simple algorithm will give useful results without a full GE model and that a partial equilibrium calculation may grossly underestimate the excess burden.

Table 8.1   Comparison of partial equilibrium and the Goulder–Williams GE algorithim calculations of excess burden

	Elasticity of demand	Tax rate	Partial equilibrium excess burden	True GE excess burden	Error	Estimate of GE excess burden	Error
Cigarettes	0.4	31.3%	0.669	1.728	61.3%	1.796	3.9%
Energy	0.9	5%	0.533	3.596	79.5%	2.698	3.9%

Table 8.1 shows the results for median own price elasticity for cigarettes and energy. The cigarette tax is 31.3 percent, equal to the existing federal plus lowest state excise tax, and the energy tax is 5 percent. The table shows that there are substantial differences between the partial equilibrium estimates of excess burden and the actual GE values for excess burden, with the partial equilibrium estimates falling below the correct GE values by 61.3 percent in the case of cigarettes and 79.5 percent in the case of energy. The Goulder–Williams algorithm, on the other hand, closely approximates the full GE value for excess burden, with an error of only 3.5 percent in both cases.

8.5   CONCLUSION

GE analysis is an extension of the partial equilibrium approach that has tended to characterize BCAs. By explicitly considering several sectors of an economy and estimating the impacts of a project on households, firms, production processes and the government budget, the potential exists for improving the quality of analysis and the reliability of results. Although GE analysis can be much more demanding in terms of the modeling and information requirements, some recent work suggests that the benefits may be worth the trouble. While a complete examination of GE modeling techniques and information requirements is beyond the scope of this text, we hope to have briefly acquainted you with the topic.

REFERENCES

Brendemoen, Anne and Haakon Vennemo (1996), 'The marginal cost of funds in the presence of environmental externalities', *Scandinavian Journal of Economics*, **98** (3): 405–22.

Goulder, Lawrence H. and Roberton C. Williams III (2003), 'The substantial bias from ignoring general equilibrium effects in estimating excess burden, and a practical solution', *Journal of Political Economy*, **111** (4): 898–927.

Harberger, A. (1964a), 'The measurement of waste', *American Economic Review, Papers and Proceedings*, **54**: 58–76.

Harberger, A. (1964b), 'Taxation, resource allocation and welfare', in *The Role of Direct and Indirect Taxes in the Federal Revenue System*, Princeton, NJ: Princeton University Press, pp. 58–76.

Kopp, Raymond J. and Michael Hazilla (1990), 'The social cost of environmental quality regulations: a general equilibrium analysis', *Journal of Political Economy*, **98** (4): 853–73.

Zerbe, R. (2005), 'Monopsony and the Ross–Simmons case: a comment on Salop and Kirkwood', *Antitrust Law Journal*, **72** (2): 717–25.

9.   Discounting and net present value

9.1   INTRODUCTION

Most projects take place over a number of years, incurring costs early on and generating benefits later. As a result, it will usually be necessary to compare monetary values at one point in time with monetary values at another point in time.

For example, a vaccination program that will prevent future cases of a communicable disease will have some immediate costs for production, distribution and injection of the vaccine. The benefits will be gained in the future, perhaps after many years, as the incidence of the disease is reduced. The immediate costs of the project need to be compared with the future benefits.

The difficulty is that comparing costs and benefits occurring at different points in time is not simply a matter of adding or subtracting. It is generally believed that the further a benefit or cost is pushed into the future, the less it is worth today. This consideration needs to be incorporated into calculations of a project's net benefits.

Consider a payment of $1000 today and a payment of $1000 at some point in the future. For most people in most situations, the payment today is worth more than the payment in the future. Similarly, a benefit you receive from a project would be worth more if you received it today rather than in the future, other things being equal.

It may be a similar question to ask whether the people living in a school district would prefer that a new elementary school be built immediately and be ready for the next school year or if they would prefer to wait for two years. Other things being equal, getting the new school immediately will be preferable to waiting.

The process of reducing the value of benefits to be received or costs to be incurred at some point in the future solely because they lie in the future is called *discounting*. This is generally done by multiplying costs or benefits by a fractional number depending on how far in the future they occur. Costs or benefits occurring further in the future are usually discounted more heavily while those occurring closer to the present are usually discounted less heavily.

Discounted values from each year of a project's life are added up to calculate the project's *net present value*, the difference between the sum of the discounted benefits and the sum of the discounted costs.

Discounting is often criticized for diminishing the importance of benefits or costs solely because they lie in the future. For example, under discounting the existence of a tree at some point in the future is less valuable than the existence of a tree of similar size and quality today. Doing this simply on the basis of timing may seem arbitrary, but this is how people behave when making their own decisions. To convince a person to give up some consumption today, you need to offer them more compensation at some point in the future.[1] In part this is because people have a time preference for earlier rather than later and in part because nature is productive, so an investment today is worth more tomorrow. Other things being the same, the marginal value of one unit of future consumption is less than the marginal value of one unit of immediate consumption.

Discounting over very long periods of time is particularly controversial. To see why, consider the difference between a project done today that will impact the current generation and a project done today that will impact a future generation. As long as the same people who pay for a project also enjoy the benefits, any discounting reflects the difference between payments at one point in their lives and benefits at another point in their lives. However, if a project has intergenerational effects, the analysis is very different. A project might impose some costs on a 35-year-old middle-class male today and generate benefits for a 35-year-old middle-class male living one hundred years from now. Should the effects on one of these otherwise identical people be considered differently from the effects on the other simply because one is living at a different point in time?

To make the question more interesting, consider a program that will generate electricity very cheaply today, but leave some deadly waste product that will escape containment far in the future. How should costs involuntarily imposed on people living hundreds of years from now be compared with benefits for people alive today? Does your answer change if the residue will escape containment after five hundred years versus one thousand years or ten thousand years? The question may be more about standing than about discounting.[2]

---

[1]   This is entirely separate from the idea of consumption smoothing in which people do some saving when income is high in anticipation of future periods when income will be lower in order to consume the same amount in all periods.

[2]   A good discussion of the issues involved and a summary of various points of view on this matter is offered in Portney and Weyant (1999).

This chapter begins by explaining why discounting future costs and benefits of public projects is appropriate. It then describes the standard techniques for discounting and calculating a net present value and discusses differences between real and nominal rates and describes when each is appropriate. The chapter then discusses two alternatives to net present value: benefit–cost ratio and internal rate of return and finally offers suggestions as to actual rates that might be appropriate for projects you are analyzing.

9.2 JUSTIFICATION FOR DISCOUNTING

There are a number of reasons why future costs or benefits are usually considered to be of lesser value than if they occurred today.

First, most economies experience some degree of inflation. If a payment of exactly $1000 is to be made, the real value or purchasing power will probably be less at some point in the future than it is now. For example, if prices increase by 5 percent annually, the real value of the payment will fall by 5 percent each year. Because it is real rather than nominal values that are of interest to economists, this effect is important. This in itself does not justify discounting but it does require taking into account inflation, which can also be done through the discounting process.

Second, if a payment is due at the end of five years, a smaller amount could be invested today, earn interest for five years and accumulate value to the end of the period. For example, a future payment of $1000 requires a smaller immediate investment to yield this amount at the end of several years. The longer the waiting period, the smaller the initial investment needs to be.[3] If there are investment opportunities available to the agency considering a project, deferring costs will reduce the amount that needs to be put aside today in order to cover them.

Third, there is some risk that a future payment will never be made or that a future benefit will not be realized. For example, imagine that a municipal recreation project to construct playfields in one city is undertaken with the understanding that the neighboring city, whose residents will also use the fields, will make a payment at some point in the future to help cover the costs. There is some risk that the neighboring city will be unable to make this payment and this risk decreases the value of the promised payment. Alternatively, a natural disaster may destroy the playfields, eliminating

---

[3] If an investment earns 10 percent annually, only $620.92 would need to be invested today to yield $1000 at the end of five years. Only $385.54 would need to be invested today to yield $1000 at the end of ten years.

future benefits that the facilities would have yielded. Either of these events presents a risk that will diminish the project's value and as the length of time involved increases, so does the risk.

Fourth, ownership of a particular asset might provide a special opportunity at some point. If receipt of this asset is delayed, the recipient might miss a rare opportunity that could have been exploited if they had received it earlier. As an example, consider a road expansion project in a suburban community. A large employer interested in expanding into the area might have a choice of locations to choose from and would be attracted to a particular community depending on the local road capacity. If the road expansion is delayed, the employer may choose to locate elsewhere and the community would have missed a rare opportunity to increase its tax base. Thus, the benefits gained from the road expansion would be reduced because the project was delayed.

Finally, most people demonstrate some degree of impatience. Put very simply, even in a situation with no inflation, no investment returns, no risk and no special opportunities, most people would rather receive something now than wait to get it, other things being the same. From a community point of view, if a project is funded by current residents, each of those residents will have some degree of impatience and will prefer to gain the benefits earlier than later. Further, over time new residents of a community will replace previous residents. If the benefits of a project occur over a long period, they will likely be enjoyed by people who did not pay for the project. If it is important that benefits of a project accrue to the people who paid for it, the sooner benefits are received, the more they are worth. This may be considered as a sort of societal impatience.

For these reasons, most economists agree that some degree of discounting is appropriate in analyzing most projects. We turn now to the mechanics of discounting.

9.3 BASIC TECHNIQUES, FORMULAE AND MECHANICS

Discounting simply means reducing the value of costs or benefits depending on how far in the future they lie. The multiple attached to a value occurring n periods in the future is the discount factor:

$$d_n \leq 1.$$

This factor is then multiplied by the value of the benefit in a future year to give its discounted value or *present value*.

While discounting may be done according to any scheme the analyst considers appropriate, the most commonly used technique, exponential discounting, uses an interest or discount rate r to calculate a discount factor of:

$$d_n = \frac{1}{(1+r)^n},$$

where n is the number of periods (usually years) after which the cost or benefit in question will occur.

The implication of exponential discounting is that a cost or benefit delayed by one period is valued at $r \times 100\%$ less than if it were not delayed. For example, $r = 0.05$ implies that being forced to wait one period for a benefit diminishes its value by 5 percent. So, other things being equal, a benefit occurring at the end of one period is worth 5 percent less than the same benefit today. A benefit occurring at the end of ten periods is worth 5 percent less than if it had occurred at the end of nine periods.

For example, imagine that a project will generate a benefit valued at $5000. The present value of this benefit will depend on when it occurs. If it occurs immediately, it will have a present value of $5000. If it occurs after one period, it will have a present value of:

$$d_1 \cdot \$5000 = \frac{1}{(1+r)^1} \cdot \$5000,$$

and if it occurs after nine or ten periods it will have a present value of:

$$d_9 \cdot \$5000 = \frac{1}{(1+r)^9} \cdot \$5000$$

$$d_{10} \cdot \$5000 = \frac{1}{(1+r)^{10}} \cdot \$5000.$$

If the interest rate used is 0.08 or 8 percent, the present values after zero, one, nine and ten periods are:

$$d_0 \cdot \$5000 = \frac{1}{(1+0.08)^0} \cdot \$5000 = \$5000$$

$$d_1 \cdot \$5000 = \frac{1}{(1+0.08)^1} \cdot \$5000 = \$4629.63$$

$$d_9 \cdot \$5000 = \frac{1}{(1+0.08)^9} \cdot \$5000 = \$2501.24$$

$$d_{10} \cdot \$5000 = \frac{1}{(1+0.08)^{10}} \cdot \$5000 = \$2315.97.$$

It should be apparent from the formula for discounting that the discount factor will decrease as either time or the discount rate increases. The effects of time and of the magnitude of the rate can be large. For example, the present value of $1000 discounted for 10 years at 8 percent is $463.19. The same $1000 discounted at the same rate for 50 years has a present value of only $21.32. Similarly, the present value of $1000 discounted for 10 years at 3 percent is $744.09 but if discounted at 15 percent is $247.18.

Net Present Value

The *net present value* (NPV) of a project is the sum of the present values of its benefits minus the sum of the present values of its costs. In an equation this is:

$$NPV = \sum_{t=0}^{T} d_t B_t - \sum_{t=0}^{T} d_t C_t$$

$$NPV = d_0 B_0 + d_1 B_1 + \ldots + d_T B_T - d_0 C_0 - d_1 C_1 - \ldots - d_T C_T.$$

If exponential discounting is used this becomes:

$$NPV = \frac{B_0}{(1+r)^0} + \ldots + \frac{B_T}{(1+r)^T} - \frac{C_0}{(1+r)^0} - \ldots - \frac{C_T}{(1+r)^T},$$

where:

B_t = benefits in period t;
C_t = costs in period t;
r = interest rate used for discounting;
d_t = discount factor for period t; and
T = number of periods the project will last.

This may be rewritten as:

$$NPV = \frac{B_0 - C_0}{(1+r)^0} + \frac{B_1 - C_1}{(1+r)^1} + \ldots + \frac{B_T - C_T}{(1+r)^T}$$

$$NPV = \frac{NB_0}{(1+r)^0} + \frac{NB_1}{(1+r)^1} + \ldots + \frac{NB_T}{(1+r)^T} = \sum_{t=0}^{T} \frac{NB_t}{(1+r)^t},$$

where:

$$NB_t = B_t - C_t = \text{net benefits in period } t.$$

So, the net present value is the sum of the present value of the net benefits in each period.

Net present value is one way of determining whether a project is worthwhile. It allows the value of a project's inputs and outputs to be compared. If the value of the outputs or benefits from a project is greater than the value of the inputs, the NPV will be positive and, from the point of view of the analysis, the project should be done. A negative NPV suggests that the value of the project's outputs is less than the value of its inputs and the project probably should not be done. The following example, Example 9A, discuss NPV.

EXAMPLE 9A   A TUTORING PROJECT

Consider a project that will provide tutors for some students for two years. The tutors will require training before they start at a cost of $10,000 over the first year. After that, they will be employed at a cost of $8000 annually. The benefits from the improved performance of the students has an estimated value of $12,000 annually. The benefits and costs in each year of the life of the project are:

Period	0	1	2
Benefits	0	12,000	12,000
Costs	10,000	8,000	8,000
Net benefits	− 10,000	4,000	4,000

Using an annual interest rate of 5 percent to discount the future costs and benefits of this project, the NPV is calculated as:

$$NPV = -10,000 + \frac{4000}{1.05} + \frac{4000}{(1.05)^2}$$

$$NPV = -10,000 + 3810 + 3628 = -2562.$$

If, however, the project is extended another year the benefits and costs will be:

Period	0	1	2	3
Benefits	0	12,000	12,000	12,000
Costs	10,000	8,000	8,000	8,000
Net benefits	− 10,000	4,000	4,000	4,000

And the NPV will be calculated as:

$$NPV = -10{,}000 + \frac{4000}{1.05} + \frac{4000}{(1.05)^2} + \frac{4000}{(1.05)^3}$$

$$NPV = -10{,}000 + 3810 + 3628 + 3455 = 893.$$

So, after the tutors are trained, extending the project one more year will increase the net benefits and make the project worth doing.

Discounting Uniform Payments

When discounting uniform payments, the discounting formula reduces to a particularly simple equation. Let A be the uniform payment to be received at the end of each period for a total of T periods or T payments. Applying the discount formula would give:

$$PV = \frac{A}{(1+r)^1} + \frac{A}{(1+r)^2} + \cdots \frac{A}{(1+r)^T}.$$

However, this stream of payments has a present value equal to:

$$PV = A \times \frac{1-(1+r)^{-T}}{r}.$$

If the payments come at the beginning of each period for T periods, these equations become:

$$PV = \frac{A}{(1+r)^0} + \frac{A}{(1+r)^1} + \cdots \frac{A}{(1+r)^T}$$

and

$$PV = A \times \frac{1-(1+r)^{-T}}{r/(1+r)}.$$

Consider the following example of uniform payments (Example 9B).

Interest Rates and Net Present Value

It is often asked how the NPV of a project will change if a different interest rate is used in discounting. This issue may be raised as a result of some dispute regarding the most appropriate interest rate or to determine the sensitivity of the net benefits to changes in the interest rate. The answer depends on the structure of the project's costs and benefits.

EXAMPLE 9B   UNIFORM PAYMENTS

Bob will receive a uniform payment of $100 per year for 30 years. What is the present value of this payment at an interest rate of 3 percent if the payments start immediately and if the payments start at the end of one year?

Starting immediately:

$$PV = A \times \frac{1 - (1 + r)^{-T}}{r/(1 + r)} = \$100 \times \frac{1 - (1.03)^{-30}}{0.03/1.03} = \$2,018.84.$$

Starting at the end of one year:

$$PV = A \times \frac{1 - (1 + r)^{-T}}{r} = \$100 \times \frac{1 - (1.03)^{-30}}{0.03} = \$1,960.04.$$

Most projects involve immediate costs and deferred benefits. In the example of the tutoring project, the cost of training the tutors was incurred early on and the initial net benefits were negative. During the later years of the project there were positive net benefits because the value of improved educational outcomes was greater than the cost of the tutors. Another example might be a road or bridge project. There will be some initial construction expenses and negative net benefits early on, but these will yield years of positive net benefits afterward.

For these traditional projects in which the costs come before the benefits, a higher interest rate will result in a lower NPV. This is because the effect of discounting at a higher rate will be very small for the early years of the project, but much larger for the later years.

Other projects have more complicated or unusual net benefit streams. You might imagine a temporary bridge that will involve construction costs followed by several years of service, then a year of maintenance work, a few more years of service, and finally demolition and removal. The effect of changing the interest rate on the NPV would be difficult to predict. Example 9C explores the effect on NPV of changing interest rate.

Terminal Values

Many projects involve construction of some sort of capital or durable asset. The lifetime of this capital may extend beyond the end of the period under which the project is being considered, the *planning horizon*. It would be incorrect to ignore the value remaining at the end of the planning horizon, so this may be included as a *terminal value*.

A primer for benefit–cost analysis

EXAMPLE 9C   A TEMPORARY AIRPORT EXPANSION

A major municipal airport is going to be replaced by a new, larger facility which is expected to open in ten years. In the interim, however, airport officials are considering a temporary expansion to alleviate crowding at the current facility. The temporary expansion would take one year to build at a cost of $5 million. It would then have to be demolished at the end of ten years at a cost of $2 million. The additional gate space would allow airport officials to bring in an additional $800,000 per year in net revenues. What is the present value to the airport authority of the temporary expansion at a rate of 3 percent and how does this change if the rate used rises to 6 percent?

The calculations are:

$$NPV_{3\%} = \frac{-\$5m}{1.03^0} + \frac{\$800K}{1.03^1} + \frac{\$800K}{1.03^2} + \cdots + \frac{\$800K}{1.03^{10}} - \frac{\$2m}{1.03^{11}}$$

$$= \$379,320$$

$$NPV_{5\%} = \frac{-\$5m}{1.06^0} + \frac{\$800K}{1.06^1} + \frac{\$800K}{1.06^2} + \cdots + \frac{\$800K}{1.06^{10}} - \frac{\$2m}{1.06^{11}}$$

$$= \$165,505$$

Note that the analysis is done from the point of view of the airport authority, and only the authority has standing. Any benefits gained by passengers in terms of having additional space or by airlines because they have additional gates are excluded.

For example, imagine that a state department of transportation is considering construction of a new highway. Department guidelines specify a thirty-year planning horizon for analyses, but it is generally believed that the highway will have some value at the end of thirty years. This residual or terminal value should be recognized in the analysis.

While it may be difficult to determine what value to attach to the asset at the end of the planning horizon, the discounting is straightforward; the terminal value should simply be discounted as other costs and benefits of the project have been discounted. It should be noted that if the planning horizon is distant, the effect of discounting may be severe. Example 9D illustrates the use of terminal values when considering a public swimming pool.

EXAMPLE 9D   A PUBLIC SWIMMING POOL

A city's department of parks and recreation is considering building a public swimming pool. Department guidelines call for a planning horizon of twenty years when analyzing projects, but it is recognized that with proper maintenance, a twenty-year-old pool has a value of about 60 percent of that of a new pool. The construction cost is $10 million, so the terminal value to be used in the analysis will be $6 million.

The present value of the terminal value will be:

$$PV = \frac{\$6\,m}{(1+r)^{20}}.$$

If an interest rate of 3 percent is used, the present value is $3.32 million while an interest rate of 6 percent yields a present value of $1.87 million.

9.4   REAL VERSUS NOMINAL

Discounting is the process of reducing the value of a future payment in order to determine its present value. One consideration in doing this may be inflation.

Most costs or benefits are specified in non-monetary terms. A project may require some amount of labor, energy or materials, the costs of which are likely to rise with inflation. A project may provide electricity, recreational opportunities or many other goods whose value will rise with inflation. Because the real value of these costs or benefits will not change as a result of inflation, the inflation rate does not need to be included in the interest rate used for discounting. Put another way, because the prices of these goods will rise with inflation, their values do not need to be adjusted for changes in the price level.

To discount costs or benefits specified in units of real goods, the interest rate used is a *real interest rate*, a rate that does not include inflation. The real interest rate simply represents such things as impatience and the expected value of lost opportunities in waiting until the payment is received.

Inflation should be considered when the cost incurred or benefit received from a project is a specified number of dollars. For example, if a project is financed with bonds, payments on those bonds are usually specified in exact monetary amounts regardless of inflation. If a project will generate revenues of known dollar amounts, perhaps due to long-term use contracts, these will also be payments specified in exact monetary amounts. In this case, the real value of the payment or benefit depends on the price level, so the expected inflation rate needs to be included in the interest rate used for discounting.

To discount exact monetary payments, the correct interest rate to use is a *nominal interest rate*, a rate including the expected inflation rate from the present until the payment is made.

Using a nominal interest rate to discount real costs and benefits will result in their present value being too small. Using a real interest rate to discount nominal costs and benefits will result in their present value being too large. In either case, the calculated present values will be incorrect, a mistake that has been made by more than one public agency.

If the real interest rate is r and expected inflation is π, the nominal interest rate is:

$$i = (1 + r) \times (1 + \pi) - 1.$$

When both r and π are relatively small, a good approximation is:

$$i^* = r + \pi.$$

For example, if the expected annual inflation rate is 3 percent and the real interest rate is 2 percent, the actual and approximated nominal rates are:

$$i = 1.03 \times 1.02 - 1 = 0.0506$$

$$i^* = 0.03 + 0.02 = 0.05,$$

a close approximation, differing by only 0.06 percent.

If, however, the expected annual inflation rate is 10 percent and the real interest rate is 8 percent, the actual and approximated nominal rates are:

$$i = 1.10 \times 1.08 - 1 = 0.188$$

$$i^* = 0.10 + 0.08 = 0.18.$$

In this case, the approximation differs by 0.8 percent and is not as good. As the rates increase, the quality of the approximation will deteriorate. Example 9E illustrates these concepts.

In most cases, costs and benefits are specified in real terms and real interest rates are appropriate. However, the difference between real and nominal interest rates is important and should be recognized in any analysis.

EXAMPLE 9E   LABOR CONTRACTS

An agency requires a real interest rate of 5 percent and an expected inflation rate of 6 percent in valuing projects. They are considering a project that will involve 6000 hours of skilled labor each year for ten years. The current market wage for this type of labor is $12/hour. Alternatively, the agency could contract with a firm specializing in this sort of work at a fixed wage of $14/hour that is guaranteed not to change for the ten-year project. Under the agency's guidelines, which is a better deal?

There are some risk issues here. Locking in a wage eliminates the probability that your costs could rise dramatically, but for this answer we will ignore these issues.

The first option specifies a wage of $12/hour, for a total cost of $72,000/year. This can be expected to rise with inflation, so the real interest rate should be used to calculate the present value:

$$PV = \$72,000 + \frac{\$72,000}{1.05} + \frac{\$72,000}{1.05^2} + \cdots + \frac{\$72,000}{1.05^9} = \$583,763.$$

The second option specifies a wage of $14/hour, for a total cost of $84,000/year. Because this will not rise with inflation, the nominal rate should be used. In this case, we will use the simplified version, $5\% + 6\% = 11\%$.

$$PV = \$84,000 + \frac{\$84,000}{1.11} + \frac{\$84,000}{1.11^2} + \cdots + \frac{\$84,000}{1.11^9} = \$549,112.$$

So, the fixed wage of $14/hour seems to be a better deal than the wage of $12/hour that will rise with inflation.

Incidentally, the more complicated calculation of the nominal interest rate, $1.06 \times 1.05 - 1 = 0.113$, generates a present value of:

$$PV = \$84,000 + \frac{\$84,000}{1.113} + \frac{\$84,000}{1.113^2} + \cdots + \frac{\$84,000}{1.113^9} = \$543,738.$$

Using a higher interest rate (11.3 percent versus 11.0 percent) generates a smaller present value.

9.5   ALTERNATIVES TO NET PRESENT VALUE

This chapter has focused on the use of discounting in the calculation of the net present value of a project. The decision rule is that if a project has positive NPV, it is, at least from the point of view of the analysis, worth doing. Although economists generally prefer NPV, in fact a number of other criteria are used and some of these quite widely. Two of the most common are the benefit–cost ratio (B/C) and internal rate of return (IRR). A third criterion, payback periods, are also used.

Benefit–Cost Ratio

The benefit–cost ratio is equal to the present value of a project's benefits divided by the present value of its costs. In a formula, this is:

$$B/C = \frac{\sum_{t=0}^{T} d_t B_t}{\sum_{t=0}^{T} d_t C_t},$$

where d_t is the discount factor for period t and T is the total number of periods under consideration.

If the calculated B/C is greater than one, the project is considered worthwhile. This is equivalent to the requirement that a NPV be positive. So, what is the value of calculating B/C if the basic decision rule is identical to that of NPV?

The answer is that B/C offers some measure of how large the benefits are relative to the costs of a project. A B/C of 1.2, for example, tells you that the estimated benefits of a project are 20 percent greater than the costs. This is likely to be important if there is some uncertainty regarding the actual value of costs and benefits. If the calculated B/C is 1.2, costs could be as much as 20 percent larger than estimated in the analysis and the project will still be worthwhile. Knowing, for example, that the NPV of a project is $5 million offers no such information.

A weakness of B/C is that it does not allow an analyst to choose between mutually exclusive projects when their costs are different. That is, when choosing between projects, the project with the higher B/C is not necessarily the one with the higher NPV.

As an example, imagine that a city department of parks and recreation has one site on which it can put either a set of tennis courts or a softball field, but not both. Costs and benefits are described in Table 9.1. The softball field has a higher NPV ($30 million versus $20 million for the tennis courts) and so is the better project. However, the tennis courts have a higher

Table 9.1 Costs and benefits of alternative uses

	Present value of benefits	Present value of costs	B/C
Tennis courts	$100 m	$80 m	1.25
Softball field	$160 m	$130 m	1.23

Table 9. 2 Reconciliation of benefit–cost ratios by budget equalization

	Present value of benefits	Present value of costs	B/C
Tennis courts	$150 m	$130 m	1.15
Softball field	$160 m	$130 m	1.23

B/C (1.25 versus 1.23). In this case, choosing the project with the higher B/C would be incorrect.

Another problem with B/C is that the ratio can be altered slightly by re-naming costs as negative benefits or benefits as negative costs. This cannot be used to make a good project look bad or vice versa, but it can change the B/C. If B/C is used to compare mutually exclusive projects, those projects must have equal costs and the categorization of costs and benefits must be consistent.

There is a variation on the B/C used above and this is ratio 2:

$$\text{Ratio 2} = (\text{B/C}) - 1 = \frac{\sum_{t=0}^{T} d_t B_t}{\sum_{t=0}^{T} d_t C_t} - 1.$$

Ratio 2 is equal to the previously stated B/C minus one. Thus the criterion for acceptance of ratio 2 is that the ratio is greater than 0.

In comparing projects by these ratios there is a technique that will give the correct comparison regardless of differing scale of the projects. This is to assign both projects the same budget and invest any left-over funds at the discount rate. Thus in the above example of the tennis court and the softball field, we give both projects the same budget, $130 million, equal to the budget of the larger project. This accounts for the $50 million difference in costs between the two projects. The additional $50 million invested at the discount rate also has a present value of $50 million so that the present value of benefits and costs are now as given in Table 9.2.

The NPVs remain the same, favoring the softball field, but the benefit–cost ratios are now 1.15 and 1.23, also in favor of the softball field.

Note that both projects have a positive NPV so that if there is a budget or financing available (as well as the necessary land), both projects would be worthwhile.

Internal Rate of Return

The internal rate of return of a project is the interest rate that will generate an NPV of zero. In an equation, this is:

$$\sum_{t=0}^{T} \frac{B_t - C_t}{(1 + i_{IRR})^t} = 0,$$

where i_{IRR} is the internal rate of return. The usual decision rule is that if the IRR for a project is greater than some target rate (the opportunity cost of capital, perhaps) then the project is desirable.

As an example, consider a project whose net benefits are as described in Table 9.3. The IRR is calculated by writing out the calculation for net present value and then adjusting the interest rate until the NPV is equal to zero:[4]

$$-200 + \frac{80}{1+i} + \frac{80}{(1+i)^2} + \frac{80}{(1+i)^3} = 0.$$

For this example, the IRR is approximately 9.70 percent. That is:

$$-200 + \frac{80}{1.0970} + \frac{80}{(1.0970)^2} + \frac{80}{(1.0970)^3} = 0.$$

Put another way, the rate of return generated on the $200 investment in this project is about 9.70 percent. If the agency considering the project has an opportunity cost of capital of less than 9.70 percent then this project will be beneficial. If the present value is calculated using an interest rate less than 9.70 percent then the project will have a positive NPV.

Table 9.3　Net benefit of a project

Period	0	1	2	3
Net benefits	− 200	+ 80	+ 80	+ 80

---

[4] As it will in general be impossible to solve for this analytically, it is usually necessary to calculate an estimate of the IRR using a calculator or computer. Microsoft Excel's goal seek tool is particularly useful for this purpose.

There are a number of problems with IRR. The first of these is that IRR may not be unique. If a project has a net benefit stream that changes sign more than once (starts out negative, then turns positive and then turns negative, for example) there may be two IRRs, both of which are equally valid. If one of these is greater than and one is less than the opportunity cost of capital then the IRRs will be of no value in assessing the project. In general the IRR may have as many positive rates of return as there are sign changes.

Consider the example of a project with the net benefit stream given in Table 9.4. The IRR for this project is both 3.73 percent and 13.0 percent. The reason for this result is that the IRR implicitly assumes that the returns are reinvested at the (in this case different) IRRs.

The second problem is that IRR may actually give the wrong assessment of a project when compared to the opportunity cost of capital. Consider the example of a slightly non-traditional project in which there are initial benefits and future costs, as described in Table 9.5. One example of a project of this type would be harvesting a forest and then replanting it.

The IRR of this project is 10 percent. If the agency considering the project had an opportunity cost of capital of 8 percent, the standard decision rule would classify the project as desirable. However, using an interest rate of 8 percent actually results in a negative NPV. So, the project should not be done, and application of IRR yields the wrong decision.

Finally, IRR is of no value in choosing between projects. Consider two projects, A and B, with net benefit streams as described in Table 9.6. The IRRs are 10 percent for project A and about 8.21 percent for project B. This has no bearing on which project should actually be chosen. The important factor is the interest rate used for discounting. If an interest rate less than 6.85 percent is used, project B is preferable because it will have a higher NPV. For higher interest rates, project A will have a higher NPV. This is demonstrated in Figure 9.1.

Table 9.4   Net benefits of a project with two IRRs

Period	0	1	2	3
Net benefits	− 190	+ 190	+ 258	− 260

Table 9.5   IRR may yield the wrong decision

Period	0	1
Net benefits	+ 100	− 110

Table 9.6   The IRR and alternative projects

Period	0	1	2	3
Net benefits of project A	− 100	+ 110		
Net benefits of project B	− 100	+ 20	+ 40	+ 60

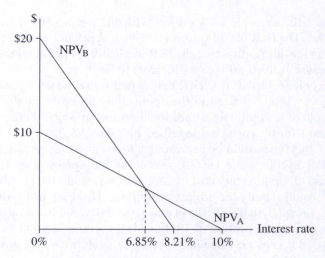

Figure 9.1   Interest rates and NPV of two projects

Both B/C and IRR are frequently used. Both have their limitations and need to be understood. At best, IRR is a slightly more complicated substitute for NPV, at worst it offers decisions that are exactly wrong. B/C does offer some measure of the reliability of the results in the face of uncertainty regarding costs and benefits, but must be employed carefully when choosing between projects. In any case, a calculated B/C or IRR should be accompanied by an NPV.

Nevertheless, the IRR must have some intuitive appeal as it is widely used in business. Also, the IRR can be modified to yield correct results by subtracting cash flow streams (Newnan et al., 2004). Perhaps people can relate better to rates of return than to pure numbers such as the NPV. The IRR may also be modified to compare projects correctly. This can be done by subtracting the cash flows of the two projects in question and calculating the IRR of the cash flows. If the IRR is above the trigger rate, the project with the larger cash flow is the better project. This technique is sometimes called the modified IRR.

Table 9.7   Payback periods

Time period in years	0	1	2	3
Project A	−100	50	50	0
Project B	−100	45	45	100

Payback Period

The payback period is the time required to recover the original investment. For example if an investment of $100 yields benefits of $50 each period, the payback period would be 2 years. The payback period is simply that time period, T, for which the sum of the cash flows, including the initial investment, equals zero. That is, it is the time period T that satisfies:

$$T : \sum_{t=0}^{T} \mathrm{NB}_t = 0.$$

This is a crude measure and can give wrong results. For example, consider the cash flows of two projects, A and B, described in Table 9.7. Project A has a payback period of 2 years. Project B has a payback period of 2.1 years. Yet project B is better. Project A has a negative NPV at any positive discount rate while project B has a positive NPV at any discount rate less than 34 percent.

If payback periods can give incorrect results, why are they used? They are used particularly in energy work. The reasons are partly historical. For energy work where cash flows are fairly regular and go far into the future, payback periods are less likely to give wrong results. Also payback periods are easily understood, a feature that is always a virtue. (See Table 9.8.) None of these yields an unambiguous yes across the board. Our recommendation is that if some criterion other than the NPV is used, NPV should also be used as a check.

9.6   WHAT RATE TO USE?

You may work for an agency that has a predetermined interest rate to use in discounting future costs and benefits. Alternatively, you may be able to generate a set of results using a range of interest rates, turn this over to your superiors and leave the tricky choices to them. In either case, this section will be of little use to you.

Table 9.8   Advantages and disadvantages of the techniques

Criterion or attribute	Gives the correct answer	Ease of use	Intuitive	Widely used
NPV	Yes	Yes	No	Yes
B/C	Yes but with adjustments when comparing projects of different costs	Yes	Yes	Yes
IRR	Not always	Not when 2 or more rates appear	Yes	Yes
Payback period	Can often give wrong answer	Yes	Yes	Yes

If, however, you are asked to choose an interest rate to use in calculating present values or are called upon to offer an opinion as to whether another person's choice was responsible, here are some guidelines.

Ideally, analysts would discount future costs and benefits using the *social rate of time preference*, which is, by definition, the rate at which society discounts future time periods. This definition is operationally useless because different people in a society have different attitudes toward the future depending on their current and expected future income, their life expectancy, whether or not they have children, risks they currently face and so on. People do not even have the same opportunity cost of current consumption as they face different rates of interest that could be earned on savings and that would be paid on loans. Moreover, people have different rates for different purposes. The rate they use to make a choice between say, purchase of a refrigerator with greater electricity saving and one with less electricity saving, will be quite different from the rate they use to make a decision about what to contribute to their 401K pension fund. It would seem that the rate that people would tend to use in conservative investment decisions would be a reasonable choice for assessing public projects. To combine the various rates of time preference of a society's members into one rate would be challenging and would generate an answer of questionable value.[5]

---

5   Harberger (1976) suggests a different procedure in which the rate is a combination of the cost of capital and the consumption rate.

A productive approach might be to ask what a project's resources would be used for if they were not employed in the project. If the resources would be used in private industry then the pre-tax, real rate of return in private industry is a reasonable rate to use in discounting future costs and benefits. If, on the other hand, the resources would be used in the public sector, the real rate of return on public projects might be an appropriate measure. This rate is in any event a reasonable estimate of the rate of time preference.

The harsh reality is that very often the rate used to discount future net benefits of public projects is zero. According to Bazelon and Smetters (1999, p. 219) many federal agencies do not discount at all, treating a dollar next year exactly the same as a dollar today. Similarly, Dively and Zerbe (1991) find that most municipalities do not use a discount rate, again considering a dollar next year (or even several years in the future) equivalent to a dollar today. While this practice is widespread, we cannot recommend it. The failure by many agencies to discount, a very basic practice, may demonstrate that BCA frequently takes a back seat to political considerations. In spite of this possibility, we offer some guidelines for choosing an interest rate.

An absolute minimum rate to use in discounting might be the effective yield on US treasury bonds of a length approximately equal to that of the project you are considering. This is the risk-free rate at which the US federal government can borrow, and represents their opportunity cost of capital. The cost of capital is probably higher for most other agencies as the risk of default is more severe in smaller agencies. From 1953 through 1999, interest rates on three and ten-year US treasury bonds averaged 6.42 percent and 6.74 percent. Over the same period, inflation rates averaged about 4.49 percent, suggesting real interest rates of slightly over 2 percent. Over the 1990s, the same interest rates averaged 6.01 and 6.66 percent while inflation was about 2.88 percent, suggesting a risk-free real interest rate of slightly over 3 percent.[6]

Beyond the federal opportunity cost of capital calculated above, a number of rates have been prescribed for use in evaluating projects. As of 1992 the Office of Management and Budget (OMB) requires that federal agencies use a 7 percent real discount rate for BCA and regulatory impact analysis. Prior to 1992 the OMB required a 10 percent discount rate.

Alternatively, it might be suggested that capital used by a project would have alternative uses in private industry.[7] In such a case, an appropriate rate

---

[6] These figures were calculated from data found in the Economic Report of the President (2001).

[7] This might be true if a country's capital markets were small relative to the amount of debt incurred by the project or if the agency doing the project has the opportunity to invest in private bonds, although either of these seems unlikely.

to use in discounting could be the private opportunity cost rate, or the real, pre-tax rate of return on corporate investments. This is the return that could be generated if, instead of being used in the project, any capital was used by the private sector. This rate is equal to the interest rate paid on corporate bonds plus the corporate tax rate. From 1958 to 1999, the average rate of return on Moody's AAA rated corporate bonds was 7.88 percent.[8] Assuming a corporate tax rate of 35 percent, this suggests a pre-tax rate of return of approximately 12.12 percent. Over the same period, the average rate of inflation of the consumer price index was 4.36 percent, suggesting a real, pre-tax rate of approximately 7.43 percent.

Finally, as suggested in the introduction to this chapter, if the project you are considering will have effects long after the current generation has died off, it might be appropriate to discount these future effects (costs or benefits) at a rate of zero or, alternatively, at different rates over different periods of the future. There may be some time-inconsistency issues, but such *differential discounting* reflects two considerations. First, there is evidence that people apply different discount rates to different ranges in the future. The rate people use to discount a payment received one year from now relative to an equal payment received immediately will likely be higher than the rate used to discount payments received after 51 relative to 50 years from now. An example from Thaler (1991) is that a person might prefer one apple today to two tomorrow, but would prefer two apples after 51 days to one apple after 50 days. This effect is referred to as the *common difference effect*. For more discussion of this effect and its implications, see Strotz (1955), Ainslie (1975, 1985), Horowitz (1988) and Benzion et al. (1989). Second, long-term effects are basically transfers from people alive now to people alive at some point in the distant future. Discounting transfers to future generations suggests diminished standing for those people more than any measure of time preference, and may argue for the use of lower annual discount rates. Example 9F discusses differential discounting.

Weitzman (1999) offers some approximate rates to use in discounting effects occurring over long periods of time. He suggests a sliding scale in which different rates are used to discount different ranges of the future. The first 25 years from the present would be discounted at 3–4 percent, periods between 25 and 75 years away would be discounted at about 2 percent, periods from 75 to 300 years away would be discounted at about 1 percent and all subsequent periods would not be discounted. So, if a project has net benefits in the 110th year of $50 million (to the extent that this could be reasonably predicted) the present value of this might be calculated using

---

8   Economic Report of the President (2001).

EXAMPLE 9F DIFFERENTIAL DISCOUNTING

Imagine that you are choosing between $1000 to be received now versus a payment to be received one year from now. How large must the delayed payment be in order to make you indifferent between the two? This implies some discount rate.

Now, imagine that you are choosing between $1000 to be received at the end of 50 years versus a payment to be received at the end of 51 years. How large must the delayed payment be in order to make you indifferent between the two? This implies another discount rate.

In experiments, people give answers that suggest they use a higher rate when discounting the nearer future than they use when discounting the more distant future.

For example, the same person who would be indifferent between $1000 now and $1100 a year from now (indicating a discount rate of 10 percent) might also be indifferent between $1000 after 50 years and $1010 after 51 years (indicating a discount rate of 1 percent).

a rate of 3.5 percent to discount the first 25 years, 2 percent to discount the next 50 years and 1 percent to discount the remaining 35 years to give:

$$PV = \frac{\$50\,m}{1.035^{25} 1.02^{50} 1.01^{35}} = \$5.55\,m.$$

In the end, the most responsible approach to the question of which rate to use in discounting future costs and benefits is to calculate the present value of the net benefits for a range of values and comment on the sensitivity to changes in the interest rate. If a project is desirable even at relatively high rates or undesirable even at relatively low rates, it may be that the rate has little to do with the economic decision. A good analysis will reveal this.

The actual decision, of course, requires an actual rate. This rate should certainly be greater than zero, especially for projects of limited duration. If the project is being analyzed from an agency's point of view, the opportunity cost of funds for that agency (the rate at which they can borrow funds) is probably appropriate. If the project is being analyzed from a societal point of view and is not particularly large or risky, a rate of between 3 and 4 percent, as suggested by Weitzman and indicated by real rates of return on US treasury bonds is probably appropriate. Under other conditions, when capital is particularly scarce or a project is especially risky, higher rates may be appropriate.

9.7 APPROPRIATE RATES AND THE SHADOW PRICE OF CAPITAL IN A SECOND-BEST WORLD WITH TAXES

In a first-best world the discount rate to use for public projects equals the market rate, the same rate that will be used by the private sector. The introduction of a tax on corporate profits and an individual income tax into this first-best world will make our analysis of the discount rate to use more realistic and more complex. Suppose the corporate profits tax is 36 percent and the marginal income tax is 27 percent. For simplicity, suppose further that only corporations undertake investment, that all investment is funded with equity capital, and that all after-tax profits are paid as dividends subject to the personal income tax. Finally, suppose that the after-tax rate of return required by investors is 8 percent. That is, we assume 8 percent is the marginal rate of time preference (MRTP).

In order that shareholders earn 8 percent after taxes they must earn 10.9 percent before taxes, and the corporation must earn about 17 percent before taxes. Shareholders that loan the corporation $1.00 for investment expect to obtain almost $1.11 for a one-year period. A $1.00 investment by the corporation yields $1.17 next year. Of the $0.17 earned, 36 percent or about $0.06 goes to taxes, leaving $0.11 to be paid to the shareholder. Of the $0.11, the shareholder pays 27 percent or about $0.03 in taxes, leaving the requisite $0.08 to the shareholder.[9]

In equilibrium the required rate of return to private investment of 17 percent must be higher than the MRTP of 8 percent. This situation is inconsistent with an optimal allocation of resources. Investments that yield more than 8 percent should be undertaken as long as they yield a return greater than the individual's MRTP. But investments will not in fact be undertaken unless they yield more than 17 percent. The level of investment will, *ceteris paribus*, be too low.

Bias against Longer-term Investments

This wedge between the rate of return and the MRTP will also create an inefficient bias against longer-term investments. Consider alternative projects A and B in Table 9.9. Investment A is shorter term than B.

---

[9]   We ignore the possible tax deductibility of interest payments.

Table 9.9   Bias against long-term investments at too high discount rates

Time	A	B
0	− 100	− 100
1	63.09	27.85
2	63.09	27.86
3		27.86
4		27.86
5		27.86
6		27.86

Both investments are just worthwhile at 17 percent interest, the market rate of return. (That is, at a discount rate of 17 percent, the $NPV_A = NPV_B = 0$.) From the MRTP standpoint, however, B is the better investment since the NPV of A at 8 percent is $12.51, while the NPV of B is $28.75. Thus use of the rate of return to private investment leads both to under-investment and a bias toward shorter-term projects.

The Conceptual Problem of a Discount Rate in a Second-best World

Given that we are not operating in an idealized economy and that there are distortions in market interest rates arising from taxes, we are in a second-rather than a first-best world. The second-best approach seeks to maximize the discounted present value of social welfare taking into account the distortions. This approach is equivalent to determining the optimal level of government spending in a second-best world. The determination of the appropriate discount rate is a by-product of the social welfare maximization process.

In a world in which there are corporate and individual taxes, the choice of interest rate for the evaluation of public projects is no longer obvious. There has been a long-standing debate over the correct rate. Some argue that the MRTP is the correct rate. Others contend that the return to private capital (opportunity cost rate: OCR) should be used. The simple argument for either of these positions is quite intuitive.

The MRTP represents the rate at which one is willing to trade present consumption for future consumption. If, therefore, an investment is worthwhile when evaluated at the MRTP, it should be undertaken because it will yield enough consumption to make it worthwhile. Yet, no private business would undertake an investment whose yield was only equal to the MRTP. It must consider taxes that it must pay, the cost of funds, and the opportunity cost of other investments. Clearly government must be the one to undertake these investments. Thus advocates of using the MRTP tend to be advocates also of more extensive government investment.

Those advocating use of the OCR rate note that public investment displaces some private investment by diverting investment funds that would otherwise go to private investment. Suppose that a dollar of public investment displaces a dollar of private investment that would otherwise yield 17 percent. If the public investment yields say 8 percent, the public investment causes a net decrease in wealth. Therefore, the argument goes, no public investment should be undertaken that yields less than the rate of return to private investment, that is, less than the OCR. Suppose the government does value investments at the MRTP. An identical investment would be worth more to the government than to private business because the present value of the earnings stream would be calculated at the lower MRTP rate by the government and at the higher OCR by private firms. So, if the MRTP is used, the government could displace investment by private businesses that had greater returns than those undertaken by the government. These arguments, which suggest that the interest rate used by government should be the one used by the private sector, were a motivating factor in the directive of the Office of Management and Budget, issued during the Nixon administration, that the discount rate for evaluating public projects was to be 10 percent in *constant* (inflation-adjusted) dollars.

In recent years, it has been realized that there is truth in both the arguments for both the MRTP and the OCR. The consumption value of investment should be discounted at the MRTP, but on the other hand the displacement of private capital should be taken into account. There is an important caveat, however to the above rule. Where a project can be undertaken by either government or private industry, and the evaluation will affect which party undertakes the project, the government evaluation should use the same discount rate as the private sector, that is, the OCR rate. Otherwise, government will tend to displace private operation even when the private operation is more efficient. The following is the approach when the government is considering whether or not a project should be undertaken.

A Correct Approach to a Discount Rate in a Second-best World

It has come to be understood, from Musgrave (1969), Bradford (1975) and others, that an approach to determining the public project discount rate involves setting out the consumption that results over time from the investment and then discounting this consumption at the social rate of time preference (SRTP). The SRTP is by definition the rate at which society is willing to trade off present for future consumption. The SRTP represents the MRTP adjusted for external effects or ethical considerations.

This approach assumes that the value of investments ultimately lies in the consumption they generate and that the willingness of society to forgo present for future consumption is measured by the SRTP.

The change of welfare occasioned by a change in consumption is then discounted by the SRTP. Thus,

$$dW = \sum_{t=0}^{T} \frac{\Delta C_t}{(1 + i)^t},$$

where ΔC_t is the change in consumption associated with the investment and i is the SRTP. Thus far it looks as if we are adopting the MRTP approach because the SRTP is closely related to the MRTP. But the effect of the OCR is taken into account in discovering the change in consumption produced by a private investment.

An investment of $1.00 in public funds displaces some private saving and investment and some consumption. The private investment displaced would itself in turn have generated later consumption. The investment of $1.00 in public funds will itself generate future cash returns. Some of these benefits will return to direct consumption, while the rest will contribute to private investment that will in turn generate additional future consumption and private investment. The trick now is to express the stream of both benefits and costs of an investment in consumption terms.

The Shadow Price of Capital

To set out the general procedure formally, we define the following variables:

K_0 = original investment at time t;
$K(t)$ = the value of the investment at time t;
s = the fraction of the proceeds of an investment that are reinvested in excess of the amount needed to maintain capital;
r = the private investment rate of returns, the OCR;
t = time;
e = the natural log, 2.718 . . .; and
i = the social rate of time preference, SRTP.

The total capital at time t from an initial investment of K_0 will be:

$$K(t) = K_0 e^{srt}.$$

The term sr can be thought of as the growth factor. For example, if the investment rate (r) was 8 percent and the fraction reinvested was 100 percent, the growth rate would be 8 percent.

The income in any year will be the interest rate r times the stock of capital. The fraction of income consumed will be $1 - s$. The consumption in any year t will therefore be found by multiplying the amount of capital in year t, ($K_0 e^{srt}$), by the returns to capital, r, to give income in year t, and then multiplying this by the marginal propensity to consume $(1 - s)$.

This gives consumption per unit of capital in any period t as:

$$C(t) = \frac{(1-s)rK_0 e^{srt}}{K_0} = (1-s)re^{srt}.$$

The present value of a future sum, P, where discounting is continuous is given by:

$$PV = Pe^{-it},$$

where i is the relevant interest rate.

The present value of consumption in each period is found by discounting it by the social rate of time preference, i. The present value of the consumption for period t only will then be:

$$PV_t = (1-s)re^{srt - it}.$$

The present value of the entire consumption stream for all time periods will be:

$$PV_c = \sum_{t=0}^{T} (1-s)re^{srt-it}.$$

This will be equivalent to using a negative discount rate where $sr > i$ and would yield infinite values where the time horizon is infinite. For the usual case $sr < i$, however, and this reduces to a simple expression:

$$PV_c = \frac{(1-s)r}{i - sr}.$$

This is a particularly useful expression. It is the present value of the consumption from \$1.00 of private investment, that is, the shadow price of private capital (SPC). We call this expression V_t (or the SPC) so that:

$$V_t = \frac{(1-s)r}{i - sr}.$$

The amount V_t is the additional amount of consumption that society would expect in place of $1.00 of private capital investment forgone. It is through SPC that the OCR is taken into account. Note that in a first-best world in which the opportunity cost of capital is equal to the social rate of time preference, SPC is equal to one. That is, if $r = i$, then replacing i with r gives:

$$V_t = \frac{(1-s)r}{r - sr} = \frac{(1-s)r}{(1-s)r} = 1.$$

SPC is the term that can be used to convert those public investments that displace private funds to consumption equivalents. That is, we simply convert all benefits and costs to consumption equivalents using SPC and discount by the social rate of time preference.

We assume that s, i and r are not functions of time so they can be treated as the same values in different time periods. This allows us to treat V_t as a constant, V, that is time invariant. This is not an unreasonable assumption but it is important because we rely on it in what follows, but we will continue to use the expression V_t rather than V to remind the reader of this assumption.

Present Value Using the SPC

Consider an investment of $1.00 in a public project. Some of the funds will come from consumption forgone. Some will come from private investment forgone. Let θ_c be the fraction of a dollar of public spending that displaces private investment. That is, this is the amount by which private capital formation is reduced as a result of financing an additional dollar of government investment. Then $(1 - \theta_c)$ will be the fraction of public investment funds that comes from consumption. Recognizing that consumption of a dollar in year t has a present value of $1.00 in year t, the present value of a dollar of costs in year t will be:

$$PV_c = \theta_c(V_t) + (1 - \theta_c).$$

The term θ_c represents the present value of the fraction of the project's costs that come from private capital displaced. The present value of this is found by multiplying it by SPC. The term $(1 - \theta_c)$ is the fraction of the costs that come from forgone consumption. Thus the present value of costs as of year t of costs C_t incurred in year t will be:

$$C_t^* = C_t[\theta_c V_t + (1 - \theta_c)],$$

where C_t is costs as ordinarily measured and C_t^* is adjusted costs.

A similar expression can be found for benefits. Let θ_b be the fraction of each dollar of returns from public investment that is returned to private capital. That is, θ_b is the amount by which private capital is increased as a result of an increase of \$1.00 in the output of the government sector. Thus in any period t the benefits B_t will have a consumption present value in that year of:

$$B_t^* = B_t[\theta_b V_t + (1 - \theta_b)].$$

The change in consumption in each year can then be expressed as:

$$\Delta Y_t = B_t^* - C_t^*.$$

We now have expressions for the present value in each year of the benefits and costs of a project that takes into account the addition to or the displacement of private capital and the consumption gained or forgone. This is done by expressing all effects in terms of the result for consumption and discounting by the SRTP. The change in welfare can then be found by plugging the above values for adjusted benefits and costs into the standard equation for NPV. The NPV of the consumption value for the project will be:

$$NPV = \sum_{t=0}^{T} \frac{B_t^* - C_t^*}{(1 + i)^t}.$$

This equation is the fundamental present value equation for benefit–cost analysis in a second-best world. It incorporates implicitly the correct interest rate for discounting the benefits and costs of public projects. This can be spelled out with all terms to give:

$$NPV = \sum_{t=0}^{T} \frac{B_t[\theta_b V_t + (1 - \theta_b)] - C_t[\theta_c V_t + (1 - \theta_c)]}{(1 + i)^t}.$$

For simplicity we will call the terms in brackets corresponding to benefits and costs F_B and F_C, respectively. When the value of $\theta_b > \theta_c$, then $F_B > F_C$, and discounting by the SRTP will understate the net present value. When $F_C > F_B$, discounting by the SRTP will overstate NPVs. When $F_C = F_B$, however, discounting by the SRTP will give a correct answer. Consider the following cases.

Case 1 $\theta_b = \theta_c$
In this case the fraction of private investment displaced by the project is equal to the fraction of benefits that contribute to private capital, and $F_B = F_C$. When $F_B = F_C$, we shall denote both by F. The equation for NPV may then be written as:

$$\text{NPV} = \sum_{t=0}^{T} \frac{F(B_t - C_t)}{(1+i)^t}.$$

In this situation F is a multiplier that affects the size but not the sign of discounted benefits and costs. This means that a project that has a positive or negative NPV when discounted by the SRTP will continue to have a positive or negative NPV when adjusted by F. Therefore in the case where a single project is being compared to the status quo, the correct result will follow from using the SRTP applied to ordinary costs and benefits as the discount rate. That is, if the project is desirable using the SRTP, it is socially desirable when $\theta_b = \theta_c$.

There are several important situations in which the use of the SRTP to discount ordinary benefits and costs is appropriate.[10] First, in an open economy in which there is a high degree of capital mobility, public investment will not crowd out private investment, nor will returns from public projects influence the amount of private investment. The supply of investment will tend to be elastic at the world interest rate. Here discounting ordinary benefits and costs by the SRTP is appropriate. Even if the supply of investment funds is not perfectly elastic, significant elasticity means that θ_c and θ_b will be small and similar. The US economy is significantly open to world capital; it appears that for most cases, θ_b and θ_c are small and similar.

Second, benefits are sometimes costs avoided whose financing is similar to initial costs. This is likely to be especially important in the case of environmental projects in which future clean-up costs are avoided. Here again the SRTP for benefits and costs should be used.

In *cost-effectiveness analysis* the goal is to compare the costs of alternative methods of reaching the same goal. As long as the financing of the various alternatives is similar, the use of the SRTP should give a correct answer.

Finally, where both benefits and costs are widely dispersed, the effect on private capital for both benefits and costs should be captured in the saving rate. Had the public investment funds remained in the private sector only, the portion likely to have been saved would have been invested privately. Thus where benefits and costs are widely dispersed, $\theta_b = \theta_c$ and the SRTP should be used to discount ordinary benefits and costs.

---

10 When comparing projects where $\theta_b = \theta_c$ within each project but not across the projects, it may be important to estimate θ_b and θ_c. The size of the NPV will be sensitive to our assumption of the size of θ_b and θ_c. When $\theta_b = \theta_c$, then the NPV will be the same as when the ordinary costs and benefits are discounted by the SRTP. When $\theta_b = \theta_c > 1$, however, the sign of the NPV does not change but the size of the NPV will be larger because the NPV will be multiplied by the SPC, which is greater than 1.

Thus, in five situations the use of the SRTP as the discount rate without further adjustment is warranted:

1.   where analysis indicates that the same portion of benefits as costs affect private capital;
2.   where there is little effect of the price on investment funds due to an open economy;
3.   where benefits are future costs saved;
4.   where a cost-effectiveness analysis is used; and
5.   where the distribution of benefits and costs are widely dispersed.

Case 2 $\theta_b = 1$; $\theta_c = 0$
This is the situation in which none of the costs of the project displace private capital but all of the returns to the project go to private capital. In this case the discounting equation is:

$$NPV = \sum_{t=0}^{T} \frac{B_t V_t - C_t}{(1+i)^t}.$$

This indicates that discounting both costs and benefits at the SRTP will *understate* the net value of the project, unless an adjustment, multiplication by the SPC, is made to the benefits of the project. This equation tells us that in this situation costs are to be discounted by the SRTP. If unadjusted benefits are discounted by the SRTP, the present value of benefits will be understated because the SPC is greater than 1. That the SPC is greater than 1 can be seen as follows. V_t may be written as:

$$V_t = \frac{r - sr}{i - sr} > \frac{r}{i}.$$

Since $r > i$, V_t will be > 1.
   Where $\theta_b > \theta_c$, and the SRTP is used to discount benefits and costs, a project with a positive NPV clearly should be accepted.

Case 3 $\theta_b = 0$; $\theta_c = 1$
In this case all the costs of the project come from private capital and none of the benefits returns to private capital. The discounting equation is:

$$NPV = \sum_{t=0}^{T} \frac{B_t - C_t V_t}{(1+i)^t}.$$

In this situation it is appropriate to discount the benefits by the SRTP but not the unadjusted costs. Using the SRTP to discount both the unadjusted costs and benefits will overstate the present value.

The SRTP is too low an interest rate in this case. (It can be shown that the return to private capital may be either too low or too high a discount rate in the case where $\theta_c > \theta_b$; see Zerbe, 1991.)

Where θ_b and θ_c are unknown, Lesser and Zerbe (1994) show that an adjustment to costs of 10 percent will cover likely cases. We call this the 10 percent rule for the adjustment of costs. That is, if the sign of the NPV remains invariant when the costs are adjusted upward or downward by 10 percent, then the sign of the NPV will usually give a correct guide. If one knew that $\theta_b > \theta_c$, costs would only be adjusted downward by 10 percent. A project that was poor even when costs were adjusted downward by 10 percent should then be rejected. When one knows that $\theta_c > \theta_b$, costs should be adjusted upward by 10 percent. A project that passed muster even when costs were adjusted upward by 10 percent will be a good project for any likely values of θ_c and θ_b given that $\theta_c > \theta_b$.

Ethics and the SRTP

As with any aggregate measure of welfare, the SRTP is ethically determined. The SRTP is the rate society 'chooses' according to some ethical theory. For example, in choosing the SRTP the Rawlsian would wish to know whether or not future generations would be less advantaged than current generations. In a utilitarian context, the SRTP will equal the MRTP or the consumption rate of interest in the idealized economy except that external effects may lead to a divergence of the MRTP from the SRTP.

The level of consumption itself may embody an external effect. Suppose, for example, that status in society is a valued good and that status is determined by relative levels of consumption. Then collectively we might wish to reduce current consumption and to increase current savings, lowering the interest rate. Where all reduce consumption, relative status from greater savings remains unchanged. Acting individually, however, we may fail to increase saving because our current status is lowered. One might then argue that in this situation, in the absence of collective action, the SRTP is less than the consumption rate of interest or the MRTP.

An external effect of particular importance is the *intergenerational effect*. A second ethical argument against using the MRTP and in favor of the SRTP is that the preferences of future generations should count in determining the SRTP, whereas only the preferences of the current generations determine the MRTP. But, the MRTP shows the rate at which an individual is willing to trade off his/her own future for his/her own present consumption. The MRTP will also determine the future wealth of later generations. One could then argue that use of the MRTP is as ethically justified as the SRTP in so far as it derives from a golden rule of treating others as ourselves. This approach gains force also if we postulate that future generations are very like ourselves. It also gains force if the family is viewed as having an indefinite lifetime, unbroken by the births and deaths of individual members. In this situation the household utility function may make considerable allowance for future generations.

Empirical Estimates of the SRTP

The SRTP has been identified with the consumption rate of interest and thus with the after-tax rate of return on safe investments. This rate will depend on the growth rate of the economy and on macroeconomic variables. There is no reason to expect that this would be the same in all time periods. Table 9.10 shows inflation-adjusted interest rates for various bonds and for various historical time periods. The range of rates is substantial, the lowest is about 2 percent, the highest about 9.4 percent. If we confine ourselves to those periods in which rates have the lowest outstanding deviation (the SD is shown for just these periods), we have a range from 3.76 to 5.24 percent. Real rates between 4 and 5 percent before taxes seem most appropriate for the period of the 1980s and the early 1990s. On an after-tax basis, they would vary from about 2.7 to about 4.25 percent.

Ideally we would like to use expected real rates. Zerbe (1991) has examined expected real rates, and these suggest a range for projects between 3 and 20 years' duration of about 3.8 to 5.5 percent, consistent with the real rates in periods of economic stability. On an after-tax basis, these range from about 2.6 to about 4.7 percent. All things considered, then, real rates from 2.5 to 5.0 percent seem to cover the range of real rates that should be used to discount public benefits and costs in a second-best world.

Estimating the SPC

The best estimates of the size of the shadow price of capital, V_t, are about 2.5 to 3.5. Table 9.11 shows our estimates of the parameters that determine the SPC. These variables give an SPC of about 3.

The Effect of the SPC

Let us consider NPV using different possible discount rates. Consider a simple example in which we wish to find the correct NPV of a project whose present value is about $41 when costs and benefits are unadjusted by the SPC and are discounted with an SRTP of 3 percent.

If θ_b were to equal θ_c, and both were equal to 50 percent, then the NPV would be about $83, using an SPC of 3. Here the adjusted NPV differs

Table 9.10 *Inflation-adjusted interest rates for various bonds and historical time periods*

Periods	Prime commercial paper (CPI adjusted)[a] percent	American railroad bonds (CPI adjusted)[b] percent	Realized real yields			
			1-year treasury notes (CPI adjusted)[c] percent	3-year treasury bonds (CPI adjusted)[c] percent	20-year treasury bonds (CPI adjusted)[d] percent	Inflation rate CPI[e] percent
1857–1860		9.38				
1865–1889		8.86				
1881–1915		4.27 [2.30]				0.16 [2.1]
1885–1893		4.62 [0.13]				0 [0]
1890–1915	5.24 [2.3]	3.76 [2.30]				0.48 [2.1]
1920–1929	5.38	5.16				
1953–1988–1989	1.96		1.90	2.23	2.46	
1977–1989	2.92		3.20	3.56	3.97	
1980–1989	4.27 [0.023]		4.19	4.69	5.17	

Note: Figures in brackets are standard deviations.

Sources:
[a] Historical Statistics of the United States, Bicentennial Edition, US Department of Commerce, Bureau of the Census, Washington, DC, 1988, pp. 996, 1001, Series X 445.
[b] Historical Statistics of the United States, p. 1002, Series X 456–465.
[c] Economic Report of the President, Washington, DC, 1988, 1990, *Federal Reserve Bulletin*, selected months.
[d] Analytic record of yields and yield spreads from 1945, Salmon Brothers, Inc.
[e] Historical Statistics of the United States, Series E, pp. 210–12, Economic Report of the President, selected years.

Table 9.11   Estimates of the parameters that determine the SPC

Variables	Expected values	Bounds (2 SDs)
i	3	2.5–4.2
r	8	6.0–10.0
s	7.2	5.5–10.0

Source: Adjusted from Ruby (1980).

considerably from the unadjusted NPV. In an open economy, however, θ_b and θ_c are unlikely to be higher than 2 to 3 percent. If $\theta_b = \theta_c = 5\%$, the NPV will be about $45. Where $\theta_b = 0\%$ and $\theta_c = 3\%$, the NPV will be about $35. Where θ_b and θ_c are less than 5 percent and usually where they are between 5 and 10 percent, a 10 percent sensitivity adjustment to costs as suggested by Lesser and Zerbe (1994) will encompass the range of possible values. Where the difference between θ_b and θ_c is larger than this, however, adjustments using the SPC are required.

9.8   A GROWTH RATE APPROACH

Moore et al. (2004) suggest using an approach developed by Ramsey and based on the concept of the optimal growth rate. This approach determines the optimal discount rate as:

$$d = i + ge,$$

where:

  d is the social discount rate to be used;
  i is the social rate of selfish time preference;[11]
  g is the expected growth rate of per capital consumption; and
  e is the (absolute value) rate at which the marginal utility of income falls as per capita consumption increases.

As before, if there is crowding out or crowding in, the rate should be adjusted by the shadow price of capital approach. Moore et al. give discount rates to use for time periods of varying length (Table 9.12). Note that these rates are not dissimilar to those we found using the straight SPC

---

[11]   The social rate of selfish time preference is the social rate of time preference without reference to moral concerns about the future.

Table 9.12   Multi-period discounting rates

Time periods in years	Discount rate to use
0–50	3.5
50–100	2.5
100–200	1.5
200–300	0.5
> 300	0

Source: Moore et al. (2004).

Table 9.13   Our suggested real rates of discount

Time periods	Suggested rates
0–50	2.5%–4.5%
50–100	1.0%–2.5%
100–150	0.7%–1.0%
>150	0%

approach. We think they are, slightly high, however. In an elegant paper by Layton and Levine (2003) using actual survey data in connection to global warming, they find that the difference between discounting at 50 years and 150 produces a rate of a bit less than 1 percent. Our reading of the evidence suggests the rates as shown in Table 9.13.

A Practical Approach

The discount rates suggested here can be regarded as practical rates derived from theoretical underpinnings. Lyons (1990) argues, correctly we think, that the expected real rate of return on treasury bonds whose length corresponds to the project in question will give reasonable approximations to the correct discount rate. Dively and Zerbe (1991) show that most municipalities that use a discount rate choose the cost of (private) capital; a majority of municipalities, however, do not use any discount rate at all.

In the context of an air pollution control problem analyzed by Ruby (1980) the uncertainty of the variables θ_b, θ_c, r, i and s were substantially less than that of certain physical variables such as morbidity and predicted concentrations of the pollution dispersion model. Ruby's results suggest that the rates recommended here should give reasonable estimates.

We have presented a conceptual framework for determining the discount rate for public projects. This framework involves first tracing the consumption flows generated by the projects' benefits and displaced by the projects' costs. These consumptions flows are then discounted by the SRTP. A general equation was developed to use in discounting public projects. We make the following recommendations (which do not consider risk) for calculating intertemporal benefits and costs:

1. We suggest that the SRTP approach be used as the basic approach.
2. The discount rate should be the SRTP.
3. A reasonable approximation to the SRTP appears to be the rate on government bonds of the same term length as the project in question. This is the same conclusion that Moore et al. (2004) reach using an optimal growth approach.
4. The SRTP appears to lie within the range of about 2.5 to 5.0 percent for projects less than 50 years (adjusted for inflation).
5. The SRTP approach suggests rates of between 1 and 2 for projects longer than 50 years but shorter than 100 years.
6. The SRTP approach suggests rates of about 0 for projects longer than 150 years.
7. Sensitivity analysis with different discount rates should be confined to the range of rates thought to represent the SRTP.
8. In many cases, discounting unadjusted benefits and costs by the SRTP will give correct results.
9. Where the contributions or displacements of private capital from benefits or costs are not known, a 10 percent adjustment of costs should be performed to cover likely cases.
10. Where projects are considered in which an issue is whether the government or the private sector should undertake the project, the private sector rate should be used.

9.9 SUMMARY

Most projects take place over a number of years and involve costs and benefits occurring at different points in time. For various reasons, it is generally considered appropriate to treat costs or benefits differently depending on when they occur.

Discounting is the practice of reducing the value of a cost or benefit that occurs in the future. Although this may be done in any way an analyst considers appropriate, the most common method is exponential discounting in which an interest rate is used, and the value of a cost or benefit decreases by that rate each period until it occurs.

There are numerous complexities in choosing an appropriate rate to use for discounting. Among the considerations are issues of real versus nominal rates, the time period over which the project is to be evaluated, the possibility of intergenerational effects, the effects of taxes on various rates of time preference and the possibility that public investment might displace private investment.

Discounting is critical in calculating the NPV of a project, the best measure of whether the project is desirable from an economic point of view. A positive NPV means that the present value of the benefits of a project is greater than the present value of its costs.

REFERENCES

Ainslie, G. (1975), 'Specious reward: a behavioral theory of impulsiveness and impulse control', *Psychological Bulletin*, **82**: 463–509.

Ainslie, G. (1985), 'Beyond microeconomics. Conflict among interests in a multiple self as a determinant of value', in J. Elster (ed.), *The Multiple Self*, Cambridge: Cambridge University Press, pp. 133–75.

Bazelon, Coleman and Kent Smetters (1999), 'Discounting inside the Washington D.C. Beltway', *Journal of Economic Perspectives*, **13** (4): 213–28.

Benzion, U., A. Rapoport and J. Yagil (1989), 'Discount rates inferred from decisions: an experimental study', *Management Science*, **35**: 270–84.

Bradford, D.F. (1975), 'Constraints on government investment opportunities and the choice of discount rate', *American Economic Review*, **65**: 887–99.

Dively, Dwight and Richard Zerbe (1991), 'The discount rate policy for municipalities', Working Paper, University of Washington.

Economic Report of the President (2001), Washington, DC.

Harberger, Arnold (1976), 'On measuring the social opportunity cost of public funds', in A. Harberger, *Project Evaluation: Collected Papers*, Chicago: University of Chicago Press, pp. 94–122.

Horowitz, J.K. (1988), 'Discounting money payoffs: an experimental analysis', working paper, Department of Agricultural and Resource Economics, University of Maryland.

Layton, David and Richard Levine (2003), 'How much does the far future matter? A hierarchical Bayesian analysis of the public's willingness to mitigate ecological impacts of climate change', *Journal of the American Statistical Association*, **98** (463): 532–45.

Lesser, J.A. and Richard Zerbe, Jr. (1994), 'Discounting procedures for environmental (and other) projects: a comment on Kollo and Scheraga', *Journal of Policy Analysis and Management*, **13** (1): 140–56.

Lyons, Randolph (1990), 'Federal discount rate policy, the shadow price of capital and challenges for reforms', *Journal of Environmental Economics and Management*, **18** (2), part 2, S29–S50.

Moore, Mark A., Anthony E. Boardman, Aidan R. Vining, David L. Weimer and David H. Greenberg (2004), 'Just give me a number! Practical values for the social discount rate', *Journal of Policy Analysis and Management*, **23** (4): 789–812.

Musgrave, R.A. (1969), 'Cost–benefit analysis and the theory of public finance', *Journal of Economic Literature*: **7**: 759–806.

Newnan, Donald G., Ted G. Eschenbach and Jerome P. Lavelle (2004), *Engineering Economic Analysis*, New York: Oxford University Press.

Office of Management and Budget (1992), Circular A-94, Guidelines and Discount Rates for Benefit–Cost Analysis of Federal Programs, Washington, DC.

Portney, Paul R. and John P. Weyant (eds) (1999), *Discounting and Intergenerational Equity*, Washington, DC: Resources for the Future Press.

Ruby, M.G. (1980), 'Cost–benefit analysis with uncertain information', PhD Dissertation, University of Washington.

Strotz, R.H. (1955), 'Myopia and inconsistency in dynamic utility maximization', *Review of Economic Studies*, **23**: 165–80.

Thaler, Richard (1991), *Quasi Rational Economics*, New York: Charles Scribner's Sons.

Weitzman, Martin L. (1999), 'Just keep discounting, but . . .', in Paul Portney and John Weyant (eds), *Discounting and Intergenerational Equity*, Washington, DC: Resources for the Future Press, pp. 23–9.

Zerbe, Richard O., Jr. (1991), 'The discount rate for public projects', working paper, University of Washington.

10. Risk and uncertainty

10.1 INTRODUCTION

The benefits and costs of any project will not be known with certainty. At the very least, calculations of costs and benefits are based on estimates, and these estimates will have some degree of imprecision. The actual values for future parameters will always depend on future events. For example, the benefits of a new highway may depend on the rate of population growth in an area, and this rate of growth may turn out to be low, moderate or high. The benefits of a flu vaccination program will depend on how severe the predominant strain of flu occurring in that year would have been in the absence of the program. Uncertainty, even in the presence of exact cost and benefit calculations, is unavoidable.

A well-expressed benefit–cost study will incorporate consideration of the uncertainty and the associated risk into the analysis. Greater certainty has its own value and it may be worthwhile even if the expected values are reduced. This is similar to individuals' consideration of risk in personal decisions. The decision to fund a public disaster prevention project may be analogous to an individual's decision to purchase insurance for his/her house. While the individual cannot expect to receive more in benefits than he/she pays in premiums to the insurance company (insurers could not stay in business if this were the case) the consequences of an uninsured house burning down are sufficiently severe that the homeowner is willing to pay more than the expected loss for financial protection. Similarly, projects that reduce the risk to which a population is exposed may be desirable even if their benefits do not otherwise justify their costs. On the other hand, projects with positive net benefits that expose populations to increased risks may be undesirable even if they offer positive net benefits before accounting for risk.

This chapter begins with a discussion of uncertainty and expected value. From there, it moves to risk and risk aversion and why expected values are really only part of the story in project analysis and why projects with negative expected values may be desirable. It then discusses how risk concepts may be practically applied in BCA, given that there will not be sufficient knowledge for straightforward application of the theoretical models. From there the chapter discusses practical approaches to dealing with the uncertainty that inevitably comes with any project.

Definitions

A couple of technical terms are important to this discussion. The *states of the world* are the random outcomes that may occur. If the amount of rainfall is important to a project's valuation, the state of the world may be wet, moderate or rainy. If financial conditions are important, it may be that the inflation rate is less than 3 percent or greater than 3 percent. In terms of analyzing flu inoculations, it may be that strain A, strain B or strain C of a flu virus hits a country.

Uncertainty refers to the idea that planners do not know for certain what the state of the world will be. While they realize that different states of the world may occur, the relative probabilities of these states of the world may be unknown.

Risk is a condition where probabilities are assigned to these different states of the world and active consideration is given to how good or bad the outcomes are in each state of the world.

Risk is not typically considered in BCA and it is a rare paper or report that explicitly considers risk in its assessment of a project. This is not a desirable state of the world. The goal of this chapter is to allow the reader to see how risk might have been discussed in existing reports and to envision how it should be incorporated into consideration of ongoing or future projects. Examples 10A, 10B and 10C provide three illustrations of the risk assessment in a project decision.

EXAMPLE 10A   CONTRASTING APPROACHES TO NUCLEAR POWER

The generation of electricity using nuclear power has met with mixed results. Ignoring the serious problems with disposal of waste products (an issue touched upon elsewhere in this text) there have been problems with serious cost overruns in construction and reliability and performance problems in operation.

Different approaches have been taken to the construction of nuclear power plants in the United States and France. The United States favored large, unique generating units that were generally designed for a specific situation and constructed once. French plants relied on smaller units that were produced in relatively high numbers and then combined in large generating facilities.

Both approaches are subject to some degree of uncertainty in terms of construction cost of an individual unit and the quantity and value of the resulting electricity. There is, however, much greater risk in the US approach of building a small number of large units rather than a large number of small units. The French approach replicates the project many times, meaning that if cost and benefit expectations are accurate, the average experience should be fairly close to those expectations.

On the other hand, because the US approach involves very large projects done once, it may result in costs that are well above or benefits that are well below reasonable expected values. The diversification of risk across multiple independent projects may make the French approach preferable to the US approach.

EXAMPLE 10B   MUNICIPAL WINTER SPORTS FACILITIES

Consider a municipal department of parks and recreation serving a city in an area known for moderately cold winters. The department is considering investments in two different winter sports facilities, each of which has benefits that depend on how cold the winter weather is.

The first project is a natural skating rink that is constructed for the winter and dismantled in the spring, and the second is construction of facilities to allow skiing on a hill that the department owns. The skating rink is a one-year project and the benefits depend on the weather in that particular winter. If the winter is cold, the ice will remain frozen on the rink for several months and residents will have a good place to skate. If the weather is warm, the ice will melt and there will be no benefits from the rink. Thus, there is a great deal of risk from the investment in the skating rink.

The second project is an investment in equipment that will allow skiing for many years. These many years will include some that are relatively cold, allowing for continuous snow coverage on the hill and good skiing, and some that are relatively warm, resulting in little or no snow and poor skiing. If each year is independent, the outcome over the project lifetime should be subject to only a small amount of risk as a result of numerous independent trials. That is, over forty years the total number of cold years and the total number of warm years should be reasonably predictable.[1] There is, of course, the possibility that large-scale climate change might result in weather patterns that are not independent from one year to the next. While the risk of one warm year is less important for the investment in a skiing facility, the risk of a warming climate is very important.

EXAMPLE 10C   FLU VACCINE

When producing a flu vaccine, public health officials must make a prediction as to which flu strain is likely to be most prominent in the coming year. Predominance of different flu strains represents different states of the world and different strains have different consequences.

Imagine that there are two possible strains with different characteristics. The first strain of flu is more likely to predominate and is relatively mild. It will result in its victims experiencing moderate symptoms for a day or two. There will be a small number of missed work days and very few deaths as a result.

The second strain of flu is much less likely to occur, but is very severe. Although the probability of seeing it is very low, if it occurs its victims will be bedridden for days and there will be many resulting deaths.

Although the cost of the second strain occurring is very high, it is so unlikely that the expected damage from the second is less than the expected damage from the first.

However, it may be that the risk of the second strain of flu occurring is sufficiently great that, facing the choice of vaccinating against either the first or the second strain, public health officials choose to vaccinate against the second.

---

[1] In probabilistic terms, the number of cold years is the outcome of a binomial experiment. For example, if the lifetime of the project is forty years and probability of any one year being cold is 0.75, then the total number of cold years will be between 28 and 32 with a probability of 0.639.

10.2   EXPECTED VALUE

A straightforward and commonly used approach to valuing projects in the face of uncertainty is to calculate the project's *expected value*. The expected value is the sum of the product of the probability of each possible state of the world and the value of the project in that state of the world.[2] If you can attach probabilities for and know what the net benefits will be in each state of the world, calculating the expected value of a project is fairly simple.

Expected value is a tool to be used in evaluating projects. A project is considered beneficial if its expected value[3] is positive. When choosing between mutually exclusive projects, the decision might be made to choose the one with the greatest expected value. This use of expected value is fairly intuitive and will yield good decisions about projects under certain circumstances. Consider the following example of rafting permits (Example 10D):

EXAMPLE 10D   RAFTING PERMITS

A city department of parks and recreation is considering purchasing permits that will allow them to operate rafting trips for children and families from the city on a nearby wild and scenic river. The permits are only valid for one year and their value depends on the amount of water available. Under normal conditions, there will be sufficient water to maintain a high rate of flow through much of the summer, allowing rafting for much of the summer. Under drought conditions, there will be insufficient water to allow such high flow rates and the amount of water flowing down the river will become too low to allow rafting fairly early in the summer.

The cost of the permits is $80,000, and the department estimates their value at $40,000 in a drought year and at $110,000 in a normal year. Drought years occur with probability 0.3 while normal years occur with probability 0.7.

---

[2]   A simple example of expected value is to consider flipping a coin once and counting the number of heads that come up. You will get zero heads with probability 0.5 and one head with probability 0.5, with the result that the expected number of heads is 0.5. This demonstrates the odd nature of expected value as you will never observe half of a head on any flip of a coin.

[3]   In this case, expected value refers to the expected net benefit, or the difference between the expected benefits and the expected costs.

The expected value of purchasing the permits is $9000, as shown in the following table:

State of the world	Probability	Net benefits of permits	Probability × net benefits
Normal	0.7	+$30,000	+$21,000
Drought	0.3	−$40,000	−$12,000
			+$9,000

Expected value accounts for probabilities of outcomes. It does not, however, account for risk preferences. It is a correct technique when people are risk neutral.

Unfortunately, people in general are not risk neutral. Because of this, expected value alone may not tell us whether or not a project should be done or which of several mutually exclusive projects is most desirable. In some situations, it is entirely possible that the option with the highest expected value is the least desirable while that with the lowest expected value is most desirable. This section will seek to explain expected value and then describe its limitations.

Basics of Expected Value

As an example of calculating expected value, imagine a one-time project that will bring a large quantity of water to an isolated farming area. The cost of doing this is known with certainty to be $20 million but the benefits depend critically on rainfall. If it is a dry year, the benefits will be $50 million, if it is a moderate year, the benefits will be $25 million and if it is a wet year the benefits will be $0. If a dry year occurs with probability 0.3, a moderate year with probability 0.6 and a wet year with probability 0.1, the calculation of the expected value is shown in Table 10.1.

Table 10.1 Expected values

State of the world	Benefits	Cost	Net benefit	Probability	Net benefit × probability
Dry	$50m	$20m	$30m	0.3	$9m
Moderate	$25m	$20m	$5m	0.6	$3m
Wet	$0	$20m	−$20m	0.1	−$2m
					+$10m

Table 10.2   Expected values

Project	Benefit if successfull	Probability of success	Expected benefit	Cost	Expected value
1	$40 m	0.6	$24 m	$15 m	$9 m
2	$40 m	0.9	$36 m	$25 m	$11 m

The expected value of this project is $10 million. This is the expected value of the net benefits or, put another way, the difference between the expected benefits and the cost.

As a second example, consider two projects intended to prevent a predicted power outage that will do $40 million worth of damage if it occurs. The first project has a cost of $15 million and will prevent the outage with a probability of 0.6. The second project has a cost of $25 million and will prevent the outage with a probability of 0.9. The expected values of these projects are shown in Table 10.2.

The analysis in Table 10.2 shows that the second project has a higher expected value. One interpretation of this result is that the greater probability of preventing the outage offered by the second project is worth its extra cost.

This analysis may be extended to calculate the expected value of doing both projects. Assuming that the projects are independent, the cost will be $15 million plus $25 million or $40 million. The probability of successfully preventing the outage will be 0.96, yielding expected benefits of $38.4 million, for an expected value of −$1.6 million. The implication is that if one of the two projects is already being done, it is not worthwhile to also do the other.

Risk Preferences

Imagine that you are given the choice between receiving $400,000 for certain or participating in a lottery that will give you a prize of $1,000,000 with probability 0.5 and $0 with a probability of 0.5. When faced with a theoretical option such as this, most people say they would take the $400,000 despite the fact that the expected value of the lottery, $500,000, is greater.

As a second example, consider the fact that most people choose to diversify most of the money that they save or invest rather than putting it into only one asset with a high expected return. By diversifying rather than concentrating their investments, people are actively choosing a lower expected return.

These violations of the simple logic of expected value reduce its effectiveness in analyzing situations and either making or predicting decisions. Expected value fails to predict how individuals make private decisions and, by analogy, simple application of expected value to public decisions should be regarded with suspicion. To better understand decisions made under uncertainty and risk, we must think beyond the idea of expected value.

10.3   UTILITY AND RISK AVERSION

In considering different aspects of BCA, we have attempted to move from individual preferences and motivations to social preferences and motivations. The net benefit of a project to a community, for example, is simply the sum of the net benefits to each person in that community. Similarly, when there is risk, we can think of individual WTP or WTA for either avoidance of or exposure to that risk. The sum of individuals' values for a change in risk (either increased or decreased risk as a result of a project) is the social value of that change in risk. Similarly, the WTP or WTA for the net benefits of a project and the risk it eliminates or creates is the social value of that project.

When economists consider individuals' decisions under uncertainty, one of the important factors is the individual's attitude toward risk. In particular, if people seek out risks, they may be referred to as *risk loving*. People who are indifferent toward risk are termed *risk neutral*. Those who seek to avoid uncertainty and risk are said to be *risk averse*. The same individual may have different risk preferences based on the activity involved. The degree to which these terms describe an individual depends not only on the individual and the activity, but also on the potential level of risk. For example, many people choose to gamble with small amounts of money while also purchasing insurance against large monetary losses such as damage to their house or car. The first of these activities, gambling, suggests an attraction toward risk when the potential losses are small while purchasing insurance suggests an aversion toward risk when the potential losses are large.

The idea that an individual's attitude toward a risk depends on the risk involved may be demonstrated by the following example. First, imagine that you have the option of receiving $1,000,000 with certainty or receiving $999,999 with probability 0.5 and $1,000,001 with probability 0.5. In this case, many people would be indifferent between having the certain amount and facing the risk and would be risk neutral. Now, imagine that you have the option of receiving the same $1,000,000 with certainty or receiving $0 with probability 0.5 and $2,000,000 with probability 0.5. In this case, most people would want to avoid the risk of getting nothing in favor of getting $1,000,000 for sure and would be labeled risk averse. The first situation involves a small potential loss while the second involves a large potential loss. People may be risk neutral in the first case but risk averse in the second.

To extend this example a bit, imagine that you were given a lottery ticket that would give you a prize of $2,000,000 with probability 0.5 and nothing with a probability of 0.5. You would be willing to trade this lottery ticket for some amount of money. The expected value of the ticket is:

$$0.5 * \$2,000,000 + 0.5 * \$0 = \$1,000,000,$$

but if you are risk averse, you would be willing to trade the ticket for something less than $1,000,000. That is, you would be willing to accept a lower expected payoff in order to avoid the risk of getting nothing. If, for example, you sell the ticket for $800,000, your expected net benefit from the sale would be −$200,000. That is, in terms of expected value, you would lose $200,000 by selling the ticket. However, if you choose to sell the ticket, avoiding the risk of getting nothing must be worth that expected loss. In effect, selling the ticket is a project with a negative expected value but which is worthwhile due to the resulting reduction in risk.

Risk aversion is consistent with *decreasing marginal utility of wealth*. This is the idea that while utility (the utility derived from the consumption of material goods) increases as wealth increases, other things being the same, the marginal increase in utility from an extra unit of wealth decreases as total wealth increases. This is intuitively appealing. To a desperately poor person, an extra $100 may be the difference between starvation and survival while the same person, under more prosperous conditions, would likely use the extra money for some less important purpose, perhaps to purchase a second DVD player for his/her home. The gain in utility may be seen as being much greater in the first case than in the second.

Figure 10.1 shows a utility of wealth, $U(W)$, function, for a person who is risk averse and facing two states of the world. In the good state of the world, the person has a high level of wealth, W_H, and in the bad state of the world, he/she has a low level of wealth, W_L. Associated with these two states of the world are utility levels $U(W_H)$ and $U(W_L)$, respectively. If these two states of the world are equally likely, then the expected level of wealth is given by $E[W]$. Similarly, if these two states of the world are equally likely, then the expected level of utility is given by $E[U]$. The wealth level associated with $E[U]$ is the *certainty equivalent* (CE) of the risk, or the amount, if given with certainty, that would make a person indifferent between facing

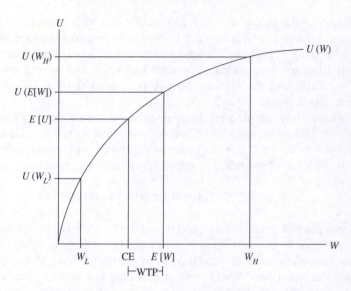

Figure 10.1   Declining marginal utility of income

that risk and getting the certain amount. Again, this individual would be indifferent between the uncertainty of having either a high or low level of wealth and having CE for certain.

The important point to note in Figure 10.1 is that the level of wealth associated with the expected utility, $E[U]$, is lower than the expected level of wealth, $E[W]$. This is because expected utility is diminished due to the risk the individual faces. If, instead, the risk was eliminated and the person received the expected level of wealth $E[W]$ with certainty, his/her utility would increase from $E[U]$ to the utility level associated with the expected level of wealth, $U(E[W])$. The person's willingness to pay for this benefit is equal to the difference between $E[W]$ and CE. Put another way, if a project eliminated the risk of W_L and simply assured that this person would get the expected value of wealth, then he/she would be willing to pay $E[W] - \text{CE}$ for the project, even though the expected net benefit of the project is zero. The implication is that projects that reduce or eliminate the risk of large losses in bad states of the world may be worthwhile even if an unsophisticated calculation suggests that they have zero or even negative net benefits.[4]

---

[4]   The program has zero net benefits because, by yielding $E[W]$ with probability 1, it reduces wealth by $W_A - E[W]$ with probability 0.5 and increases wealth by $E[W] - W_L$ with probability 0.5. If $W_H - E[W] = E[W] - W_L$, the expected net benefits of the project are zero.

Expressed in a slightly different way, the willingness to pay is an amount p such that:

$$U(E[W]-p) = U(CE).$$

That is, people would be willing to pay an amount to eliminate a risk that would leave them just as well off as they would expect to be if they were facing the risk.

As a numerical example, consider a person with utility of wealth given by $U(W) = W^{1/2}$, as shown in Figure 10.2. This person faces two states of the world. In the good state of the world, which occurs with probability 0.5, he/she has wealth of $1,000,000 and utility of wealth of 1,000. In the bad state of the world he/she has wealth of $100 and utility of 10. His/her expected utility is:

$$E[U] = 0.5 * 1,000 + 0.5 * 10 = 505.$$

His/her expected wealth is:

$$E[W] = 0.5 * \$1,000,000 + 0.5 * \$100 = \$500,050.$$

The utility that this person would get from having his/her expected level of wealth with certainty is:

$$U(\$500,050) = 500,050^{1/2} = 707.14.$$

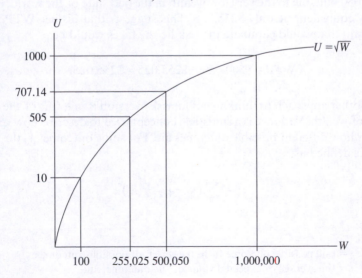

Figure 10.2 Expected utilities

This is higher than the expected utility he/she gets facing the risk of a devastating loss.

Now, imagine that a project will eliminate the probability of this loss and leave the person with his/her expected level of wealth for certain. If there are many people facing such a risk independently of one another, this may be a program that redistributes money from those who find themselves in the good state of the world to those who find themselves in the bad state. If it is a simple redistribution program, there will be no net benefits and may even be some administrative costs, suggesting that a straightforward analysis would likely reject it as failing to have positive net benefits. However, this program would eliminate the risk. The person's WTP for this elimination of risk is given by the difference between his/her expected wealth, $500,050, and the certainty equivalent of the risk he/she faces:

$$U(\text{CE}) = E(U)$$

$$U(\text{CE}) = 505$$

$$\text{CE}^{1/2} = 505$$

$$\text{CE} = 505^2 = \$255{,}025.$$

The person facing the risk described above has expected wealth of $500,050 but, due to the very low wealth in the bad state of the world, a certainty equivalent of only $255,025. This suggests that his/her WTP for a program that would eliminate the risk he/she faces would be:

$$\text{WTP} = \$500{,}050 - \$255{,}025 = \$245{,}025.$$

Another approach to thinking about risk aversion is in terms of the variance of wealth. Variance is a statistical concept used to describe how spread out or how different possible outcomes are. For some outcome, X, the variance is defined as:

$$\sigma_x^2 = \sum_x (x_i - \mu_x)^2 f(x_i),$$

where:

x_i = one possible outcome from the set of all possible outcomes;
μ_x = the average or expected value of the outcome; and
$f(x_i)$ = the probability of outcome x_i.

Table 10.3   Risk and probabilities

	State of the world	Probability	Wealth
Risk A	1	0.3	$20
	2	0.7	$500
Risk B	1	0.3	$230
	2	0.7	$410

If two situations involve some risk and have the same expected value of wealth, a risk-averse person will prefer the situation in which his/her wealth has the smaller variance.

For example, imagine the risks described in Table 10.3. There are two states of the world, State 1 and State 2. They occur with probabilities 0.3 and 0.7, respectively. If a person is subject to Risk A, he/she has wealth of $20 in State 1 and wealth of $500 in State 2. If a person is subject to Risk B, he/she has wealth of $230 in State 1 and $410 in State 2. In both states of the world, the expected level of wealth is $356.

The variance of wealth associated with Risk A is calculated as:

$$\sigma_w^2 = (20 - 356)^2 \times 0.3 + (500 - 356)^2 \times 0.7$$
$$= 48{,}384.$$

The variance of wealth associated with Risk B is calculated as:

$$\sigma_W^2 = (230 - 356)^2 \times 0.3 + (410 - 356)^2 \times 0.7$$
$$= 6804.$$

Without knowing anything about the relationship between wealth and utility, we can say that a risk-averse person would prefer to face Risk B rather than Risk A.

At the root of risk aversion is a sense that the damage suffered from a loss of some amount of money is greater than the benefit gained from receiving an equal amount. Losing $100,000 might be personally devastating while winning that same amount would be only moderately satisfying. The extra happiness I might gain from receiving an additional house would be much smaller than the sadness I would suffer at losing the one I currently own.

As an example, imagine that a person has initial wealth of $200,000 and utility of wealth given by the function $U(W) = \ln W$. If this person suffered a loss of $100,000, his/her utility level would fall from:

$$U(200{,}000) = 12.206$$

to:

$$U(100,000) = 11.513,$$

a decrease of 0.693. If, on the other hand, this person were to receive $100,000, his/her utility level would rise to:

$$U(300,000) = 12.612,$$

an increase of only 0.406. The increase in utility from the gain does not offset the decrease in utility from the loss. As a result, this person has a WTP to avoid this risk.

In general, the willingness to pay to avoid risk will be larger as the size of the potential loss increases. Losses that are small relative to a person's wealth present only a small risk. Potential losses that are large relative to a person's wealth present a significant risk and leave open the potential for a willingness to pay for avoidance.

Conversely, a project with positive expected benefits that exposes the affected population to significant risks should be regarded with healthy skepticism.

Example 10E briefly discusses risks faced by farmers in making crop choices.

Recent research into individuals' attitudes toward risk (Slovic et al., 1979 and 1999) suggests that issues beyond expected value and certainty equivalents affect the extent to which people would be willing to pay to avoid or willing to accept to incur various risks. In interviewing people about various actual or potential risks, Slovic et al. found that several characteristics of the risk itself were more important in people's assessments of the risk than the probability of occurrence or the expected loss of lives. Among the qualitative factors that seemed to matter were the potential for major disaster, the extent to which a risk was voluntary, the extent to which a risk was familiar and the extent to which a particular risk was seen as increasing or decreasing over time. Any of these factors could affect the relative importance attached to a risk and greatly distort the ranking relative to what a more straightforward analysis based on expected damages of loss of life might yield. Even more importantly, many people attach dramatically distorted numbers to the probabilities of certain disastrous events and to the typical number of lives lost to those events. Such distortions can put the policy maker in a difficult position if the public mistakenly attaches great value to the reduction in one risk when, in fact, proper analysis reveals a different risk to be much more important. In such a case, a BCA of a public education program might reveal such a program to be worthwhile. However, when public evaluation of the importance or relative importance

EXAMPLE 10E   FARM CROP CHOICES

Pity the poor farmer. He is uniquely exposed to unpredictable weather patterns. Poor weather can wipe out his crop and leave him broke while good weather can result in a bumper crop, driving prices down and leaving him broke.

One opportunity that farmers have employed over the years is to grow a variety of crops simultaneously, allowing for diversification against threats of weather, pests and low crop prices.[5] A farmer, perhaps in a developing country, may be able to increase his expected income by exclusively producing a particular cash crop (a crop that can only be sold for cash rather than eaten) but this comes with a great increase in risk. Such specialization, though potentially lucrative, exposes a farmer to financial ruin and his family to starvation if weather, pests or the market turn against him. If, indeed, an entire agricultural community is convinced to turn from its traditional set of crops to specialization in one cash crop, the results are potentially devastating.

of a particular risk is based on accurate perceptions about the likelihood of occurrence and expected loss, then the specific nature of the risk and its characteristics could appropriately enhance a more straightforward assessment and valuation.

10.4   DIVERSIFICATION: CONSIDERATION OF MULTIPLE PROJECTS

One important consideration in analyzing multiple projects is whether or not their outcomes are independent and, if they are not independent, how they are correlated. Independence suggests that the outcome from one project (or one part of a large project) is not dependent on the outcome of any other project. For outcomes that are not independent, positive correlations suggest that a good outcome in one project makes a good outcome in another project more likely and, conversely, a bad outcome in one project makes a bad outcome in another more likely. Negative correlation suggests

---

[5]   The benefits to the soil associated with crop rotation should also not be ignored, but they are not the main focus of this section.

that a good outcome in one project makes a bad outcome on another more likely. Positive correlations between projects' outcomes increase risk while negative correlations decrease risk.

For example, if fire safety regulations require installation of certain equipment in a large number of buildings scattered across a country, the experience of any two buildings is likely to be independent because a fire in one building has nothing to do with a fire in another building. In such a case, the variance of the project's net benefits will be very small and consideration of risk may be unnecessary.

On the other hand, the construction of a series of dams in a region will yield net benefits that depend on the quantity of rainfall. If the quantity of rainfall is consistent across the region, the net benefits of the dams will be positively correlated. In this case, the variance of the project's net benefits will be very large and, as a result, it may be very important to consider the risk involved.

10.5 PRACTICAL APPLICATIONS

The material presented in this chapter establishes the theory behind the consideration of risk in benefit–cost analysis. People prefer to have less rather than more variance in their wealth and will be willing to pay to reduce this variance. This WTP can be calculated given a mathematical relationship between wealth and utility, but such a relationship cannot usually be written down or analyzed. Despite this, there are situations in which consideration of risk should be incorporated into an analysis.

Consideration of risk will be important under several circumstances. First, the project being analyzed should be associated with a risk whose potential impact on a member of the affected population is large relative to his/her income or wealth. Exactly how large cannot be said with any precision, but the reader might consider how large a loss, in terms of his or her income, would be sufficient to induce consideration of the risk and an asymmetry between a gain and a loss of equal size. Impacts of ten or twenty dollars per household per year are probably not worthy of risk analysis. Potential, though perhaps unlikely, impacts of ten thousand or one hundred thousand dollars, even if they will occur to only a small number of households, are probably worthy of some sort of risk analysis.

Second, the potential loss should be uninsurable. If the people affected by the risk of the program can buy insurance against its effects, the risk can be distributed among many people and its effects reduced or eliminated. Put another way, people already have a way of eliminating the effects of insurable risks. Insurable risks include the risks against which people generally purchase insurance: automobile theft or damage, injury, disability, some types of damage to a house and so on.

Uninsurable risks differ in important ways from insurable risks. It may be that the insured individual has too much control over the outcome of the risk for a private insurer to offer insurance against it. Private unemployment insurance is not generally available because the people that would most want to buy it are either those who expect that they will become unemployed or those who intend to take actions that will leave them unemployed. It may be that the event associated with a risk would generate losses that are so large that no private insurer will choose to assume the risk. Insurance against losses from large-scale natural disasters such as floods, earthquakes or tsunamis may be prohibitively expensive or unavailable not because the expected loss is large, but because a private insurer is not able to spread the risk of the coverage among many independent individuals. If one person in a city suffers earthquake damage, it is likely that many others will as well. This is different from the effects of a burglary or a house fire that are likely to occur independently across households.

An example of an uninsurable risk that may affect a large portion of a person's wealth is the risk of declining property values in the area where he/she owns a home. This is not a loss against which insurance may usually be purchased and such a decrease in property values will likely involve a large percentage of an individual's wealth. A project that will stabilize property values, street improvements, the establishment of a park or the construction of a new school, may, in addition to their other benefits, reduce the risk homeowners in the area face of declining property values.

Another example is retirement investment. People make investments during the years that they are working in the hope that these investments will increase in value and provide them with income during their retirement. Strict reporting and disclosure requirements for the firms in which people invest may be costly in terms of compliance and enforcement, and may reduce the expected return on these retirement investments if firms must spend large amounts of money for auditing and reporting. However, if the probability of fraud and the accompanying variance in returns that people may expect is reduced, strict reporting standards may be worthwhile.

Losses that may be insurable in industrialized economies may not typically be insured in developing countries. Homeowners in industrialized countries will generally have some insurance against a house fire, but this may not be true in a rural area of a developing country. A program to replace an expensive but non-flammable building material with a cheaper but flammable building material in a rural village may seem to offer positive net benefits. However, if the risk to which flammable building materials would expose the homeowner is taken into account, the more expensive building materials may be worthwhile, even if an analysis based solely on expected value suggested otherwise.

Incorporation of some analysis of risk into a benefit–cost analysis need not be complicated. The technicalities of risk aversion and the relationship between utility and income or wealth are important only in establishing the principles of risk aversion. Simple discussion of the level of risk faced by the affected population and the effect that the considered project may have on that risk should serve as a guide in looking beyond the expected net present value of a project.

10.6   DEALING WITH UNCERTAINTY – SOURCES OF UNCERTAINTY

It is useful to distinguish between two types of uncertainty: (1) uncertainty caused by the unpredictability of future events, and (2) uncertainty caused by limitations on the precision of data. The first type of uncertainty is a consequence of our inability to foretell the future. An agricultural policy analyst cannot know with certainty what the weather will be in Kansas, Manitoba or the Ukraine during the fall harvest season and thus cannot be sure how much wheat will be produced. Of course, he/she will be able to make an estimate based on historical weather patterns, but historical patterns offer no assurance for any single year. The analyst can attempt to cope with this type of uncertainty by using forecasts, but there is no way to completely eliminate the uncertainty caused by our inability to predict future events.

The second type of uncertainty is a consequence of the inability to measure many variables with a high degree of precision at a reasonable cost. It is theoretically possible to precisely measure many variables of interest to policy makers: For example, many types of aid provided by the US federal government are allocated to states and localities based on population. The share of aid given to the city of San Diego is based on the Census Bureau's 1990 estimate of the city's population, which was 1,110,549. The probability that San Diego's population in 1990 was really 1,110,549 is essentially zero; the Bureau undoubtedly missed some individuals and probably counted some people twice. Thus, information on the exact population of San Diego is uncertain, which may affect the federal government's ability to administer policies in the way that was intended. Uncertainty of this type can be reduced by more accurate measurement, but the virtues of this accuracy are often outweighed by the time and expense required to get better information. In some cases it will be appropriate to invest the resources necessary to get more precise data; in other cases, it will be better to utilize the available data and assess the resulting uncertainty using the techniques described in this chapter.

10.7 COPING WITH UNCERTAINTY

Once it is recognized that uncertainty is an important issue for policy analysis, the obvious next question is how to deal with such uncertainty. There are three possible approaches to this problem. First, uncertainty can simply be ignored. This is appropriate in cases where the uncertainty is small, the time span of importance is short, or where the benefit–cost calculations are intended only as rough estimates. Unfortunately, uncertainty is often, probably usually, ignored by policy analysts in cases that do not fall into these categories. A second approach is to reduce uncertainty to levels at which it can safely be ignored. This usually involves gathering additional data or more accurate information on which to base the BCAs. The final approach is to recognize the uncertainty and factor it into the benefit–cost calculations. Three techniques to do this are described later in this chapter. Besides providing additional quantitative information on the benefit–cost calculation, these methods often yield several other advantages, including:

1. *Recognizing uncertainties*   The explicit recognition of uncertainties helps policy makers understand the quality of information used to support a particular decision and gives them an idea of potential problems in the analysis.
2. *Identifying information needs*   Analyzing the impacts of uncertainty on a benefit–cost calculation often highlights subjects for which better information is needed.
3. *Exploring causes of potential success or failure*   The use of methods to analyze uncertainty usually reveals factors that have the greatest influence on the possible results of a project. Once these factors are recognized, it may be possible to modify or influence them to increase the project's chances for success.
4. *Identifying options once a project is underway*   If uncertainties are analyzed before a project is begun, it is frequently possible to identify strategies to be pursued after the project is underway. In particular, the analysis may suggest conditions that indicate when the project should be terminated.

10.8   ANALYTICAL TECHNIQUES

Many techniques have been developed for dealing with uncertainty. Some of these techniques were developed with public policy analysis in mind, while others have been adapted from uses in other fields. In general, the most important analytical techniques fall into three categories:

1.   sensitivity analysis;
2.   simulation; and
3.   decision trees.

We do not consider here the third category, decision trees. The interested reader is referred to Zerbe and Dively (1994). The sections below describe these techniques and their advantages and disadvantages.

   In addition, it should be noted that both sensitivity analyses and simulations may be facilitated using the Fast Environmental Regulatory Evaluation Tool (FERET), which is described in greater detail in Chapter 12. This tool, developed specifically for analysis of environmental regulations, uses values from a variety of published environmental analyses to analyze the effects of uncertainty on the value of proposed environmental projects and offers an excellent example of how techniques for coping with uncertainty might be used elsewhere.

10.9   SENSITIVITY ANALYSIS

Sensitivity analysis is the simplest and most frequently used method for analyzing uncertainty. In essence, sensitivity analysis measures how sensitive the result of a BCA is to a change in one of the variables. The analyst would generally calculate the costs and benefits using his/her best estimate of each of the relevant factors. A more complete analysis would go a step further and test the sensitivity of the result to changes in each of the factors. There are two basic approaches to sensitivity analysis:

1.   The variable-by-variable approach, which treats each variable separately.
2.   The scenario approach, which treats variables in groups.

Variable-by-variable Approach

One common method of sensitivity analysis is to treat each individual variable separately. This method involves three analytical steps:

1.   List all variables that are important for the analysis.

2. For each variable, identify a range of possible values. In the simple problems we have considered so far in this book, we have assumed that each variable has only one possible value. When sensitivity analysis is employed, we consider the different values each variable might have. It is usually appropriate to consider three to five values for each variable, unless the range of possible outcomes for that variable is more restricted. The most common approach is to prepare 'optimistic', 'pessimistic' and 'most likely' estimates for each of the variables. The optimistic and pessimistic values can be defined in terms of a number of standard deviations above or below the mean value, if such information is available. The range of values used in the analysis is often derived from previous experience or from the experiences of other agencies with similar projects.

3. Calculate the appropriate result (such as the net present value or benefit–cost ratio) using each possible value of the variable, holding all other variables at their expected or most likely values.

If a calculation of NPV involves three variables labeled A, B and C, the analysis would begin by listing the variables and developing optimistic, pessimistic and expected values for each variable. Table 10.4 shows what this would look like.

Note that optimistic values can be either higher or lower than expected values. The optimistic value will be higher for benefits, as for items B and C, since we hope that benefits exceed our best estimate. The optimistic value will be lower for costs, as for item A, since we hope that costs are lower than our best estimate. The reverse patterns hold true for pessimistic values. Note also that there need not be a fixed relationship among the optimistic, expected and pessimistic values; for example, the optimistic value for variable B is 500 more than the expected value, while the pessimistic value is only 300 less than the expected value.

Once the values of the variables are established, the usual calculation of NPV would be made using the expected values of each of the variables. A sensitivity analysis then requires several additional calculations. First, the NPV would be calculated using the optimistic estimate for variable

Table 10.4 Range of variable values

Variable	Optimistic	Expected	Pessimistic
A	15	20	30
B	1000	500	200
C	14	13	11

A and the expected values of variables B and C. The calculation would then be repeated using the pessimistic value of A and the expected values of the other variables. These results would show how sensitive the NPV is to changes in variable A. The entire process would then be repeated using the alternative values of variable B and the expected values of variables A and C, and would be repeated again using the range of estimates for variable C along with the expected values of variables A and B. The final result illustrates the sensitivity of the NPV to changes in each of the variables. Examples 10F and 10G demonstrate sensitivity analysis.

EXAMPLE 10F   VARIABLE-BY-VARIABLE SENSITIVITY ANALYSIS

A new public hospital is expected to cost $175 million to build. The contractor says the building may cost only $160 million if conditions are ideal, but costs could escalate to $210 million if the weather is bad and materials are delayed. The benefits of the hospital for the first five years are given below in millions of dollars:

Year	1	2	3	4	5
Optimistic	45	55	55	55	55
Expected	40	50	50	50	50
Pessimistic	35	47	47	47	47

Assume the benefits in subsequent years can be ignored at this time. The appropriate discount rate is 8 percent. Using variable-by-variable sensitivity analysis, determine the NPV of this project under different combinations of variables.

Step 1:   List all important variables. In this case, these have already been combined into overall costs and benefits.

Step 2:   Identify a range of possible values. A range of costs is given above as $160 million in the optimistic case, $175 million in the most likely case and $210 million in the pessimistic case. The present value of the benefits can be found as follows (using the optimistic data as an example):

$$PV_B = \frac{\$45\,m}{1.08} + \sum_{t=2}^{5}\frac{\$55\,m}{1.08^t} = \$210.3\,m.$$

The other two possibilities are calculated in the same way. This produces the following ranges:

	Optimistic	Expected	Pessimistic
Cost	$160m	$175m	$210m
Benefits	$210.3m	$190.4m	$176.5m

Step 3: Calculate the appropriate result. In this case it is the NPV. For the expected or most likely values:

$$NPV = \$190.4 - \$175 = \$15.4 \text{ million}.$$

Similar calculations are made for the optimistic and pessimistic cases.

Optimistic case: NPV = $210.3m − $160m = $30.4m.

Pessimistic case: NPV = $176.5m − $210m = −$33.5m.

Thus, the project is desirable in all cases except when the construction costs are high. The project managers should carefully monitor these costs.

EXAMPLE 10G   BEACH IMPROVEMENTS

The Seaside City Council is considering a project to improve the community-owned beach for the coming year. The city's engineering department expects to take 45 days to complete the project, but the time could vary between 40 and 55 days depending on construction conditions. Each day of work will cost the city $2000. The city estimates that 20,000 people will use the beach this summer and that the improvements will increase the value of their experiences by an average of $5 each. However, historical data indicate that beach usage could range from 17,000 to 22,000 people. Assume that no benefits of the project will carry forward to future years. Using sensitivity analysis, identify which combinations of variables will produce an attractive benefit–cost ratio.

Step 1: List all important variables. For this analysis, construction days and beach usage are the only important factors.

Step 2: Identify a range of possible values:

	Optimistic	Most likely	Pessimistic
Days	40	45	55
Usage	22,000	20,000	17,000
Costs	$80,000	$90,000	$110,000
Benefits	$110,000	$100,000	$85,000

Step 3: Calculate the appropriate result. In this case, we will use the BCR. Note that discounting can essentially be ignored since all costs and benefits are accrued in a short time period.

	Costs		
	Optimistic	Most likely	Pessimistic
Benefits			
Optimistic	1.375	1.222	1.000
Most likely	1.250	1.111	0.909
Pessimistic	1.062	0.944	0.773

Scenario Approach

Variable-by-variable sensitivity analysis is useful for many relatively simple analyses. However, this approach assumes that variables operate independently. In our earlier example, we assumed that an optimistic value of variable A could exist with the expected values of variables B and C. In the real world, however, variables are often interdependent, and the optimistic value of variable A may only exist when variable B also assumes an optimistic value or when variable C assumes a pessimistic value.

A good example of this interdependence involves energy demand estimates prepared for the Pacific Northwest region of the United States in the early 1970s. Utility analysts noted that the demand for electricity was rising by about 7 percent per year and calculated that the region's inexpensive hydroelectric power would soon be used up. These analysts suggested that a series of new nuclear and coal-fired power plants were needed. As construction began on these plants, the cost of power began to rise, which in turn reduced demand. The eventual result was that the region had a surplus of power, higher electricity prices, and several abandoned partially completed nuclear reactors. The analysts had generally overlooked the relationship between price and demand and had assumed that rapid growth in demand would continue to exist even with higher prices. In other words, they had combined variables in ways that were not realistic.

Problems such as this can be avoided by using alternative scenarios for sensitivity analysis. Rather than using combinations of variables based upon optimistic, pessimistic and expected values, several consistent combinations of variables are studied. These combinations are known as scenarios. This type of sensitivity analysis involves two basic steps:

1. Identify several possible consistent combinations of variables.
2. Compute the result (such as the NPV) for each scenario.

The analyst can then see which scenarios are likely to produce favorable or unfavorable results and can make decisions about the project accordingly. Example 10H explains this idea using a work-incentive program.

EXAMPLE 10H   A WORK-INCENTIVE PROGRAM

A state government is considering a new work-incentive program for people receiving public assistance. The program would pay participants $1000 if they received instruction in job search techniques. The total cost per participant is $2000, which includes the cost of the instruction and the payments to individuals. Each individual who obtains a job will save the state $10,000 in public assistance costs. No one is certain, however, how many individuals will participate in the program and what percentage will get jobs, but the general belief is that the more people who participate the lower the percentage getting jobs will be. Several scenarios are possible:

Scenario	Participants	Percentage getting jobs
1	10,000	22%
2	15,000	15%
3	25,000	12%
4	37,000	10%

Calculate the NPV of this program under each scenario. Assume that all costs and benefits occur simultaneously so no discounting is needed.

Step 1:   Identify several scenarios. These are listed above.

Step 2:   Calculate the NPV under each scenario. Since no discounting is needed, the NPV is simply the difference between the costs and the benefits.

For Scenario 1:

$$NPV = (10,000)(0.22)(\$10,000) - (10,000)(\$2,000) = \$2,000,000.$$

This shows 22 percent of 10,000 people getting jobs worth $10,000 each, minus the cost of providing training for 10,000 people at $2000 each.
  Similarly,

Scenario 2: NPV = −$7,500,000
Scenario 3: NPV = −$20,000,000
Scenario 4: NPV = −$37,000,000.

Thus, the program has a positive NPV only if it is relatively small and has a high placement rate. This suggests that the program might benefit from restricting the size, screening applicants and selecting those that seem most promising. Note, however, that there may be other benefits from the training that are not included in this financial analysis.

Advantages and Disadvantages

Sensitivity analysis has several advantages as a technique for analyzing uncertainty. It gives some information about possible outcomes under different circumstances and therefore allows more informed decisions to be made. It forces recognition of key variables and their possible implications, and in scenario analysis it recognizes the interactions among variables. The results may indicate areas in which further research should be conducted to get better data before a project is undertaken.

Sensitivity analysis is subject to important limitations, however. First, there are no definite rules for choosing values for variables or for selecting pessimistic and optimistic estimates for variables, so the meaning of the results is not entirely clear. Second, it is often difficult to get information about alternative estimates for each variable, and it is likewise hard to develop consistent scenarios. Third, the variable-by-variable approach overlooks interaction among the variables and may therefore lead to the analysis of impossible combinations of variables. Finally, the scenario approach is limited in that usually only a small number of scenarios are considered.

These strengths and weaknesses suggest that sensitivity analysis is best suited for relatively simple problems or for problems where rough accuracy is sufficient. Sensitivity analysis is best used to illustrate the range of possible outcomes and to identify variables for which better information or more precise controls are needed.

Extended Example: The Applewhite Reservoir[6]

Plans to build the Applewhite Reservoir near San Antonio, Texas, have existed since the 1970s and have been a major political issue in the area during the last decade. Voters have rejected construction proposals twice; the first time (Applewhite I) was after construction had already been underway for six months.

General Applewhite I project description
This reservoir would be located along the Medina River and would hold water to be used by the City and part of the capital cost would be for a water treatment plant and additions to the City's water. The water from Applegate would, however, be of lower quality than the existing water due to many polluted sources in the reservoir's watershed.

Applewhite's estimated capital and operation and maintenance (O&M) costs are shown in Table 10.5. These numbers were estimates subject to error (historically, water projects have cost much more than original estimates). For many harmful project effects, there was no effort to make even rough estimates. These include the effects of reduced flows into coastal bays and estuaries and the costs of ostensibly mitigating habitat loss.

Table 10.5   Costs of Applewhite's

Year	Capital costs	O&M costs
1989	$ 7.894m	$3.44m
1990	$19.054m	$3.44m
1991	$32.246m	$3.44m
1992	$68.170m	$3.44m
1993	$52.404m	$3.44m

---

[6]   This example is based on Merrifield (1997).

There were no official estimates of the project's benefits. Proponents asserted that the benefits would be greater than any reasonable costs. Here benefits are estimated from published projections and from data in the 1988 Water Statistics.

Sources of controversy and uncertainty

For Applewhite I, the key uncertainty factors were: (i) The appropriate discount rate. (ii) The life of the project; the time until the project would be shut down unless major new capital outlays were made. (iii) The rate of increase in demand, which depends on future population growth and per capita water use. (iv) The yield of the project. (v) The scarcity of water; rainfall and the availability of water from other competitive sources. (vi) Other costs (distribution, lowered overall water quality and so on) associated with delivering the Applewhite water to San Antonio City Water Board (SACWB) customers. (vii) Environmental impacts. (viii) Except for the management option that maximizes the water yield (where water yield is the only benefit), project benefits other than increased water supplies (largely recreational) to the SACWB.

Interpretation of the results of reinvented BCA

The most probable scenario is the starting point for the sensitivity analysis. Advocates of Applewhite I believed it would have an average annual yield of 48,000 acre-feet (af)[7] and that demand for water from the SACWB would increase at least 1.11 percent per year. The annual benefits from the project would have been the yield (Q) multiplied by the difference between the price (P) at which users consume that yield plus any additional less expensive available water and other (non-project related, not covered in the projected costs) water service costs. The latter are called non-production costs (NPC). In equation form, annual benefits are: Annual Benefits $= Q *$ ($P -$ NPC). Assume that 400,000 af of water are available annually from sources that are cheaper than the proposed water project and that the annual yield of the water project would be 50,000 af. P is the price that would cause the amount purchased to be 450,000 af/year. (Note also that the SACWB was reorganized and renamed the San Antonio Water System [SAWS] not long after the demise of Applewhite I.) Price measures WTP for the marginal water delivered to ratepayers' homes. Since Applewhite I costs are for extra water available to the distribution system, the price (P) paid by ratepayers would be an overestimate of marginal benefits (MB) of additional water. Since average revenue (AR) was used as a proxy for P and

---

[7] An acre-foot is the quantity of water required to cover one acre of land to a depth of one foot.

since the SACWB was using increasing block rate pricing, $(P - NPC)$ is an underestimate of MB. However, to value a large addition to supply, an underestimate of MB is appropriate.[8] It was assumed that the San Antonio Water System (SAWS: the new name) would retain access to the pre-existing Edwards Aquifer at least at historic use levels prevailing through 1988 and that NPC would be at least $100/af (NPC = $258/af in 1988) for the life of the project. It was assumed that the project life would be 30 to 50 years, and based on Hoehn and Randall (1987), it was assumed that 3–9 percent was the relevant range of sensible, inflation-adjusted discount rates.

Tables 10.6–10.9 present samples of NPV and BCR results. The informative result of the proposed revision of formal BCA practices is the totality of the information in those tables. The general size of the numbers is quite important. The tables also reveal factors that produce switch points (where NPV goes from positive to negative or where B/C goes from greater than one to less than one). Most of the interpretations of the data would be evident to any reader, a big plus.

The figures in Tables 10.6–10.9 show many more BCRs that are less than one than are greater than one. Certainly if this is the reasonable range of variables, its project does not have a financial justification. One might reasonably argue, however, that 3 percent is the best estimate for the relevant public project interest rate. Still to justify the project, one would also need to maintain that the low-cost scenarios were more likely. This might be difficult to do. These tables make it clear that proponents would need to justify a low cost, low interest rate and at least a 40-year life scenario to provide quantitative support for the project.

Table 10.6   Low demand growth (growth = 1.11%), low cost ($100/af)

Discount rate %	Ratio of benefits to costs		
	30-yr life	40-yr life	50-yr life
3	0.87	1.03	1.17
4	0.78	0.90	1.00
5	0.69	0.79	0.85
6	0.62	0.69	0.74
7	0.56	0.61	0.64
8	0.51	0.55	0.57
9	0.46	0.49	0.50

---

8   See Hoehn and Randall (1987) for details.

Table 10.7   High demand growth (1.78%), low cost (100/af)

Discount rate %	Ratio of benefits to costs		
	30-yr life	40-yr life	50-yr life
3	0.98	1.21	1.42
4	0.87	1.04	1.19
5	0.78	0.90	1.00
6	0.69	0.79	0.85
7	0.62	0.69	0.74
8	0.56	0.61	0.64
9	0.50	0.54	0.56

Table 10.8   Low demand growth (1.11%), high cost ($200/af)

Discount rate %	Ratio of benefits to costs		
	30-yr life	40-yr life	50-yr life
3	0.50	0.62	0.72
4	0.44	0.53	0.60
5	0.39	0.46	0.51
6	0.35	0.40	0.43
7	0.31	0.35	0.37
8	0.28	0.31	0.32
9	0.25	0.27	0.28

Table 10.9   High growth (1.78%), high cost ($200/af)

Discount rate %	Net present value		
	30-yr life	40-yr life	50-yr life
3	0.61	0.80	0.97
4	0.54	0.67	0.79
5	0.47	0.58	0.66
6	0.42	0.49	0.55
7	0.37	0.43	0.46
8	0.33	0.37	0.40
9	0.30	0.33	0.34

Comparison of traditional and reinvented BCA

In a traditional BCA (done honestly), the authors would make a serious effort to select the best data, calculation methods, and assumptions and then go to great lengths to justify and defend selections. They would then compute a single NPV and BCR, make recommendations based on those computations, and then put a table in an appendix that shows how sensitive that result is to one or two of the key uncertainties.

Suppose that for Applewhite I, that process led the analyst to pick a discount rate of 6 percent, project life of 40 years, demand growth of 1.11 percent per year, and NPC of $200/af. The project return is 40 cents in benefits for each $1 spent, for a total loss of $116.9 million 1989 dollars over the 40-year life of the project.

Without the sensitivity analysis (SA) presented in Tables 10.6–10.9, it would not be difficult for a determined project advocate to dismiss the results by generally criticizing the data inputs used or to base dismissal on a disagreement with just one of them. The SA makes such criticism much less likely, especially if the project proponents conduct or sponsor the BCA. The SA indicates that it would take major departures from the BCA authors' most probable scenario, or huge unquantified benefits, for the project to be feasible. Indeed, the SA identifies the switch points that bound the range of conditions under which the project is feasible. Project proponents will have to defend the future plausibility of such conditions to justify a decision to proceed – a much more difficult process than dismissing a traditional BCA by criticizing a single set of assumed conditions and practices.

10.10 MONTE CARLO SIMULATION

The second important technique for dealing with uncertainty is simulation. Simulation is an outgrowth of sensitivity analysis that considers many possible combinations of variables, rather than a few estimates or a few scenarios. It can thus be a very powerful analytic tool. This power comes at the expense of requiring a great deal of information. Here we consider Monte Carlo simulation, probably the most widely used simulation.

Monte Carlo simulation relies on a computer to perform a large number of calculations that reflect many possible combinations of variables. This technique requires three major analytical steps:

1. Develop a computerized model of the project's cash flows (or other factors of interest). The model should include equations showing the relationships among the different variables.

2. Specify the probabilities for different results for each of the variables.
3. Sample the probability distributions and calculate the resulting cash flows.

The analyst must conduct the first two steps, while the computer performs the calculations required in the third step. Hundreds or thousands of combinations of variables are tested by the computer in a typical simulation.

The result of the simulation is a probability distribution of the project's cash flows and probable NPVs over a wide range. We recommend using a program such as Crystall Ball. These are generally easy to use and quite powerful. The result of the simulation is a probability distribution of the project's cash flows. This distribution reveals the range of possible cash flows resulting from the project and shows which results are more likely than others. The expected value of the cash flow, which is found from the mean of the probability distribution, can be used to calculate the NPV, the B/C or other results of interest. The variance of the simulated distribution can also be determined.

The example below shows how Monte Carlo simulation can be used for a very simple problem. In practice, a problem such as this would never be solved through simulation, but it does illustrate the basic approach in an understandable way. Most simulation problems are considerably more complex than the one described in the example. This complexity usually stems from one or more of the following characteristics:

1. *More variables with more interrelationships*   The example includes only three variables, and only two of them are related. In most real simulation problems, there are more variables and the variables are often related in complex ways.
2. *More complex probability distributions*   The probability distribution in the example is very simple. Only four discrete values for N are possible and each of the possibilities has a fixed probability. Usually, each variable can assume a wide range of values.
3. *Variability over time*   Example 10I, the relationships among variables and the probability distribution for N do not change over time. This allows us to use the same result for B for each of the eight years of the project's lifespan. In many simulation problems, however, the relationships among variables and the probability distributions do change in successive years. If fact it is common to have problems where the results in a particular year are dependent upon the results of previous years.

EXAMPLE 10I   HIGHWAY LIGHTING

A state highway department is considering a plan to improve light-
ing on a dangerous section of a rural highway. The improvements
would cost $5,000,000 and would last for eight years. The lighting
would help to reduce accidents, but the department's planners do
not know exactly how many accidents would be prevented. Based
upon experience at similar sites, they have prepared probability
estimates for the number of accidents that would be prevented
each year.

Accidents prevented	Probability
9	30%
10	40%
11	20%
12	10%

Each accident that is prevented will yield $100,000 in benefits. If the
discount rate is 10 percent, is this project a worthwhile investment?
   This problem can be solved using Monte Carlo simulation. It is
a relatively simple problem and could be solved using other techniques, but it will help to illustrate the approaches used to solve
more complex simulation problems.

Step 1:   Develop a computer model. There are only three variables involved in this problem: costs (C), benefits (B) and the
number of accidents prevented (N). The costs are fixed:

$$C = \$5,000,000.$$

The benefits are a function of the number of accidents prevented:

$$B = \$100,000 \times N$$

This equation is the only one necessary for the computer model.

Step 2:   Specify the probabilities. The probabilities for N are
shown in the table above. The same probabilities apply to each of
the eight years of the project's lifespan, so only one set of calculations needs to be made.

Step 3: Sample the distribution and calculate cash flows. The computer now uses the equation relating *B* and *N* and the probability distribution for *N* to calculate values for *B*. It chooses values for *N* in proportion to their probability; that is, the computer is four times more likely to choose an *N* of 10 than an *N* of 12 since the probability of *N* being 10 is four times greater than the probability of *N* being 12. For each choice of *N*, the computer calculates *B* and stores the result. After several hundred or thousand calculations, the computer produces the following probability distribution for *B*:

Value of *B*	Probability
$ 900,000	0.30
$1,000,000	0.40
$1,100,000	0.20
$1,200,000	0.10

Based upon these results, the expected value of *B* is $1,010,000. The NPV will then be the present value of this over 8 years at 10 percent minus the costs of $5,000,000 for an NPV of $388,275.

Advantages and Disadvantages

Simulation is an extremely powerful technique that allows many combinations of variables to be explored. A simulation analysis produces information about the range of likely results, along with an estimate of the expected value. Simulations often reveal combinations of variables that produce unexpected outcomes, allowing the project to be redesigned to accommodate these outcomes. For all these reasons, simulation can be very valuable in analyzing complex projects.

However, simulation suffers from three disadvantages. First, it is often difficult to prepare good probability estimates for each of the variables. Second, it is also often difficult to develop equations that reflect all the possible interactions among variables. Third, preparing a computer model can be expensive and time consuming, although the availability of powerful computers and standardized statistical software packages have made this problem less significant.

A review of these advantages and disadvantages suggests that simulation is best suited for relatively complex projects and for projects that need to be very carefully analyzed. In these cases, the time and expense involved in preparing a simulation are usually justified. For simpler projects or projects that do not require detailed uncertainty analysis, simulation is usually unnecessary.

10.11   CONCLUSION

All projects are conducted under some level of uncertainty. Any number of factors may be uncertain and may lead to a project being unexpectedly desirable or undesirable. Under some conditions, examining a project using expected value will yield a good decision about whether or not it should be undertaken. However, if there are relatively large potential losses for some members of the affected population, either as a result of doing or not doing a project, some consideration of risk may be appropriate. A variety of approaches is available for attempting to understand the importance of uncertainty regarding various aspects of the project to its ultimately being desirable or not. Use of these techniques can offer insights into the likelihood of a project being beneficial.

REFERENCES

Hoehn, John P. and Alan Randall (1987), 'A satisfactory benefit cost indicator from contingent valuation', *Journal of Environmental Economics and Management*, **14** (3): 226–47.

Merrifield, John (1997), 'Sensitivity analysis in benefit–cost analysis', *Contemporary Economics Policy*, **15** (3): 82–92.

Slovic, Paul, Baruch Fischhoff and Sarah Lichtenstein (1999), 'Facts and fears: understanding perceived risk', in Kenneth G. Willis, Kenneth Button and Peter Nijkamp (eds), *Environmental Valuation, Volume 1: Methods and Anomalies*, Cheltenham, UK and Northampton, MA, USA: Edward Elgar, pp. 319–52.

Slovic, Paul, Sarah Lichtenstein and Baruch Fischhoff (1979), 'Images of disaster: perception and acceptance of risks from nuclear power', in G.T. Goodman and W.D. Rose (eds), *Energy Risk Management*, London: Academic Press, pp. 219–45.

Zerbe, Richard and Dwight Dively (1994), *Benefit–Cost Analysis in Theory and Practice*, Chapter 17, New York: Harper & Row.

11. Case studies

11.1 INTRODUCTION

We now offer two case studies in benefit–cost analysis that deal with important contemporary policy issues: the ethanol tax exemption and a ban on the use of cell phones while driving. The purpose of these case studies is to indicate some of the richness that is present when addressing actual cases in the real world. The cases are written from a broad perspective in which distributional effects and other considerations play a role. In this regard they combine benefit–cost analysis with policy analysis. Readers should ask themselves at least the following questions: (1) what are the technical limitations of the case studies? (2) What are the other limitations? (3) If in a decision-making position, what should one do on the basis of the information provided? (4) What additional information would one desire before making a decision? (5) How should the information be provided (that is, in what form) to decision makers?

The ethanol case study attempts to parse a complex and difficult policy proposal into a benefit–cost, policy analysis. The cell phone example was motivated by the fact that one of the authors suspected that the study that was done might have mis-estimated costs of the ban, and perhaps overestimated benefits. No conclusion about this is reached. Both of these cases involve on-going public policy questions so that the interested reader can follow the events in the public sector as they unfold.

11.2 ETHANOL CASE STUDY: A BENEFIT–COST ANALYSIS OF THE FEDERAL MOTOR FUELS ETHANOL TAX EXEMPTION

Ethanol is a gasoline substitute or additive that is derived from agricultural products, most commonly corn. The cost of producing a gallon of ethanol is generally higher than the cost of producing a gallon of gasoline. For this reason, it is unlikely that large quantities of fuel ethanol would be produced, except that there is a federal gasoline tax exemption granted to blends of gasoline and ethanol. Production of ethanol is largely due to this tax exemption, essentially making the tax exemption a program to promote the use of corn and other agricultural products for the distillation of ethanol in the United States.

The ethanol tax exemption takes a somewhat unusual and complicated form. The exemption applies to fuels containing 10 percent ethanol and amounts to $0.052 of the $0.184 per gallon federal gasoline tax. That is, the blending of ethanol with gasoline in a ratio of 1:9 lowers the federal tax on a gallon of the resulting gasoline blend by $0.052, implying a tax exemption of $0.52 per gallon of ethanol used. This tax exemption has the effect of increasing ethanol production by an estimated 1.2 billion gallons per year and virtually all of the ethanol produced is blended with gasoline in this way.

The question that this case study will address is whether the tax exemption and resulting increase in ethanol production result in positive or negative net benefits and how large these net benefits might be. Further, we will attempt to describe how the benefits and costs of the exemption are distributed, as some people would use this as an argument to either sustain the program in spite of net losses or terminate it in spite of net gains.[1] Ideally, BCAs would be performed from a societal or universal perspective in which all individuals would have standing, but for illustrative purposes, this case study will consider how a change in assumptions regarding standing would change the results.

This case study begins with the simplest assumptions and most concrete numbers regarding ethanol production. An assessment of the program will be offered based on this simple scenario. Then some of the myriad complexities and distortions surrounding ethanol will be considered and their impacts on the overall assessment calculated. The ultimate goal is to provide as correct and complete a consideration of the ethanol tax exemption as possible in the hope of guiding future policy in this area.

In particular, there are several complications that will be considered. The first is that the ethanol tax exemption has a large impact on tax revenues. How these are treated in an analysis depends critically on assignments of standing. The second is that the primary inputs into ethanol production (corn and other grains) are produced under federal price support programs that may distort the prices of these inputs but, in the context of an analysis of ethanol, should be taken as exogenous. The third is that the blending of ethanol with gasoline, though resulting in several externalities, may generate environmental benefits. The fourth is that gasoline and ethanol are produced by firms that have market power, with the implication that market prices may be above the marginal costs of production. The fifth is that the

---

[1] Of course, wealth redistribution should usually be handled through programs specifically intended to redistribute wealth and not through other public projects.

benefits and costs of this ethanol support program are not evenly distributed, so there are distributional implications to consider.

Finally, there will be some consideration of intangible effects of the ethanol exemption. Given the more easily quantified figures from the preceding sections of the analysis, readers might ask themselves how the intangible effects of the ethanol exemption compare with the quantified net benefits.

The analysis presented here is based on descriptions, facts and figures presented in 'Fuel Ethanol: Background and Public Policy Issues' (hereafter referred to as 'the report') prepared by Brent D. Yacobucci and Jasper Womach of the Congressional Research Service.[2] Other sources are as noted.

The Basic Model

A basic assessment of ethanol production should examine the costs of production and the value of the ethanol and by-products produced. In the simplest sense, the value of the ethanol produced is limited by the value of a gallon of gasoline, a substitute for ethanol. Given that one bushel of corn generates approximately 2.7 gallons of ethanol, the simplest analysis would compare the cost of a bushel of corn divided by 2.7, plus the average production cost for ethanol, minus the value of any by-products of ethanol production, with the wholesale price of a gallon of gas. According to the report, 'the average price (for corn) received by farmers is forecast by USDA to average about $2.10 per bushel for the 2003/04 marketing year'. This means that the value of the corn in a gallon of ethanol is about $0.78. This may be compared with the wholesale price for gasoline, which ranges from $0.65 to $1.03, not including taxes. The value of the corn that goes into a gallon of ethanol, even at the relatively low price of $2.10/bushel, may exceed the cost of gasoline.[3]

In addition to the cost of the raw material, there will be costs incurred to convert (through distillation) the corn into ethanol. The report does not say what these costs are, and they are likely to vary from one producer to another. However, if the market for ethanol production is sufficiently competitive, the wholesale price for ethanol should approximate the marginal

---

2   The version of this report upon which the analysis is based was released in September of 2003. The report is updated occasionally and may be found at the National Council for Science and the Environment's National Library for the Environment web site, http://www.NCSEonline.org/NLE/CRS/.

3   In fact, provisions of the 2002 Farm Bill (details at www.doa.gov) set a target price of about $2.60 for corn, suggesting that approximately $1.00 worth of corn goes into a gallon of ethanol.

cost of production less the marginal value of saleable by-productions. Similarly, if the wholesale market for gasoline is sufficiently competitive, the price should approximate the marginal cost of production for gasoline. The wholesale price for ethanol ranges from $0.94 to $1.33, generally about $0.30 higher than the price of gasoline, suggesting that the marginal cost of ethanol is greater than the marginal cost of gasoline.

If a benefit of producing ethanol is a reduction in the production of gasoline, the net value of this benefit is equal to the marginal cost of producing a gallon of gasoline minus the marginal cost of producing a gallon of ethanol. Because the marginal cost of producing ethanol is likely greater than the marginal cost of producing gasoline, the net benefits of producing ethanol are negative. While some producers of ethanol may have a comparative advantage, on average producing ethanol consumes more resources than producing gasoline, perhaps by as much as the difference in the price of the two fuels, or about $0.30/gallon. If, as stated in the report, the ethanol tax exemption results in the additional production of 1.2 billion gallons of ethanol each year, this is equivalent to an annual loss of $360 million.

This result, under these simple assumptions, is a confirmation of the efficiency of markets. In the absence of taxes and the ethanol exemption, ethanol production would be dramatically reduced because the cost of private inputs used to produce ethanol is greater than the cost of the private inputs used to produce gasoline. If both products were taxed equally, gasoline would maintain its cost advantage and ethanol production would be reduced. The differential taxation of gasoline and ethanol distorts the decision from what would otherwise prevail in an efficient market, with the result being that too many resources go into ethanol production. If the tax exemption for ethanol is to be justified, it must be on the grounds that there are sufficiently large problems with the markets surrounding agricultural products, energy and the environment, or perhaps that there are important distributional considerations that cannot be addressed in any other way.

Before we turn to these issues that may or may not justify the ethanol exemption, let us first consider the effects of the ethanol exemption on federal tax revenues.

Effects on Tax Revenues and Why Standing Matters

One effect of the federal exemption for ethanol is a reduction in federal tax revenues. How large an impact the exemption might have depends on assumptions about what would happen to gasoline production if the ethanol exemption were removed and ethanol production fell. More importantly, the classification of the reduction in federal taxes as a cost, a transfer or a benefit of the ethanol exemption depends on the point of view taken in an analysis.

Assuming that in the absence of the exemption gasoline production would expand to compensate for lost ethanol production, federal motor fuel tax revenues would rise by 1.2 billion gallons (the amount of ethanol production attributed to the exemption) multiplied by $0.52/gallon, or about $624 million annually.

How this $624 million reduction in tax revenues should be considered depends on who is granted standing in an analysis of the ethanol exemption. If the analysis is done from the point of view of the federal government, reduced tax revenues are a cost of the ethanol tax exemption. If the analysis is done with universal standing, these tax revenues are simply a transfer and are irrelevant to an analysis of the program. Finally, if the analysis is done from the point of view of ethanol producers and consumers, this $624 million is an annual benefit of the exemption.

Effect of Corn Price Support Programs

The usual assumption in BCA is that markets are working efficiently and that marginal value and marginal cost are at least roughly equated. However, in the US prices for some agricultural products are supported at levels above what might dominate in the absence of support or protection programs. If price supports are in place, caution should be exercised in using market prices as a measure of either the marginal value or the marginal cost of agricultural products used as inputs into ethanol production. Further, if an analysis of ethanol is done with the assumption that agricultural support programs exist and are unchangeable, then the effect of the ethanol exemption on agricultural support payments should be incorporated into the analysis.

The effect of the ethanol tax exemption is to increase demand for some agricultural products, primarily corn. It results in the consumption of more corn than would otherwise be consumed and in higher prices for corn and potentially greater production in domestic markets.

If the ethanol exemption results in increased corn production, the cost of the extra corn produced should be the marginal cost of its production, and this should be equal to the average of the price that producers receive with the ethanol exemption in place and the price that they would receive were it not in place.

The difference between the market price and the price received by producers for a bushel of corn depends on the exact form of the price support program that is in place. The US Farm Bill of 2002 establishes an effective price floor of $2.10 per bushel of corn. This is done through a loan program in which farmers may receive loans equal to $2.10 multiplied by their total expected number of bushels produced. The collateral offered for the loan is the crop itself, so if the price of corn turns out to be below $2.10, farmers can retire the loan by surrendering the corn. So, corn producers receive at least this price for their product and, according to economic theory, will produce additional output until their marginal cost rises to this level.

The effect of federal price supports is complicated by the fact that the ethanol program increases the demand for corn and, thus, makes corn prices higher than they otherwise would be. According to the report, 'Economists estimate that when supplies are large, the use of an additional 100 million bushels of corn raises the price by about 4 cents per bushel. When supplies are low, the price impact is greater'. According to the report, without the tax exemption, ethanol production would fall by about 80 percent, suggesting a reduction of about 736 million bushels in the demand for corn, resulting in a decrease of about $0.29 in the price. Total corn production is about 9.6 billion bushels. If support payments were necessary to maintain the price floor of $2.10 per bushel, eliminating the ethanol exemption would increase transfer payments by about $0.29 for all bushels produced, potentially as much as $2.8 billion. When no support payments are required to preserve the price floor, the ethanol exemption has no impact.

Proper treatment of ethanol's effect on support payments depends on standing. If both taxpayers and farmers have standing, then support payments to farmers are simply transfers and any reduction in these payments resulting from the ethanol tax exemption would simply be a reduction in a transfer and would count neither as a cost nor as a benefit. If taxpayers have standing but farmers do not, then a reduction in transfer payments would be a benefit of the ethanol exemption. Finally, if farmers have standing but taxpayers do not (perhaps because the analysis is prepared on behalf of a major beneficiary of the ethanol subsidy) then any reduction in transfer payments would be a cost of the ethanol tax exemption.

Environmental Benefits of Ethanol

Ethanol production has several environmental impacts. While these are probably prohibitively difficult to value accurately, they do deserve mention here.

First, if ethanol production displaces gasoline production, it will have the effect of reducing negative externalities associated with refining crude oil into gasoline. This will be a benefit as long as the negative environmental impact of gasoline production is greater than the negative environmental impact of ethanol production. However, if there are significant negative externalities associated with ethanol distillation, then the exemption may increase external damages associated with fuel production.[4]

Second, ethanol is an oxygenate, used in the Midwest during certain times of the year either as a component in reformulated gasoline (RFG) or on its own to improve the efficiency with which gasoline combusts, reducing formation of carbon monoxide (CO) and volatile organic compounds (VOCs) and improving air quality. In addition, ethanol can replace methyl tertiary butyl ether (MTBE), a component of reformulated fuels that has been linked to groundwater contamination. However, while ethanol may be environmentally beneficial, its use in RFG or as an oxygenate is largely the result of federal mandate and would likely persist if the tax exemption were eliminated. Attributing these environmental benefits to the tax exemption is probably inappropriate.

Effect of Imperfect Competition in the Production of Ethanol and Gasoline

The appropriate value to attach to the additional resources used to produce ethanol instead of gasoline is the difference between the marginal cost of producing ethanol and the marginal cost of producing gasoline. If ethanol and gasoline markets were sufficiently competitive, the market price would be a close approximation of the marginal cost and could be used to value these extra resources. Unfortunately, both gasoline and ethanol are produced in markets that exhibit some degree of concentration, so it may be the case that wholesale market prices are above the marginal cost of production. If, however, the degrees of concentration of the ethanol distillation and petroleum refining markets in the relevant geographic area are roughly similar, then the percentage by which the price of each product exceeds its marginal cost should be approximately equal.

If it were the case that gasoline production was perfectly competitive and ethanol production was highly concentrated, then the higher price of ethanol might simply be attributed to a markup above marginal cost and it would be possible that the marginal cost of producing ethanol could be equal to the marginal cost of producing gasoline. The higher price attached to ethanol would be a cost to consumers of ethanol and a benefit to producers of ethanol. If an analysis of the exemption adopted universal standing (or, at the very least granted standing to both consumers and producers)

---

4 There is anecdotal evidence that ethanol production can result in significant negative externalities. See 'Air pollution uncovered at ethanol plants . . .', *Lancaster New Era*, March 11, 2004, p. A-1, and 'St. Paul residents protest ethanol plant emissions . . .', *Minneapolis Star Tribune*, September 12, 2000, p. 1B.

then the markup would simply be a transfer and there would be no extra cost associated with production of ethanol instead of gasoline.

Distributional Considerations

Distributional effects should not generally be used to justify a program that is not purely redistributional. It would always be more efficient to levy a lump-sum tax on the general population and make a direct transfer to the people that might be helped. However, a discussion of the ethanol tax exemption should discuss who is gaining and who is losing.

Costs of the ethanol tax exemption are imposed on non-ethanol corn consumers, gasoline producers and US taxpayers.

Because the ethanol tax exemption increases demand for corn and, depending on the price floor established by price support programs, the price of corn, other consumers of corn may be hurt by the ethanol exemption. These may include people who raise corn-fed livestock as well as people who more directly consume corn and corn products such as corn syrup.

The ethanol tax exemption reduces the demand for gasoline. This will reduce the profits of companies involved in extracting and refining crude oil and in wholesaling and retailing gasoline. To the extent that this affects domestic oil companies, the stockholders of those companies suffer losses. It may also be that the oil producers hurt are nationalized foreign oil companies. In this case, residents (or, perhaps, governments) of those countries suffer a loss.

Benefits of the ethanol tax exemption go to corn producers, ethanol producers, ethanol consumers and, to the extent that the ethanol exemption reduces corn price supports, US taxpayers.

Because the ethanol tax exemption raises the price of corn by at least $0.29/bushel, corn producers benefit from the exemption. These producers may be small family farmers or may be large agribusiness corporations, so the benefits may be distributed to small family farmers or to stockholders of these corporations. However, if the ethanol exemption simultaneously raises the price of corn and reduces support payments to corn producers, ethanol offers no benefit to these people.

The tax exemption directly benefits ethanol producers, a concentrated industry in which the four largest producers, topped by Archer Daniels Midland (ADM), control about 44 percent of the production capacity. The exemption benefits these producers or, more specifically, their stockholders.

The tax exemption also has the potential to benefit ethanol consumers to the extent that the exemption is reflected in the retail fuel price. Because ethanol cannot be transported through petroleum pipelines its distribution is somewhat limited, meaning that ethanol consumers are generally people who live in corn-producing regions. Most commonly they are residents of metropolitan areas in the Midwest. Of course, the extent to which consumers benefit from the exemption depends on how much of the value of the exemption is passed along to consumers. Depending on the structure of the fuel market it may be that suppliers (or their stockholders) enjoy these benefits. So, benefits of the ethanol exemption accrue to corn producers in the rural Midwest and, perhaps, to urban residents of Midwestern states, suggesting the potential for a concentration of benefits.

The remaining effect is on US taxpayers. The ethanol exemption is a burden on taxpayers as there must be either increased taxes or reduced government services to compensate for the lost federal fuels tax revenue. However, if corn prices are low enough that support payments would otherwise be made, the ethanol exemption may raise the corn price enough to prevent these payments and reduce the burden on US taxpayers.

Overall, the ethanol exemption benefits stockholders in agricultural and ethanol-producing corporations while hurting stockholders in oil companies and other corn-using industries. The exemption benefits farms and farmers who produce corn while hurting ranchers and livestock companies that use corn. It usually hurts taxpayers, but may help them when corn prices are unusually low. It also helps people living in a small number of cities in the Midwest, both by slightly reducing motor fuel costs and, perhaps, by improving air quality. It is not clear that costs and benefits of ethanol are distributed in such a way as to particularly degrade or improve equity in the United States, so a straightforward analysis of the net benefits with no further consideration of distribution is probably sufficient.

Intangibles

There are a number of issues related to ethanol that defy quantification. They will be discussed here in qualitative terms not because they are unimportant, but rather because they lie outside the scope of what might ordinarily be considered in a BCA. Because none of these issues is related to goods traded in markets, one approach to assessing their value might be through contingent valuation: asking people about the value that they attach to these issues, either in the context of ethanol or, more simply, on their own.

Thermodynamic efficiency

One criticism of ethanol production is that it is not thermodynamically efficient. That is, it may be the case that a gallon of ethanol contains less energy than was used to grow, harvest and transport the grain, produce the fertilizers and pesticides used, and to distill and transport the resulting ethanol.[5] From an economic point of view, thermodynamic efficiency is irrelevant. If the marginal value of the energy coming out of the process is greater than the marginal value of the inputs, the process is economically beneficial even if it is thermodynamically inefficient. However, while this is not an economic issue, it may be that people somehow suffer from a production process that actually consumes more energy than it delivers.

National energy security

One argument presented in favor of ethanol production (and, indirectly, in favor of the tax exemption) is that it promotes national energy security by reducing reliance on foreign oil. Again, this is not necessarily an economic issue, but to the extent that energy security matters to people who have standing, it may have a place in a BCA of the program. It should be noted, however, that if ethanol is not thermodynamically efficient, then it is more likely to hurt rather than help national energy security. Plainly stated, we may use more petroleum producing ethanol than the ethanol will replace.

Renewable energy

Agricultural products are a renewable resource while fossil fuels, for all practical purposes, are not. If development of renewable replacements for fossil fuels is important to people who have standing, this aspect of ethanol may be important in a BCA. However, as before, this is not an economic issue and if ethanol is not thermodynamically efficient, it is not a viable renewable energy source.

Summary and Conclusion

The most quantifiable effects of the ethanol tax exemption may be divided into additional fuel production costs, reduced federal tax revenues and potentially reduced price support payments to corn producers. Effects that are less easily quantified include the environmental effects of ethanol production, both directly and through the potential for reduced gasoline production, as well as a variety of intangible benefits.

Reaching a conclusion about the net benefits of the tax exemption granted motor fuels that contain ethanol depends critically on assumptions about standing (Table 11.1).

---

[5] This is a somewhat controversial point. See Hosein Shapouri, James A. Duffield and Michael S. Graboski, USDA, Economic Research Service, *Estimating the Net Energy Balance of Corn Ethanol*, July 1995 and T.W. Patzek, 'Sustainability of the corn–ethanol biofuel cycle', UC Berkeley Report, June 2004.

Table 11.1   Annual benefits and costs of ethanol tax exemption

Standing	Universal	Government	Corn and ethanol producers and consumers
Increased fuel production costs	−$360 m	−$360 m	−$360 m
Federal motor fuel tax revenues		−$624 m	+$624 m
Reduced support payments if corn prices would otherwise be below the $2.10 floor		As much as +$2800 m, depending on corn prices	
Net tangible benefit	−$360 m	(−$984 m, +$1816) depending on corn prices	+$264 m

It is most correct to apply universal standing to the analysis. When this is done, effects of taxation and transfer payments fall out of the calculation and the one critical consideration is the cost disadvantage of ethanol. The exemption results in the production of 1.2 billion gallons of ethanol. If the cost of producing a gallon of ethanol is $0.30 greater than the cost of producing a gallon of gasoline and if ethanol production displaces gasoline production, the value of the extra resources consumed as a result of the exemption is $360 million annually. Any changes in tax revenues or agricultural transfer payments are irrelevant because they are simply seen as transfers.

There are several remaining considerations. The environmental impacts of ethanol displacing petroleum refining are a potential benefit that is difficult to value and depends on the specifics of where and when the displaced petroleum refining would have occurred. The distributional effects of the ethanol exemption seem to be of no great importance as there is no great benefit or cost to any particularly disadvantaged group. The intangible effects listed here may be important to consider, but quantifying these effects would likely involve contingent valuation studies that are beyond the scope of this analysis.

In the end, the most critical consideration in assessing the ethanol tax exemption is also the most basic, standing. The most correct assumption, universal standing, suggests that the ethanol tax exemption is economically inefficient.

11.3 CELL PHONE CASE STUDY: USING BENEFIT–COST ANALYSIS TO EXAMINE CELL PHONE USE WHILE DRIVING

Often, BCAs provide only point estimates of benefits, costs and net present values. The usefulness of these point estimates is reduced when little or no information is provided as to their reliability. Sometimes simply a brief discussion of uncertainty suffices to render the point estimates convincing. In some cases additional statistical information is necessary. In the following study on cell phone use while driving, an intermediate path is followed. In considering this case, imagine that you are a staff person for a committee for the state of California in connection with Assembly Bill 1828,[6] which was introduced in January 2004. You are aware that a ban has been or is being considered elsewhere. The question you face is the reliability of the benefit–cost estimates.

Accidents related to cell phone use while driving have led to a consideration of a ban. The city of Brooklyn, Ohio[7] instituted a ban in 1999. In 2001, New York State banned the use of hand-held phones while driving for all drivers in all vehicles. In January 2004, New Jersey banned the use of hand-held phones following the ban in New York.[8] The District of Columbia also passed a bill in early 2004 banning the use of hand-held phones while driving. All three permit the use of hands-free devices. As of May 2004, there were 23 active bills in 12 states considering some ban on cell phones.[9] Other countries have instituted bans or limitations on cell phone use of various sorts.[10]

---

6   See http://info.sen.ca.gov/pub/bill/asm/ab_1801–1850/ab_1828_bill_20040120_introduced.html.

7   Brooklyn, Ohio was the first city to implement a ban on cell phone use and the first city to mandate use of seatbelts.

8   The NJ legislation, however, only allows drivers to be ticketed when stopped for another infraction. The New Jersey law was to take effect on July 1, 2004. AP Wire, January 20, 2004.

9   Some of the states are considering banning hand held (AL, AZ, CA, DE, IL, RI, SC, VT), one is a total ban including hands free (VT), some are only for teenagers (CA, DE, IL, MI, MN, RI, SC, TN) and some are only for school bus drivers (CA, DE, PA). National Institute for Highway Safety.

10 Of the 29 countries that belong to the OECD, eight countries: Australia, Japan, France, Italy, Portugal, Spain, Sweden and Switzerland have legislation

The ban on cell phone use may be supported by the growing evidence of the number of drivers who use their cell phones while driving. In a poll of Washington state residents, over 58 percent of drivers admitted to talking on the phone while driving. They also rated this behavior as a danger rating of 4 on a scale of 1 to 5, 5 being 'very dangerous'. The poll also found that 'the more drivers admitted to performing a distracting activity, the less dangerous they saw the activity'.[11] Users may not correctly evaluate their own risks and certainly not the risks they impose on others.

BCA has been a part of this debate in the form of a 1999 study by Hahn and Prieger at the AEI–Brookings Joint Center for Regulatory Studies. You are attempting to decide if the information in the benefit–cost study is sufficiently convincing that you should recommend against a ban, even though a voter poll shows that a small majority favors a ban. The Hahn and Prieger study reports, as a basic finding, that the economic costs of a ban on cellular phone use in vehicles far outweigh the benefits. Therefore they argue against a ban. The reason is simple – cellular phone use in vehicles provides substantial benefits to users but does not appear to contribute to a large number of accidents. Next they make calculations addressing a more difficult issue – whether particular regulations mandating cellular phone innovations would represent a relatively low-cost way of reducing accidents. As an example, they consider the case of mandating a hands-free device that is similar to a phone headset used in office environments. While the results are not as clear-cut as a ban, they suggest that such regulation is probably not warranted on benefit–cost grounds.

The study's calculation of benefits and costs are shown in Table 11.2. The study shows that the costs of a ban exceed its benefits by $20 billion per year. Thus the point estimate suggests that a ban is not a good investment. These results can be questioned.

Benefits

The benefits of a ban on cell phone use are measured by the costs that would be avoided by the ban plus the willingness to pay to reduce risk of accidents. The direct costs consist of lost lives, property damage, and loss productivity in the workplace and direct medical expenses. Most important of these are lost lives and the costs of injury. The report estimates the

---

that prohibits the use of hand-held phones while driving. The UK has quasi-legislation that restricts cell phone use, but it falls in the area between formal legislation and mere administrative rule making.

11. PR Newswire, May 10, 2004.

Table 11.2   Benefits and costs of a cell phone ban

Study	Benefits	Costs	Net benefits or costs
A ban on cell phone use while driving (Hahn et al., 2000)	$4.6 bn/year	$25 bn/year	−$20 bn/year
A requirement of a hands–free device (Hahn et al., 2000)	$700 m/year	$1.4 bn/year	−$700 m/year

total annual cost of all motor vehicle accidents at roughly $630 billion (1999 dollars). This figure includes the willingness to pay for reduced mortality and morbidity risks along with lost productivity in the workplace and direct medical expenses. The Hahn et al. (2000) study estimates that cell phone use in vehicles causes 300 fatalities a year and 38,000 accidents involving injuries[12] and concludes that cellular phone use contributes to approximately 0.74 percent of accidents. To find the cost of cell phone accidents then they simply take 0.74 percent of total accident costs, and find that the benefits of a ban would be $4.6 billion.[13]

Costs

The costs of a ban are determined either by the willingness to pay (WTP) to avoid such a ban or by the amount needed to compensate drivers who use phones for the ban (willingness to accept or WTA). The former (WTP) is appropriate if we assume that there is no right to cell phone use, in which case we ask users what they are willing to pay to use the phone while driving. The latter (WTA) is the correct figure if we assume there is such a right, in which case we ask what would have to be paid to users to give up

---

[12]   The range of estimates ranges from 10 to 1000 fatalities a year and 1300 to 130,000 accidents involving injuries. *Regulation*, **23** (3), p. 49.

[13]   0074*$630 billion = $4.6 billion. Note that in the Full Report, the authors use a figure of 0.002 so that the benefits of a ban are $1.2 billion. This does not change the qualitative aspects of the report that conclude that a ban does not pass the benefit–cost test. Figures for costs avoided are based on NHTSA's estimation of the economic costs of accidents and Viscusi's estimate for WTP for reduced mortality and morbidity.

their right. The Hahn et al. study assumes the WTA measure but measures the welfare loss to consumers by examining industry-wide demand functions for cell phone service. The measure is in fact liable to fall somewhere between the two WTP and WTA measures.

The price elasticity of industry-wide cell phone demand is estimated at − 0.51, so that a 10 percent reduction in price would increase the amount demanded by 5.1 percent. From this elasticity figure, the study estimates the consumer surplus that would be lost were consumers to be entirely deprived at $41 billion (1999 dollars). That is, this is the required compensation for consumers to be indifferent to an entire ban on cell phones. Finally Hahn et al. multiply the total proportion of calls occurring in vehicles to calculate the cost of a ban while driving. They find that 60 percent of calls are made in transit. Using the figure of 60 percent as the proportion of cell phone calls occurring while in a vehicle,[14] they find that customers would need $25 billion in compensation.[15] The 60 percent figure is obtained by asking cellular users what percentage of cell phone minutes were used while in transportation versus minutes made at home, office or other locations. Calls in transport may be calls made in a taxi, bus, subway, train or plane. This figure is thus an overestimate of the calls placed in vehicles while driving.

Uncertainty

The Hahn et al. study notes that there is a great deal of uncertainty for many of the parameter values used in the model. The question is how robust are their conclusions? To address this the authors applied sensitivity analysis to account for uncertainty. The key parameters are number of lives saved, the contribution to risk of cell phone usage (relative risk) and demand elasticity. A range of 10 to 1000 for lives saved is used. A range of 40 percent to 70 percent is used as the percentage of time cell phone users use the cell phone while driving. Demand elasticity estimates are varied from −0.17 to −0.84.

Tables 11.3 and 11.4 show the benefit–cost results including sensitivity estimates.[16]

The particular contribution of the uncertainty of the various parameters is shown in Figure 11.1.[17]

---

[14] This 60 percent figure is from the 1999 *Mobile Users Survey* conducted by the Yankee Group.
[15] 60%*$41 billion.
[16] Tables from *Regulation*, **23** (3), p. 50.
[17] Figure from *Regulation*, **23** (3), p. 51.

Table 11.3   Ban on the use of cellular phones while driving

	Best estimate	Range
Benefits	$4.6 bn	$110 m to $21 bn
Costs	$25 bn	$10 bn to $87 bn
Net benefits	−$20 bn	−$87 bn to $6.8 bn

Table 11.4   Mandate for hands-free devices

	Best estimate	Range
Benefits	$690 m	$0 to $6.3 bn
Costs	$1.4 bn	$100 m to $7.6 bn
Net benefits	−$710 m	−$7.6 bn to $6.2 bn

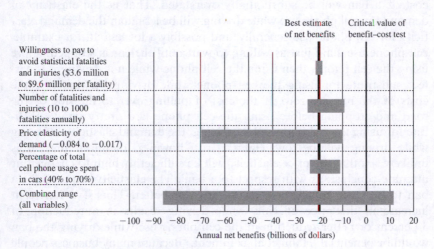

Sources: Hahn et al. (2000) and authors calculations.

Figure 11.1   Sensitivity of best estimate to key variables

Discussion

The range of estimates allows for the possibility that a ban is beneficial. When all uncertainties are considered together, there are net benefits from a ban only in the upper ranges of the parameters. Hahn et al. note (p. 50): 'The qualitative nature of our ranges does not allow us to provide precise confidence intervals'. Should we have confidence in that a ban is unwarranted?

The most problematical estimate is the demand for cell phone use while driving. The value of the call while driving can be no more than the cost of making the same call while not driving. Thus a better measure of value might be the value of the extra travel time that would be involved if they stopped the vehicle during the call. What is desired is the value of the time saved by not stopping during the call. In this case, it would be 60 percent of the value of the time that people spend on cell phones, which could be much lower than the value of the call. That is, the estimate of benefits that Hahn et al. determine for the use of a cell phone while driving may be a substantial overestimate.

Yet what we are given is not the value of time saved but, in fact, the value attached to the calls. If cell phone use (or phone use generally) while *not* driving is a good substitute for use while driving, the estimate of the cost of a ban will be substantially overstated. That is, the elasticity of demand for cell phone use while driving will be less than the demand elasticity for cell phone use generally, and possibly a lot less. If, for example, cell phone users are just as willing to wait until the car is stopped before using the cell phone, then using the cell phone while not driving is a perfect substitute for using the cell phone while driving. In this case the costs of the ban are zero. If the cost of pulling over to the side of the road and stopping before using the cell phone is a pretty good substitute for using the cell phone while driving, the demand elasticity for using while driving will be low. Hahn et al., however, maintain that 'it is unlikely . . . that the price elasticity will be sufficiently high to change our ultimate conclusions with respect to a ban'. The elasticity required for a ban to pass the benefit–cost test is three or better. Thus if a 1 percent increase in the price of calls while driving results in a reduction of 3 percent or better reduction in the cell phone use while driving the ban would be beneficial. Hahn et al. comment, 'Because many business people place a high value on their time, however, calls made while commuting to work are unlikely to be dramatically affected by a 1% increase in this price'.

But this is an assertion, not a fact based on evidence. We have no estimate for the portion that non-business calls while driving represent of the total. If this is large enough and if calling while not driving is a good substitute for calling while driving, the costs of a ban will be some fraction of the estimated costs. It may be of course that more information would provide additional support against a ban. The BCA has been suggestive and has pinpointed the area in which further information is needed. But, it does not seem definitive.

REFERENCES

Hahn, Robert and James Prieger (1999), 'The impact of cell phone use on accidents', working paper, AEI–Brookings Joint Center for Regulatory Studies, Washington, DC.

Hahn, Robert, Paul C. Tetlock and Jason K. Burnett (2000), 'Should you be allowed to use your cellular phone while driving?', *Regulation*, **23** (3), 46–56.

NHTSA (1997), various research reports, www.nrd.nhtsa.dot.gov.

EXERCISES

Questions

1. Do you find the benefit–cost analysis sufficiently persuasive to make a policy decision based on it?
2. Why or why not?
3. What could be done to make the benefit–cost analysis more persuasive?
4. Do you get angry or irritated when you see people driving using a cell phone? If so would you be willing to pay for a ban?
5. Do you find that this sort of third effect is taken into account by the Hahn et al. study?.

Answers

1. This depends on how important you find the limitations to the study that we pointed out.
2. The cited limitations seem potentially important.
3. Reduce the magnitude of the cited limitations.
4. Well, I do and I would.
5. No, they did not take this into account. Should they?

12. Resources

12.1 INTRODUCTION

Benefit–cost analyses require both theory and data. While it is impossible to anticipate all of the data that might be required for analyses, there are several types of information that may be more generally applicable. This chapter offers some resources to which an analyst might turn for supporting numbers.

12.2 GENERAL SOURCES

There are a number of resources that provide a wide variety of data. While they may not have the exact information needed, they might be a good starting point.

Economic Report of the President (ERP) This report is published annually and generally contains reports on a number of issues relating to the US economy. The more useful part is an extensive set of tables in the appendix describing numerous aspects of the economy, including national income, employment and wages, production, prices and price indices, interest rates and government expenditures, in addition to numerous other series. It is available on-line at http://www.gpoaccess.gov/eop/.

Bureau of Labor Statistics (BLS) BLS is the principal fact-finding agency for the federal government in the broad field of labor economics and statistics. As such, they assemble data on a wide variety of things. Among the data available on their web site are wages by occupation and region, numerous price indices, employment and unemployment figures and injury and illness rates. Their web site is http://www.bls.gov.

Census Bureau The Census Bureau collects a wide variety of demographic and business information. In addition to measuring the population, they also measure the level of business activity and can offer some measures of the sizes of different industries, either nationally or regionally. Their web site is http://www.census.gov/.

Energy Information Administration   Official energy data is available from the US government through the web site of the Energy Information Administration at http://www.eia.doe.gov/. This site offers a wide variety of information about all types of energy at the national, state and even individual plant levels.

A truly impressive collection of shadow values is assembled in Boardman et al. (Anthony E. Boardman, David H. Greenberg, Aidan R. Vining and David L. Weimer (1997), '"Plug-in" shadow price estimates for policy analysis', *The Annals of Regional Science*, **31**, 299–324). These include previously published shadow values for human life, injuries, various crimes, travel time, recreational activities, endangered species preservation and pollution. As discussed in Chapter 7, these shadow values are inferred in various ways and may be applied in situations where no market price is available.

12.3   ELASTICITY ESTIMATES

Estimates of income and own price elasticities of demand are available for broad consumption categories and for more specific food categories for a large number of countries from the Economic Research Service of the US Department of Agriculture. This is available on-line at http://www.ers.usda.gov/Data/InternationalFoodDemand.

12.4   TAXES

Taxes are levied on most transactions in most economies. If standing in a CBA is universal, taxes should be excluded from the cost of inputs such as materials, energy and labor.

One good resource for a wide variety of taxes is the Federation of Tax Administrators web site at http://www.taxadmin.org/.

Information on federal, state and local taxes that might be applicable to the inputs into a project can be found at a variety of sites including the Tax and Accounting Sites Directory at http://www.taxsites.com.

Information on US federal income taxes is available through the Internal Revenue Service at http://www.irs.gov. Information on Canadian taxes can be found at the Canadian Tax Foundation web site at http://www.ctf.ca.

12.5 ENVIRONMENTAL DATA AND ANALYSIS – FERET AND BENMAP

Two tools for valuing environmental effects are FERET and BENMAP.

The Fast Environmental Regulatory Evaluation Tool (FERET) is a computerized template that facilitates analysis of the impacts of environmental regulations. It includes data and values from a variety of pre-existing studies and automates the process of sensitivity analysis over these values. The software and supporting documentation for FERET is available through the Center for the Study and Improvement of Regulation web site at http://www.epp.cmu.edu/csir/index.htm.

The great value of FERET is its ability to simplify and streamline the process of BCA. FERET includes values and assumptions from a number of existing studies that may be used in either a straightforward analysis of a proposed project or in a Monte Carlo analysis to investigate the effects of uncertainty surrounding values. FERET includes an EPA model for cost estimation (PROJECT) that simplifies the process of computing the present value of fixed, operating and maintenance costs of a project. It is both transparent and flexible, allowing a wide variety of assumptions to be changed and clearly demonstrating the impacts of these assumptions.

BENMAP is a program to map and value the benefits of air quality improvements that was developed by the US Environmental Protection Agency (EPA). The program uses peer-reviewed EPA models to move from changes in environmental regulations to changes in ambient air quality to predictions of health effects and, finally, valuation of these effects. Information on BENMAP is available at http://www.epa.gov/ttn/ecas/models/benmapfactsheet.pdf and the program itself may be downloaded at http://www.epa.gov/ttn/ecas/benmapdownload.html.

Subject index

Name index